PSYCHOANALYSIS IS AN ANTIPHILOSOPHY

PSYCHOANALYSIS IS AN ANTIPHILOSOPHY

Justin Clemens

EDINBURGH
University Press

© Justin Clemens, 2013

Edinburgh University Press Ltd
22 George Square, Edinburgh EH8 9LF

www.euppublishing.com

Typeset in 10.5/13 Sabon
by Servis Filmsetting Ltd, Stockport, Cheshire

A CIP record for this book is available from the British Library

ISBN 978 0 7486 7894 5 (hardback)
ISBN 978 0 7486 8577 6 (paperback)
ISBN 978 0 7486 7895 2 (webready PDF)
ISBN 978 0 7486 7896 9 (epub)

Contents

Acknowledgements

This book has been a long time coming, and I have acquired a large number of debts along the way – for which a mention of my creditors in an Acknowledgements page is hardly a minimal down-payment. I am grateful to the School of Culture and Communication and the Faculty of Arts at the University of Melbourne for giving me time off to work on this book in 2008 and 2012. The publication of this book was supported by the Faculty of Arts Publication Subsidy Scheme. I will be forever indebted to my copy-editor Cathy Falconer, whose corrections have not only significantly improved this book, but have saved me from some embarrassing errors. Haydie Gooder has been, as ever, an impeccable indexer. I would like to thank Birkbeck College London for hosting me as an Honorary Fellow in January 2012. Among the many staff and students who discussed some of the points made here, I would particularly like to thank Anton Schütz and Thanos Zartaloudis for their incisive comments and suggestions. I must thank Richard Bell and his gallerist Josh Milani for permission to reproduce Bell's stunning image for the cover of this book. I would like to acknowledge Deakin University's Psychoanalytic Studies programme, and those I worked with there when a member of staff, especially Douglas Kirsner and Ron Gilbert. I would like to thank everyone involved in the Lacan Circle of Melbourne; if it is not too invidious to celebrate an individual in this context, I would especially like to thank Susana Tillet, whose return to Argentina several years ago has been a great loss to Australian psychoanalysis. I would like to thank my colleagues, friends and students, notably Marion Campbell, Lorenzo Chiesa, Anna Cordner, Oliver Feltham, Nicholas Heron, Helen Johnson, Sigi Jöttkandt, Adam Nash and Jessica Whyte for their discussions and support. I am especially indebted to John Frow, whose intellectual support, structural interventions and editing suggestions have greatly improved this book. There are, however, two people I would like to acknowledge above all. First, my comrade A. J. Bartlett, without whom there would hardly be any point in continuing with – as Ezra Pound puts it in his parody of W. B. Yeats's 'Lake Isle' – 'this damn'd profession of writing'. Second, Russell Grigg, whose impact on my thinking about psychoanalysis has been incalculable. It is to Russell that I dedicate this book.

Much of the material in this book has been previously published, often in very different forms. I would therefore like to acknowledge the editors and publishers of the following texts: 'To Rupture the Matheme with a Poem', in J. Freddi, M. Noonan and M. Sharpe (eds), *Trauma, History, Philosophy* (Newcastle: Cambridge Scholars Publishing, 2007), pp. 308–12; 'The Jew's Two Noses: Freud, Addiction, Cocaine', *The UTS Review*, 7:2 (2001), pp. 144–62; 'The Field and Function of the Slave in the *Écrits*', *European Journal of Psychoanalysis*, 32 (2012); 'The Abandonment of Sex: Giorgio Agamben, Psychoanalysis and Melancholia', *Theory and Event* (2010); 'Love as Ontology: Psychoanalysis against Philosophy', in R. Brassier and C. Kerslake (eds), *Origins and Ends of the Psyche* (Leuven: Leuven University Press, 2007), pp. 185–201; 'The Slave, The Fable', in P. Morrissey and G. Reifarth (eds), *Aesopic Voices* (Newcastle: Cambridge Scholars Press, 2011), pp. 45–73; 'Man is a Swarm Animal', in D. Hoens, S. Jöttkandt and G. Buelens (eds), *The Catastrophic Imperative: Time, Subjectivity and Memory in Contemporary Thought* (Basingstoke: Palgrave-Macmillan, 2009), pp. 83–113; Review of Giorgio Agamben's *The Sacrament of Language* in *Symploke*, 19:1–2 (2011), pp. 414–16.

Introduction: Psychoanalysis is an Antiphilosophy

without the pursuit of I worship you
which is a French boxer
maritime values as irregular as the depression of Dada in the blood
of a bicephalous animal
 Tristan Tzara, 'Manifesto of Monsieur AA the Antiphilosopher'[1]

WHY ANTIPHILOSOPHY?

Psychoanalysis is an antiphilosophy. Despite the precision of this concept and this claim, their implications remain controversial. This book thus introduces the concept of antiphilosophy, speaks of its constitution and pertinence with respect to psychoanalysis, and examines the consequences of such a determination through a sequence of case-studies. Although the concept has some highly abstract aspects and a somewhat forbidding intellectual history, it is deployed here, first, as a kind of corrosive of received ideas, and, second, as an affirmative means of characterising psychoanalysis that captures something essential, if often elided, about the peculiar status of the practice.

'Antiphilosophy' is, as the most cursory research reveals, a word in common use. It is for the most part deployed to designate an intellectual hostility – that is, a hostility within thought itself – to 'philosophy' more or less broadly conceived. Hence one finds accounts of how this or that religious thinker or theologian, Buddhist, Christian, Jewish, Islamic or what have you, self-consciously arrays their thought against the propositions and methods of philosophy. According to this general, essentially religious acceptation, philosophy is constitutively incapable of thinking what is most crucial, above all, the revealed truths of this

---

[1] T. Tzara, *Seven Dada Manifestos and Lampisteries*, trans. B. Wright, illustrations F. Picabia (London: John Calder, n.d.), p. 19.

or that religion or ethical practice. As Pascal once famously put it, 'the heart has its reasons which reason cannot know'. Against reason, then, one arrays revelation: the God of Abraham, Isaac and Jacob, not the *logos* and its logics. Religion is antiphilosophy insofar as revelation trumps reason. An ethics of submission subordinates epistemology.

But there is also an assault on philosophy from the other side, as it were. Modern scientists are also typically antiphilosophers, insofar as philosophy for them turns out to retain too much revelation, too much disavowed unreason. To the extent that philosophy has anything to say in the realm of knowledge, or has played a role in saying so, it has been supplanted or superseded by the post-Baconian sciences: observational, experimental, mathematisable as they are. One could invoke any number of contemporary popularising science texts in this regard, from Stephen Hawking to Richard Dawkins, in and for which science has incontrovertibly become the only acceptable source of true knowledge about the world.[2] Science is antiphilosophy insofar as experiment trumps argument. Ethics is submission to epistemology.

'Antiphilosophy' also functions as an emblem of affiliation, a polemical declaration, and a statement of method according to a strong line in the study of literature and art. As F. R. Leavis asserted in a late essay, 'I think of myself as an anti-philosopher, which is what a literary critic ought to be.'[3] The key here – and I will return to this below, as it will prove to be an indispensable aspect of my characterisation of psychoanalysis – is the conviction that, in Leavis's own words, 'philosophers are always weak on language', and that, concomitantly, the role of the critic is to attend to art with a kind of logological ethical fervour. Such an attention is antiphilosophical, not so much in its objects (both philosophy and antiphilosophy can share 'language' as their object) as in its methods and results. Antiphilosophy is not antiphilosophical in the sense of being 'non-philosophical'; on the contrary, the antiphilosopher is not out to evade or destroy philosophy, but to draw attention to forms of knowledge that philosophy cannot know, by affronting philosophy and subverting its claims. In doing so, the antiphilosopher also

---

[2] Scientists are not, of course, above crowing about this state of affairs. As Hawking puts it, 'in the nineteenth and twentieth centuries, science became too technical and mathematical for philosophers, or anyone else except for a few specialists . . . What a comedown for the great tradition of philosophy from Aristotle to Kant!', *A Brief History of Time* (New York: Random House, 2011), p. 209.

[3] F. R. Leavis, *Thought, Words and Creativity: Art and Thought in Lawrence* (London: Chatto and Windus, 1976), p. 34; see also the posthumous volume *The Critic as Anti-Philosopher*, ed. G. Singh (London: Chatto and Windus, 1982), in which one finds essays dealing expressly with the relationship between the teaching of literature and philosophy, such as 'Mutually Necessary'. See, further, C. Joyce, 'The Idea of "Anti-Philosophy" in the Work of F. R. Leavis', *The Cambridge Quarterly*, 38:1 (2009), pp. 24–44.

trumps philosophy without simply condemning it. This recurrent aspect of self-denominated critical antiphilosophy is confirmed by a recent book by Boris Groys which takes up the term in a related context, that of contemporary art. Here Groys even goes so far as to compare 'antiphilosophy' to a form of Duchampian 'readymade'.[4] Just as the readymade, in its very displacement from the context of the everyday to that of art, not only exposes the operations that establish context as such, but, under such description, shows that all and any objects can be art, antiphilosophy does the same for thought. For Groys, one of the key operations of antiphilosophy is the undermining of the 'claims of self-evidence' of philosophy itself, by showing that the latter's putative truth-claims and special operations were themselves always-already conventional, that is, cultural automatisms with pretensions – this being the very heart of every cultural activity *tout court*. In this sense, antiphilosophy enacts the submission of epistemology to ethics, but in a different way from religion. The ethics of such antiphilosophy would rather be an ethics of demotic citational depersonalisation.

Finally, there is a sense in which philosophers themselves are integrally engaged in antiphilosophy or at least struggle with the questions that it raises. Even if we leave aside the particular, peculiar 'anxiety of influence' that cannot not affect the philosophical enterprise in its heart – for instance, to pick up a classicising image of Hannah Arendt's, philosophy is the work of Penelope, unpicking at night the work she has done during the day – philosophy, particularly post-Romantic philosophy, has tended to turn from the allegedly untenable metaphysical ambitions of classical philosophy, towards more modest proposals. So we find in the work of Friedrich Nietzsche, Ludwig Wittgenstein and Martin Heidegger a kind of clinical diagnosis of the ills of metaphysics, to the extent that Wittgenstein will even hold that philosophy is what happens when language goes on holiday, or Heidegger will assert that philosophy is dangerous in its own self-unknowing pretensions.[5] As Theodor Adorno said of Walter Benjamin, his was 'a philosophy directed against philosophy'.[6] Even the putative defenders of philosophy seem only to be able to do so by precisely denominating rival philosophical enterprises as 'not real philosophy' (one thinks here especially of the analytical dismissals of 'continental philosophy'). Philosophy would therefore be the first antiphilosophy, or antiphilosophy would

---

[4] B. Groys, *Introduction to Antiphilosophy*, trans. D. Fernbach (London: Verso, 2012).
[5] See L. Wittgenstein, *Philosophical Investigations*, trans. G. E. M. Anscombe et al. (Oxford: Wiley-Blackwell, 2009); M. Heidegger, *Poetry, Language, Thought*, trans. A. Hofstadter (New York: Harper and Row, 1971).
[6] T. Adorno, *Prisms*, trans. S. and S. Weber (Cambridge, MA: MIT, 1995), p. 235.

itself be the first philosophy, insofar as it is nothing but savage, unremitting auto-critique of its own processes of critique. Philosophy is antiphilosophy insofar as it is neither ethics nor epistemology.

I do not, however, intend the declaration that 'psychoanalysis is an antiphilosophy' to be taken in such broad senses. Rather, and against this rather general background of hostility to philosophy from both 'outside' and 'within', I want to take up the term in a far more specific and precise way. More specific, because it is necessary to investigate some of the salient historical and intellectual circumstances in which psychoanalysis arises; its 'situation' as such. Contingency is irreducible in the ambit of antiphilosophy. More precise, because I also wish to consider the term as a genuine concept, a concept which attempts to capture something about the new relation forged by psychoanalysis between ethics and epistemology, experiment and argument, theory and practice.

THE CONCEPT OF ANTIPHILOSOPHY

In 1975, Jacques Lacan, speaking at Vincennes University in Paris, invoked the necessity of a training in antiphilosophy for would-be psychoanalysts.[7] Although this reference is brief and allusive (as are so many of Lacan's critical remarks), its obscurities have been leavened by a variety of commentators. As Alain Badiou has noted:

> We know that, among the disciplines contributing to the training of analysts, Jacques Lacan attributed a pre-eminent place to antiphilosophy. He thus opened up a new career for this old word, which in the eighteenth century designated the position of all the enemies of the Enlightenment. In fact, his position is a reversal of the conservative sense of the word. For, if it was expedient that analysts be antiphilosophers, this was precisely in the name of the Enlightenment, philosophy being assigned by Lacan to an essential 'not-wanting-to-know'.[8]

I will return to this 'not-wanting-to-know' shortly but for the moment wish to mark something else: the counter-institutional movement of Lacanian antiphilosophy, which seeks to reinvigorate an ancient, even moribund term, and, in doing so, to invert its sense. In this movement, the essential traits of institutionality itself are exposed, marked and rebuked, 'philosophy' being the exemplum for Lacan of learned institutional trans-cultural ignorance, and thus also a metonym not

---

[7] J. Lacan, *Autres Écrits* (Paris: Éditions du Seuil, 2001), p. 314.
[8] A. Badiou, *The Adventure of French Philosophy*, trans. B. Bosteels (London: Verso, 2012), p. 53.

only for psychiatry but for 'the master's discourse' more generally.[9] There are then three further points to be made, which I can only mark here, but which will be taken up in greater detail in subsequent chapters of this book. The first is that the relation between the institution and forms of thought is at the centre of this denomination: for Lacan, 'antiphilosophy' denominates, as Badiou underlines, a 'form of training'. Institutional forms should be modelled and remodelled on the basis of the discoveries made by psychoanalytic practice, in a kind of 'permanent revolt'. Second, it implies that psychoanalysis must seek to be a new and different kind of 'institution' from those whose matrix remains philosophical (even if they are allegedly 'non-philosophical' themselves). Indeed, psychoanalysis historically has marked itself as a radically anomalous anti-institutional institution: the notorious squabbles, shifts, splits, dissolutions and reformations are integral to its practical becoming, not simply accidents or failures that have befallen it from internal corruption or external happenstance. Third, in announcing antiphilosophy as a programme, Lacan implicitly marks how difficult it is not to be 'philosophical', that is, conceptually hypocritical: philosophy, the very discipline allegedly founded on 'knowing', becomes the epitome of the obscure drive to ignorance. In fact, it is strictly speaking impossible not to be philosophical in Lacan's sense, even for psychoanalysis – a feature to which I will also return. Yet, in accordance with Lacan's own declarations, the struggle for antiphilosophy must be an attempt at the liberation of philosophy from itself.

Emerging as a reactionary response to Enlightenment and Revolution, reconfigured in Tristan Tzara's Dadaist rantings as a kind of heteronym, then taken up by Lacan in the course of a polemic against the institutional captivations of philosophers, 'antiphilosophy' has recently been given its strongest conceptual freighting by Badiou himself. For Badiou, antiphilosophy is, in general, defined by the following features:

- a *subordination* of philosophical categories to language, and the concomitant destitution of philosophy's pretensions to truth and system;
- the *diagnosis* of such pretensions as evidence of a philosophical will to power;

---

[9] I have not found any significant references in the commentary to another phenomenon that the name clearly alludes to in this context. A few years earlier, speaking in late 1971 at the Chapelle Sainte-Anne, in a transcription now available in the brief collection published as *Je parle aux murs*, Jacques Lacan invokes 'antipsychiatry'. He proceeds to distinguish *psychiatrie* and *psychiatrerie*, and adds, 'Antipsychiatry is a movement whose meaning is the liberation of psychiatry, if I dare to express myself so'; J. Lacan, *Je parle aux murs* (Paris: Éditions du Seuil, 2011), pp. 13–14.

- the *affirmation* of an extra-philosophical ethics that escapes such strictures.[10]

'Antiphilosophy' therefore doesn't mean a simple 'repudiation of' or a 'having nothing to do with' philosophy; on the contrary, antiphilosophy tends to confront the claims of philosophy and philosophers sometimes more, sometimes less directly. If Nietzsche and Wittgenstein are for Badiou the modern antiphilosophers *par excellence*, there is something special about psychoanalysis as a kind of antiphilosophy.[11] For the Freudian intervention does not emerge as a countervailing tendency from within philosophy itself, unlike the Nietzschean and Wittgensteinian programmes. Rather, psychoanalysis proper emerges when Freud crosses – 'short-circuits' – two very different discourses, the discourse of science and the discourse of the literary. To be still more precise, psychoanalysis emerges at the point where a rigorous contemporary scientific programme (neurology and psychology) can only be sustained by being interrupted by the literary (Freud's famous *Krankengeschichte*):

> The fact is that local diagnosis and electrical reactions lead nowhere in the study of hysteria, whereas a detailed description of mental processes such as we are accustomed to find in the works of poets enables me, with the use of a few psychological formulas, to obtain at least some kind of insight into the course of that affection.[12]

It is thus on the basis of these experiences with hysterical women that Freud, who begins as a scientist trained in the best institutions of his day, recognises that he can only continue to practise as a psychologist if he radically forces the volatile linguistic inventiveness of literature into the law-governed world of science. This is precisely so that he will be able to listen to the complaints of suffering women, to their accounts

---

[10] See A. Badiou, *Wittgenstein's Antiphilosophy*, trans. B. Bosteels (London: Verso, 2011); 'Who is Nietzsche?', *Pli*, 11 (2001), pp. 1–11; 'Antiphilosophy: Lacan and Plato', in *Conditions*, trans. S. Corcoran (London: Continuum, 2008), pp. 228–47; *Logics of Worlds*, trans. A. Toscano (London: Continuum, 2009), p. 540.

[11] With this claim, I depart from Badiou's own presentation of the concept, as well as from the common claim that it 'is quite difficult, if not impossible' to reconstruct Lacan's own use of the term. See B. Bosteels, ' Radical Antiphilosophy', *Filozofski Vestnik*, 29:1 (2008), p. 158. On the contrary, as I maintain here, Lacan's deployment of the term can be given a rigorous sense, and Badiou is the thinker who has done this most powerfully. See, however, the countervailing accounts of B. Cassin, *Jacques le sophiste: Lacan: Logos et psychanalyse* (Paris: EPEL, 2012); J.-C. Milner, *L'Oeuvre claire: Lacan, la science, la philosophie* (Paris: Éditions du Seuil, 1995); F. Regnault, 'L'Antiphilosophie selon Lacan', *Conférences d'esthétique lacanienne* (Paris: Agalma, 1997); C. Soler, 'Lacan en antiphilosophie', *Filozofski Vestnik*, 28:2 (2006), pp. 121–44; A. Johnston, 'This Philosophy Which Is Not One', *S*, 3 (2010), pp. 137–58.

[12] J. Breuer and S. Freud, *Studies in Hysteria*, in *The Standard Edition of the Complete Psychological Works of Sigmund Freud*, Vol. II (1893–1895), ed. J. Strachey et al. (London: The Hogarth Press, 1955), pp. 160–1.

of pain that are at once physiologically inexplicable yet absolutely real. Suffering is at the heart of the psychoanalytic experience, where trauma is constitutive of subjective existence. But this suffering cannot be heard and this trauma cannot be captured, let alone treated, by any existing means. Not by science, not by philosophy, not even by literature alone.

Science cannot do it: 'local diagnosis and electrical reactions' are incapable of unlocking the secrets of hysteria, precisely because of the delocalised mutability of the symptom and its metastatic effects. Yet one cannot give up on the scientific worldview without throwing knowledge to the wolves. Philosophy cannot do it: because it functions by excluding unreason from its purview, it dismisses hysterical provocations insofar as the latter remain patently refractory to the operations of philosophical pedagogy (logic, argument, evidence). Literature cannot do it: at least, literature cannot do it alone. Certainly, only literature is able to provide some of the tools necessary for the requisite psychological investigations; these tools not only enable us to discern the inconsistent ambivalence or equivocity at the heart of every linguistic presentation, they also provide a non-reductive way of reattaching such equivocations to the putative 'life' of the organism 'itself'. (It is therefore precisely the literary element that the contemporary scientistic enthusiasm for evolutionary theory in the humanities must directly target, and attempt not only to curb, but to obliterate altogether.) Yet literature is constantly on the verge of losing the referential value of its descriptions through an over-emphasis on formal or generic questions, and through its hostility to being normed according to procedures of the sciences. If our sufferers are to be heard, then, it will have to be by something genuinely new, by a new discourse that interrupts science with literature.

THE IMPORT OF THE LITERARY TO PSYCHOANALYSIS

From *Studies in Hysteria* onwards, Freud develops a theory of mind that takes the problem of language as fundamental, under an extraordinary diversity of headings (symptoms, dreams, parapraxes, art, etc.). *The Interpretation of Dreams* opens with a demonstration of the necessity to situate its eponymous project beyond the distinctions of myth and science: on the one hand, every human culture has placed an enormous stress on the interpretation of dreams; on the other, almost every scientific investigation to date has dismissed such interpretations; psychoanalysis will therefore retain the ideals of science in confirming the necessity of dream-readings. Freud's attention is thereby forced towards those extreme yet quotidian forms of language-use usually

denominated 'literary'. But such a position is radically antiphilosophical, in its topics, methods and results.

Freud acknowledges poets as the first, most powerful analysts of
human behaviour.[13] Literary allusions, references and quotations are
found everywhere in his work. The epigraph to *The Interpretation of
Dreams* is from Virgil's *Aeneid*: 'Flectere si nequeo superos Acheronta
movebo' – 'If I can't sway the heights, I'll shake up Hell'. Literature is
clearly both a support and model for Freud's own style. And the central,
most famous concept in all Freud's work – the Oedipus complex –
derives from a classical tragedy in which a myth is restaged. It is often
also suggested that Freud transplants literary tropes to the domain of
psychology: the unconscious is a great and inventive writer, for instance.
In the attention that they pay to tiny linguistic details, psychoanalysis
and literature are very similar. There is no detail too small to be possibly
of significance: repetitions, peculiar rhythms, puns, nominal mistakes,
slips of the tongue and so on all become grist to the literary and the psychoanalytic mills. Literature is, moreover, necessarily anamnesiac and
amnesiac simultaneously. If it purports to speak of the world, it does
so by speaking incessantly of itself and its relation to its bearers, and it
does this from an arcane and archaic place – which is also the place of
the archaic and the anachronistic. Science – observational, experimental, formalisable – concerns itself with knowledge in the present, the
contemporary; indeed, knowledge is only knowledge in science if it is
forever young, eternally revising itself. Literature, in contrast, speaks
above all of chthonic things, things that stick or have stuck beyond their
time, at once abundant and mortificatory. Freud, finally, with the technique of 'free association', places a radical language-based principle at
the very centre of therapeutic practice.

There are thus at least four crucial ways in which the relation of
psychoanalysis to the literary is directly at stake:

- Literature provides the material support for analysis, in the same way
  as, or at least as continuous with the way in which, dreams, jokes and
  symptoms are also material for analysis;

---

[13] In a letter to Arthur Schnitzler dated 14 May 1922 on the occasion of the writer's 60th
birthday, Freud extends a familiar hand: 'I think I have avoided you from a kind of reluctance to meet my double. Not that I am easily inclined to identify myself with another, or
that I mean to overlook the difference in talent that separates me from you, but whenever
I get deeply absorbed in your beautiful creations I invariably seem to find beneath their
poetic surface the very presuppositions, interests, and conclusions which I know to be my
own . . . all this moves me with an uncanny feeling of familiarity . . . I have formed the
impression that you know through intuition – or rather from detailed self-observation –
everything that I have discovered by laborious work on other people'; *Letters of Sigmund
Freud 1873–1939*, ed. E. L. Freud (London: The Hogarth Press, 1961), pp. 339–40.

- Literature provides examples or analogons, *illustrations*, for analytic theory;
- Literature is an unscientific forerunner or inspiration for analysis; if unsystematic and unscientific, it is replete with valuable insights to which analysis gives a firm theoretical grounding;
- Literature provides a model, perhaps *the* model, for the writing of analysis itself.

In other words, Freud at once considers literature a parent, teacher, colleague and analysand of psychoanalysis – which is clearly a complex, overdetermined and psychoanalytically fraught relationship.[14]

Yet there is also something else crucial to mark here: if he is very attentive to the limits of literature, Freud is also very attentive to the limits of psychoanalysis with respect to literature. As he wrote in 1928, apropos of 'Dostoyevsky and Parricide', 'before the problem of the creative artist analysis, alas, must lay down its arms'.[15] Noting in passing Freud's symptomatic deployment of metaphors of armed struggle, I find this 'surrender' of psychoanalysis to the enigmatic powers of creative genius extraordinary. For the founder of psychoanalysis to speak of creative genius as essentially unanalysable has serious consequences for analysis itself. If psychoanalysis is to be a genuine theory of human behaviour, how and why is it that something as central to human existence as imaginative invention eludes explanation?

Freud's ironic surrender enables us to add a fifth heading to our list: the literary presents itself as an irreducible *zone of opacity* to analysis. So literature is at once a support, an illustration, a precursor, a model and a *limit* to analysis. This 'limit' is, we need to underline, a *scientific* limit. One must continue to assemble evidence, generate new hypotheses and essay new generalisations, in accordance with the exigencies of scientific research. Yet, precisely to the extent that literature presents singularities, it frustrates totalisation, and this limit is, furthermore, a provocation to further research. Thus Freud treats literature: as a *precursor* to psychoanalysis; as providing *material* and *illustrations* for psychoanalysis; as supplying *models* for psychoanalysis; as a *limit* and

---

[14] For a different but in some ways consonant interpretation of Freud's relation to aesthetics, see J. Rancière, *The Aesthetic Unconscious*, trans. D. Keates (Cambridge: Polity, 2009).

[15] S. Freud, *The Standard Edition of the Complete Psychological Works of Sigmund Freud*, Vol. XXI (1927–1931), ed. J. Strachey et al. (London: The Hogarth Press, 1961), p. 177. As Lacan puts it in *Seminar XI*, 'Freud always stressed with infinite respect that he did not intend to settle the question of what it was in artistic creation that gave it its true value. When he is dealing with painters and poets, there is a point at which his appreciation stops'; *Seminar XI: The Four Fundamental Concepts of Psychoanalysis*, trans. A. Sheridan, intro. by D. Macey (London: Penguin, 1994), p. 110.

as a *provocation* to psychoanalytic knowledge. Literature is a parent, patient, colleague, teacher, physician and, finally, an Other to psychoanalysis. This incoherence destabilises psychoanalysis; but, if analysis attempts to reduce this incoherence, it fails as psychoanalysis and becomes just one of a genre of indifferently differentiated psychotherapies, a hermeneutics or a scientism.

THE APORIA OF LOVE IN PSYCHOANALYSIS

What holds together the aforementioned list – which, on the face of it, is incoherent – is that they are instances and signs, sign-instances, of what psychoanalysis itself theorises as transference, that is, of love.[16] This leads me to a fundamental proposition about psychoanalysis as an antiphilosophy: *if psychoanalysis is in love with literature, literature is not in love with psychoanalysis.*[17] This asymmetry can lead to certain difficulties. As Freud himself comments, 'there is so often associated with the erotic relationship, over and above its own sadistic components, a quota of plain inclination to aggression. The love-object will not always view these complications with the degree of understanding and tolerance shown by the peasant woman who complained that her husband did not love her any more, since he had not beaten her for a week.'[18] These complications also go some way to explaining why commentators cannot agree on just how psychoanalysis treats literature: for Lionel Trilling, psychoanalysis ultimately views literature with contempt; for Michel de Certeau, literature functions as an authority and authorisation for psychoanalysis; for Richard Wollheim and Alain

---

[16] There are of course other ways of understanding this relationship. As Adam Phillips remarks: 'One could feel that poets are being recruited, perhaps a bit desperately, as allies. Clearly for those people who like poetry, or who like the idea of poets (which is not the same thing), their transference to poets is a remarkable thing. Indeed, so remarkable is it that it is perhaps the one thing that could be said to unite the increasingly disparate schools of psychoanalysis. Freud, Jung, Lacan, Winnicott, Bion, Meltzer, Milner, Segal, among many others, all agree in their privileging of the poetic. Psychoanalysis may not have mattered quite as much as it would have liked to poetry, but poetry has certainly mattered to psychoanalysis'; A. Phillips, *Promises, Promises: Essays on Psychoanalysis and Literature* (London: Faber and Faber, 2000), p. 6. Phillips goes on to claim, not altogether correctly I believe, that the 'privileging of poetry and poets is a counter-force to the fear that language and meaning don't work. Or don't work in quite the ways we might want them to', and that 'the research scientist has always been an easier ego-ideal, or model, for the analyst, than the poet'; p. 6.

[17] I owe the first part of this formulation to Sigi Jöttkandt (personal communication), the second half to an interpretation of an utterance by Jean Baudrillard: 'Gombrowicz, Nabokov, Svevo, Schnitzler, Canetti. Why is it that the greatest are more or less violently hostile to psychoanalysis? And, at bottom, towards the end, Freud himself?'; *Fragments: Cool Memories III 1991–1995* (Paris: Éditions Galilée, 1995), p. 20.

[18] S. Freud, *Civilization and its Discontents*, trans. J. Riviere, rev. J. Strachey (London: The Hogarth Press, 1963), p. 106.

Badiou, psychoanalysis is ultimately indifferent, in an Aristotelian kind of way, to the charms of literature, and so on.[19] In the end, what renders these accounts insufficient is that they can't seem to countenance, first, that psychoanalysis can – and *must* – coherently treat literature in so many diverse ways, and, second, that the issue of *love* is crucial in accounting for this relationship.

If psychoanalysis has a very close ongoing if fraught relationship with science, analysis doesn't love science. We could phrase this as a maxim: *psychoanalysis would love to be a science in love with the literary*. Psychoanalysis doesn't repudiate explanation by cause and law; on the contrary. Science remains – and must remain – a kind of ideal for psychoanalysis. Scientific procedures are indispensable; indeed, it has been widely suggested that, whatever its results, psychoanalysis ought to show that these are not incompatible with those of contemporary science. It is rather that psychoanalysis recognises that, in the realm of the unconscious, one needs to acknowledge causal overdetermination, lacking causes, explanatory complications, experimental failure and temporal paradoxes.

When psychoanalysis remembers literature, then, it risks losing itself in this relationship; but whenever it forgets literature, it forgets itself as well. It is in this regard that psychoanalysis is integrally imbricated with the literary. Without the literary, analysis would not be analysis at all (but psychology or psychiatry or psychotherapy), but analysis cannot remain in love with the literary either, since it literally loses itself in pursuing such a love (and we end up with psychoanalysis as just another form of literary criticism, rhetorical studies, etc.). We can now give another, aporetic sense to the 'impossibility' to which Freud often alludes vis-à-vis analysis: psychoanalysis must be in love with the literary to be itself, but, insofar as it is in love, it fails to be itself.

THE PECULIARITY OF PSYCHOANALYSIS AS AN ANTIPHILOSOPHY

One can at once see how and why psychoanalysis is so routinely compared to the other discourses which I began by invoking (religion,

---

[19] See L. Trilling, 'Freud: Within and Beyond Culture', in *Beyond Culture: Essays on Literature and Learning* (Harmondsworth: Penguin, 1967), pp. 87–110; M. de Certeau, 'The Freudian Novel: History and Literature', in *Heterologies: Discourse on the Other*, trans. B. Massumi, foreword by W. Godzich (Minneapolis and London: University of Minnesota Press, 1986), pp. 17–34; R. Wollheim, 'Freud and the Understanding of Art', in J. Neu (ed.), *The Cambridge Companion to Freud* (Cambridge: Cambridge University Press, 1991), pp. 249–66; A. Badiou, 'Art and Philosophy', in *Handbook of Inaesthetics*, trans. A. Toscano (Stanford: Stanford University Press, 2005), pp. 1–15.

science and art), whether the claims are made with a positive or negative inflection, or whether psychoanalysis is thereby considered to be
wittingly or unwittingly, speciously or effectively so. I would much
rather hold, in a fashion analogous to Badiou's own circumscription of
certain fundamental discourses, that these are four quite different kinds
of practice. Of the major possible modes of conceiving the relationship
between two putatively different discourses, namely,

1. fusion (two discourses are really one and the same);
2. exclusion (one discourse must be excluded absolutely from genuine
   knowledge);
3. subsumption (one discourse must be subordinated to the dictates of
   the other); and
4. dissension (two discourses are irreducible),

only the last named of these is adequate to any examination of psychoanalysis, at any level. It is necessary to affirm the evidence of antagonism and polemic integral to psychoanalysis's experiences, theories
and histories, without believing or presuming from the start that such
antagonisms can or should be pacified. So if, as I wish to maintain,
the aforementioned discourses are indeed irreducible, it must also be
admitted that they are irremediably entangled. It is indubitable that
religion, science, art and philosophy constantly take each other up, mix
with each other, confront each other, confound each with each. Yet
this entanglement shouldn't inveigle us into capitulating to a thought of
their confusion or dissolution. Rather, as I am arguing here, there is a
fundamental sense in which philosophy and psychoanalysis are, unlike
their relatives, secondary, derivative discourses. They follow after and
are parasitic on the others. By the same token, they are also more fragile
and more sophisticated, and, as I have noted, unsustainable to the point
of impossibility. They both repudiate religion, as they couple art and
science – but this coupling takes place, as aforementioned, in different
directions.

Moreover, it is its special relationship with literature that renders psychoanalysis the most thoroughgoing form of antiphilosophy. According
to Badiou, Plato is properly the origin of philosophy insofar as he interrupted the claims of poetry (qua paradigm of mysterious unveiling) by
the claims of the matheme (qua paradigm of rigorous knowledge).[20]

---

[20] On this point, see A. Badiou, *Being and Event*, trans. O. Feltham (London: Continuum,
2005), and *Conditions, passim*. Note that one does not necessarily have to agree with
Badiou's characterisation in order to affirm its value as a heuristic device. Moreover,
if Badiou famously identifies four different discourses as the necessary conditions for

Rational knowledge (exemplified for Plato by geometry) curbs and supplants the irrational inspirations of literary effusion. For Freud, however, the situation is precisely the reverse. If philosophy interrupts the poem with the matheme, psychoanalysis interrupts the matheme with the poem. Psychoanalysis is therefore literally the *inversion* and *other side* of philosophy.[21] As it happens, both discourses are centrally concerned with science and literature – which is why they do indeed tend to share certain features – but they go in opposed directions. The ancient quarrel between philosophy and poetry of which Plato speaks in the *Republic* is here given an unprecedented twist. Philosophy interrupts literature with science, psychoanalysis science with literature.

This situation has another very important consequence. If both philosophy and psychoanalysis consider 'man' the speaking being *par excellence*, the conclusions they draw from this are radically different. This difference is perhaps clearest in their therapeutic aims – that is, their relation to the pedagogy of love. If philosophy has usually presented itself as the science of happiness insofar as it curbs the pathos of *poiesis* with the impassivity of *logos*, psychoanalysis, on the contrary, tries to tear the mask from *logos* and testify to the deranging suffering of the animal subjected to language. If the biological body is the basis for subjectivity, this hardly entails that the subjective causality psychoanalysis uncovers is reducible to the biological. Only literature is able to provide some of the tools necessary for exposing and analysing this.

So the question 'Why the literary?' for psychoanalysis can be given a psychoanalytic answer: the literary integrally engages the question of an enduring love which is, for psychoanalysis, precisely the cause of psychic-trouble. Symptoms are always symptoms of a disorder of love, love as disorder itself, a disorder that afflicts the pure biological body as it afflicts the expressions of that body. Even at its most therapeutically effective, psychoanalysis only promises to turn, as Freud says, neurotic misery into ordinary unhappiness. Lacan's version is just as funny: it is the phallus that is happy, not human beings. Perhaps this is better as a slogan: only psychoanalysis can make you *really* unhappy!

philosophy, namely art, science, love and politics, what is critical at this precise point is that it is art and science – in distinction from love and politics – that first and foremost make integral claims to a kind of knowledge that exceeds their own sites (in his terms, the Platonic struggle between sophistry as licensed by poetry and philosophy as licensing itself as a counter-discourse through mathematics).

21 This claim is consonant with the account given in Jacques Lacan's *Seminar XVII: The Other Side of Psychoanalysis*, trans. R. Grigg (New York: W. W. Norton & Co., 2007). For Lacan, philosophy is a support for the master's discourse, of which psychoanalysis, the analyst's discourse, is the *envers*, the 'other side'. Note, too, that philosophy's relation to literature might be, as Badiou has also noted, one of rejection and exclusion; as Badiou adds, rejection and exclusion nonetheless remain forms of relation.

Psychoanalysis is thus an antiphilosophy in the strongest possible sense of the word, and all the more because it is so by default, not by aim. Psychoanalysis doesn't begin with a negative programme of critique, of preliminary ground-clearing, but of affirmative clinical construction which, in the course of its elaboration, curbs the idealisms of philosophical beatitude.

This formula seeks not only to capture something essential about the *emergence* of the discourses of philosophy and psychoanalysis, but also to say something non-trivial about their *definition* (they both require science and literature) and their *antagonistic complicity* (they require science and literature in different ways). It also says something about the *resilient volatility* of both psychoanalysis and philosophy: precisely because both discourses live at the crossroads of incommensurables, they constantly run the risk of collapsing into one or the other, one into the other. It suggests why they share certain peculiar obsessions: above all, as I will try to show in the rest of this book, the themes of slavery, alienation and love. Finally, it suggests why, as has also been the case with philosophy, the history of the psychoanalytic movement has been marked by its ceaseless lapse into scientism, on the one hand, or a hermeneutic aestheticism, on the other. Such lapses are unavoidable, if deleterious. Yet they also enable one to see the really strong, still-operative forms of psychoanalysis that haven't given way on the scandal that is the unconscious insist on sustaining a relationship to both science and literature at once, even if they try to do this in their very different ways.

The seven chapters of this book were all originally published as stand-alone essays in collections and journals, over the first decade of the twenty-first century. Despite being marked by manifold contingencies, the red thread of antiphilosophy should nonetheless be evident throughout. The chapters deal expressly with major psychoanalytic or para-psychoanalytic thinkers, from Freud himself through Lacan to Jonathan Lear and Giorgio Agamben, in the service of identifying certain singular phenomena. In each chapter, I begin by outlining a basic intellectual-practical situation for psychoanalysis, in order to draw out some essential psychoanalytical themes, concepts and operations. The themes examined here include the phenomena of addiction-slavery, alienation-sexuality, transference-love and their avatars which, although central to both philosophy and psychoanalysis, are routinely overlooked by the experts and partisans of contemporary forms of learned ignorance. What will hopefully also become clear from this sequence of chapters is how a psychoanalyst or philosopher is enabled to certain insights or constrained to certain blindnesses, depending on the ways in which he or she, implicitly or explicitly, consciously or

unconsciously, configures the relationship between science and literature in attending to the matters of slavery, sexuality and love.

As a result, and perhaps surprisingly, many of the topics, concepts
and technical jargon familiar from the many schools of psychoanalysis, whether still active or long-defunct – such as 'fantasy', 'defence',
'paranoid-schizoid position', 'the Other' or what have you – do not
appear as such here. Rather, and despite the fact that my language and
terms are often not any the less technical or rebarbative, I attempt to
transduce many of the staple concepts of psychoanalysis into a different
set of references. Despite the polemical nature of several of my claims,
I wish to avoid internecine warfare insofar as that is possible. As psychoanalysis began by acknowledging, no one can ever really convince
anybody of anything – certainly not through reasoned argument.

Yet this very necessity introduces several irresolvable difficulties,
not least the problem of partiality. As the reader will have noticed, my
major psychoanalytical references are Lacanian. Yet my central thesis
here is not especially or restrictedly Lacanian: on the contrary, if this
study is clearly and crucially influenced by his work, the articulation
between literature and science that I outline holds across the diverse orientations of psychoanalysis. My account seeks to be clarifying but not
deterministic; if it has a discriminating function, it neither elaborates
taxonomies nor demands identification papers. Unfortunately, this
immediately raises another problem, for the form of the presentation
thereby comes to undermine its own arguments – the very clarity and
organisation of the propositions bespeaking the determinations of that
same philosophy I claim that psychoanalysis is against. This would be
bad enough in any case, but the vital rift that opens in the course of this
book is particularly unfortunate. For if psychoanalysis is an antiphilosophy, its only justification is that it does something other discourses
don't and can't. This justification is, finally, its non-intrusive therapeutic attentiveness to matters of slavery, sexuality and torture – much
more pressing and distressing in their patency than the academicism
of my central thesis can contain. The major problem in what follows
is therefore for the reader to act as Bruce Lee suggests in *Enter the
Dragon*, against an unavoidable tendency of the text itself: to look at
what the finger points to – and not just the finger itself. This, however,
is not a criticism of academicism; on the contrary, it is possibly only
through such academicism that certain deleterious aspects of slavery,
sexuality and torture can be discerned and exposed at all.

So the major aim of this study is to expose and justify the antiphilosophical singularity of psychoanalysis in its rickety auto-localisation
between science and literature. Psychoanalysis must always be a

radically unstable enterprise, and the literary is what keeps it so. As Tzara concludes the aforecited 'Monsieur AA', a provocateur and *litterateur* addressing the sensible *savants*:

> I'll eat your fingers a bit
> I'm renewing your subscription to the celluloid love that creaks like
> metal gates
> and you are idiots

Full stop.

1. *Listening or Dispensing? Sigmund Freud on Drugs*

> Indeed, if we find that an organ normally serving the purpose of sense-perception begins to behave like an actual genital when its erotogenic role is increased, we shall not regard it as improbable that *toxic* changes are also occurring in it.
>
> Sigmund Freud[1]

THE ORIGINS OF PSYCHOANALYSIS AS ANTIPHILOSOPHY

In this chapter, I will reread an overdetermined and complex event in the prehistory of psychoanalysis: Sigmund Freud's so-called 'cocaine episode' from the 1880s, in which, prior to entering private practice as a psychiatrist, Freud attempted a kind of reputational 'get-rich-quick' scheme, staking his scientific credentials on what has appeared to many subsequent commentators as unethical drug experimentation. While I re-examine this event by drawing on the requisite historical facts and secondary literature, my aim is different from that of a standard revisionist account. In fine, I wish to show something quite counter-intuitive: how Freud came to imagine the possibility of the isolation of language itself as a force for self-transformation, evading the problems of treating human psychology as if it were reducible to physiology. My argument is this: the alleged contemporary supplantation of talking cures by psychopharmacology is in no way scientific but rather takes place in the register of ethics; that the various ethical questions can be best staged by reconsidering the 'debate' in terms of 'listening' versus 'dispensing'; that attending to the situational emergence of this opposition in Freud

---

[1] S. Freud, 'The Psycho-Analytic View of Psychogenic Disturbances of Vision', in *The Standard Edition of the Complete Psychological Works of Sigmund Freud*, Vol. XI (1910), trans. J. Strachey et al. (London: The Hogarth Press, 1957), p. 218.

enables us to see that psychoanalysis is not a pre-pharmacological or pre-scientific enterprise, but in fact a post-pharmacological enterprise; that this inversion of the usual narrative also reveals certain themes in psychoanalysis that are usually underestimated if not entirely occluded, including addiction, an attention to non-standard orifices, the uses and abuses thereof, and a conceptual basis essentially articulated with political submission and subversion. I will conclude the chapter by drawing out some of the implications of its odd conception and birth for psychoanalysis considered as an antiphilosophy more generally.

THE PSYCHOPHARMACOLOGY OF EVERYDAY LIFE; OR, LISTENING VERSUS DISPENSING

Recently there have been a number of authorities who – from the inside of psychoanalysis itself – have suggested that the most forceful threat to psychoanalysis as a clinical practice is the present efflorescence and dominance of drug-based psychotherapies. Indeed, the astonishing public success of a physician such as Oliver Sacks – whose entire career would have been impossible without illicit pharmaceutical experimentation upon uninformed patients in the guise of authentic Hippocratic care – can stand as a particularly ambivalent index of just such a crisis. The case-study, a genre which Freud is often said to have invented and to which he certainly gave the decisive impetus, has become in Sacks's hands an unreflective celebration of the radiant sovereign power that legal access to, and distribution rights over, synthesised psychoactive substances can bequeath to the duly authorised representatives of the pharmaco-medical institution.[2] Sacks aside, John Forrester characterises this shift thus:

> the introduction of the psychotropic drugs in the 1950s, a new generation of tranquilizers shortly after (Librium, Valium), the anti-depressants of the 1960s and 1970s, and the mood-altering drugs of the 1980s, has entailed a significant shift in the practice of psychiatry. Yes, the new psychiatry went hand in hand with a shift of theoretical focus from psychological and psychoanalytical theories to neurological and psychopharmacological concerns.[3]

Forrester is concerned to show how psychoanalysis effectively functioned in the United States as, among other things, a kind of vanishing

[2] See, for instance, O. Sacks, *The Man Who Mistook His Wife for a Hat* (London: Picador, 1985).

[3] J. Forrester, 'Lessons from the Freud Wars', unpublished manuscript. All further references to Forrester's paper will be noted in the body of the text. I am grateful to David Bennett for bringing this text to my attention.

mediator in the 'shift from asylum- to office-based psychiatry'. Or, as he more memorably puts it, 'the real Freudian revolution was to bring psychiatrists out of the asylum'. It should probably be added that such a revolution would of course have been very different without the peculiarly ego-bolstering project of American psychoanalysis, against which someone like Jacques Lacan never ceased to polemicise. Nevertheless, despite the variety of historical, methodological and theoretical complicities, there is at least one apparently irreducible, foundational difference: under the psychopharmacological dispensation, the physician only talks to the patient in order to ensure that the drugs are having some kind of beneficial effect – and thus no longer has to *listen*, insofar as there is no longer any unconscious to be discerned in the pathological symptoms and inaudible interruptions of the subject's auto-verifications. Perhaps, as many have suggested, the 'talking cure' of the Viennese Witch-Doctor is thereby finally blown to quack heaven by the magic bullets of techno-pharmaceutical wizardry.[4]

Forrester's analysis has been echoed by other major psychoanalytic theorist-practitioners, such as Bruce Fink, Elie Ragland and Elisabeth Roudinesco, all of whom naturally deplore this situation, even if their condemnations take different forms and identify different causes.[5] Yet their different analyses come down to this: why listen when you can simply dispense? This is certainly one of the great mental health questions of our era. Take Peter Kramer's massive bestseller *Listening to Prozac*, whose success is itself one of the indices of the massive public shift towards the normalisation of drugs in the 1990s. Note how the very title attempts to reconfigure the distinction between 'listening' and 'dispensing', in favour of dispensing: Prozac is a wonder drug precisely because it is the drug that overcomes the very distinction – to the point that one now listens to it as if it were the true subject of depression.[6]

---

[4] Derrida's famous reading of Plato's *Phaedrus* is still an indispensable reference here, in its analysis of the etymological, historical and speculative links between the *pharmakon* (drug, remedy, poison), *pharmakeus* (magician) and *pharmakos* (scapegoat). See J. Derrida, *Dissemination*, trans. B. Johnson (Chicago: University of Chicago Press, 1981), pp. 61–171, and 'The Rhetoric of Drugs: An Interview', *differences*, 5:3 (1993), pp. 1–25.

[5] See E. Roudinesco, 'Anti-Freudian Revisionism Triumphant in the United States', trans. A. Lewis, *Virtuosity: The Newsletter of the Australasian Society for Continental Philosophy*, 4 (March 1997), p. 4; E. Ragland, *Essays on the Pleasures of Death: From Freud to Lacan* (New York: Routledge, 1995), esp. p. 106; B. Fink, *A Clinical Introduction to Lacanian Psychoanalysis: Theory and Technique* (Cambridge: Harvard University Press, 1997), p. 116. See also p. 252, n. 70.

[6] Kramer's book (and others like it) has inspired some bilious responses. See, among others, the dialogue between Zoë Heller and Roy Porter, 'The Chemistry of Happiness', in S. Dunn et al. (eds), *Mind Readings: Writers' Journeys Through Mental States* (London: Minerva, 1996), pp. 165–75; and D. Healy's *Let Them Eat Prozac: The Unhealthy Relationship between the Pharmaceutical Industry and Depression* (New York: New York University Press, 2004).

Certainly, as Mikkel Borch-Jacobsen has noted in the context of the new drug-therapies:

> Admittedly, SSRIs sometimes lead to diminished libido and even, among men, to impotence, but that is surely a small price to pay for a restored capacity for happiness. Twenty million people worldwide are thought to be taking Prozac, and we are hearing reports of a new era of 'cosmetic psychopharmacology,' in which drugs will be used to treat not only depression, but daily mood swings and existential angst. So farewell Kierkegaard and Heidegger.[7]

Instead of psychoanalysis, then, it is 'Big Pharma', the *DSM-V* (the planned fifth edition of the American Psychiatric Association's *Diagnostic and Statistical Manual of Mental Disorders*, impending at the time of writing), cognitive behavioural therapy and rigorous cost-efficiency exigencies which determine mental health delivery in the first world. This doesn't just mean that there won't be any more free analyses for poor people, but marks a decisive shift in the conception, development and provision of psychological care: belief in the transformative and therapeutic powers of talk now appears thoroughly archaic if not simply deluded. Why talk – or, indeed, listen – when you can get yourself irradiated, do your six sessions of CBT homework, and pop pills? Rather than listening to patients, why not 'listen to Prozac', which undoubtedly has much happier things to say and cheerier news to convey than sufferers themselves? And rather than relying upon such notoriously unfalsifiable theoretical constructs as 'the Oedipal complex' or 'the anal character', the elementary particles of our acronymic mental universe have morphed into SSRIs, MRIs and PETs. As for subjectivity, who needs it when you can see people's brains grinding away in full living colour on a plasma TV? The effects of brain lesions caused by accident or disease – some of which, until recently, could only be revealed by autopsy, too late for the sufferers – can now be watched on-screen. Changes in electrical conductance, potentials and magnetic fields in the brain can be registered, monitored, recorded and analysed with unprecedented accuracy in real time. Developments in molecular neurobiology permit the 'knock-out' of particular genes in order to test physical and psychological consequences.

What these new technologies enable is not only the visualisation of previously invisible phenomena, nor just their depiction in greater detail, nor simply their recording with greater accuracy than previously – although all of this is the case. Nor is this just a quantum leap in the capacity to correlate results in one discipline with those in another,

---

[7] M. Borch-Jacobsen, 'Psychotropicana', *London Review of Books*, 11 July 2002, pp. 17–18.

to bring together disparate research from all over the globe with an unprecedented rapidity. Rather, for the first time, brain, mind and behaviour can be studied simultaneously, *in situ*. It is this synchronisation of the study of material, consciousness and activity that conditions the most exciting developments. As Antonio Damasio puts it, 'The organism's private mind, the organism's public behavior, and its hidden brain can thus be joined in the adventure of theory, and out of the adventure come hypotheses that can be tested experimentally, judged on their merits, and subsequently endorsed, rejected, or modified.'[8] The discoveries these technologies have permitted about the development, structure, function and activity of the brain have rendered older hypotheses obsolete, as they have suggested radical new ones. When individual psychological disturbances or singular behaviours start being traced to brain lesions or to mutant genes, we are no longer in a world of humanistic concerns, but in the regime of biological determinism. As Mark Solms notes, 'The modern neuroscientific quest to solve the mystery of consciousness . . . involves an attitude to human subjectivity directly antithetical to the psychoanalytic attitude.'[9]

In lieu of psychoanalysis, then, we get such cognitive psychological propositions as the following, in Jonathan Lear's acerbic characterisation of this phenomenon:

- That we can find out all we need to know about human behaviour and motivation by conducting polls, examining democratic votes, choices made in the market-place, and changing fashions. In short, human motivation is essentially transparent.
- That all human disagreements are in principle resolvable through rational conversation and mutual understanding.
- That we have reached the 'end of history'.
- That all serious psychological problems will soon be treatable either by drugs or neurosurgery.
- The only form of psychotherapy that is needed is rational conversation.[10]

And, finally, that:

- 'Freud is dead': his account of a 'talking cure' – psychoanalysis – has about as much validity as invoking Zeus.[11]

[8] A. Damasio, *The Feeling of What Happens: Body, Emotion, and the Making of Consciousness* (New York: Random House, 2000), p. 15.
[9] M. Solms, 'What is Consciousness?', JAPA, 45:3 (1996), p. 682.
[10] J. Lear, *Freud* (New York and London: Routledge, 2005), p. 2.
[11] Lear, *Freud*, p. 3.

Is, however, the difference between listening and dispensing really as irreducible as psychoanalysts' and psychopharmacologists' investments in their own respective projects compel them to assert? A number of possible procedures for reconfiguring this apparent discord can immediately be conceived. It might, for instance, be possible to demonstrate how various notions ultimately consonant with that of the 'unconscious' remain entirely acceptable, and are even explicitly welcomed, in the work of the psychopharmacologists themselves – even if, for whatever reasons, they cannot accept this very particular name. Or one could compare the actual procedures of both psychiatrists and psychoanalysts, in order to show that, whatever they may say about their own work, their conceptual differences are subtended by a fundamental similarity of practice. Or one might attempt to show that, philosophically speaking, all such differences are, finally, 'co-supplementary' and irresolvable, certainly, but nevertheless unthinkable and impracticable except when conceived in the hostile intimacy of their adversarial relationship.

Yet the confusion of the current situation tends to elide the fact that the coupled motifs of drug-treatment and addiction have always been central, not only to Freud himself, but consequently also to the discipline which he founded. Furthermore, this centrality has, for the most part, and for a number of reasons, most often been ignored, forgotten, repressed or foreclosed by writers in and on psychoanalysis, even before the explosion of modern drug-treatments for mental (and addictive) disorders. For psychoanalysis has its origins in a cocaine scandal. These scandalous origins are not simply of the order of Freud's early anatomical work on, say, sexing eels. This is because the residues of the cocaine scandal continue to determine Freud's life and work in the key moments in his development of psychoanalysis, to the point where the dream of Irma's injection – psychoanalysis's 'dream of dreams' – circulates around Freud's scandalous failure.[12] That psychoanalysts have problems with this relation is indicated by the fact that Freud's cocaine papers never made it into the *Standard Edition*, and, indeed, remained untranslated and scattered until 1963.[13]

[12] For a far less positive account of Freud's cocaine daze, see E. M. Thornton, *The Freudian Fallacy* (New York: The Dial Press, 1983).

[13] R. Byck, 'Introduction: Sigmund Freud and Cocaine', in S. Freud, *Cocaine Papers*, ed. R. Byck (New York: Stonehill Publishing, 1974), p. xvii. Byck continues: 'Freud shows himself to have been a far more astute observer than many other physicians of his time. He was correct in his prompt classification of cocaine as *both* a central nervous system stimulant and an euphoriant' (p. xxiv); and 'all of Freud's papers on cocaine can be said to be thorough in their review, accurate in their physiological and psychological experimentation, and almost prescient in their consideration of points which have become major issues in modern psychopharmacology' (p. xxvi).

These motifs bear integrally on the very foundations, limits, status and legitimacy of the Freudian and post-Freudian corpus, and in ways that are necessarily – if for very Freudian reasons – inconsistently accessible and almost unthematisable within that corpus itself. My argument will thus have recourse to details, events and structures that are at once empirical, biographical, historical, technological and philosophical, in order to demonstrate the critical role that drugs and addiction have played in the genesis of psychoanalysis, and thence to trace some of their subsequent effects. I will suggest that:

1. historically speaking, without drugs having been made a problem for Freud, psychoanalysis would not and could never have been invented;
2. as a result, a kind of fantasmatic 'Other Scene' of unspeakable 'addiction' provides the covert a priori motivation, material and support for psychoanalysis;
3. to the extent that it remains necessarily unanalysed, this non-place of addiction continues to affect, in an often illegible and subterranean form, the subsequent re-elaborations of psychoanalysis itself.[14]

FREUD ON DRUGS

It would, of course, be impossible to speak of Freud's relation to drugs without mentioning his own notorious penchant for cigars. A keen smoker throughout his life, he also periodically tried to give up and was continually in anguish over the smoking-addiction that he evidently couldn't shake. As Peter Gay notes of Freud's cigars:

> He was fatally addicted to them; when in the early 1890s Fliess – after all, a nose and throat specialist – proscribed them to clear up Freud's nasal catarrhs, Freud was in despair and pathetically pleaded for relief. He had begun smoking at twenty-four, at first cigarettes, but soon only cigars. He claimed that this 'habit or vice,' as he called it, greatly enhanced his capacity for work and his ability to muster self-control.[15]

Despite the manifold physical problems that this vice inflicted upon Freud, it didn't at all prevent him from proselytising for smoking: there

---

14 As Avital Ronell asks, 'What if "drugs" named a special mode of addiction, however, or the structure that is philosophically and metaphysically at the basis of our culture?'; *Crack Wars: Literature, Addiction, Mania* (Lincoln: University of Nebraska Press, 1992), p. 13. Hereafter referred to as 'CW'.

15 P. Gay, *Freud: A Life for Our Time* (New York: W. W. Norton & Co., 1988), p. 169. Hereafter referred to as 'LT'.

is a story of him offering a cigarette to his seventeen-year-old nephew Harry, which was refused; whereupon Freud avuncularly declared, 'My boy, smoking is one of the greatest and cheapest enjoyments in life, and if you decide in advance not to smoke, I can only feel sorry for you.'[16] Smoking even became a topic for scholarly reflection: at the first session of the Wednesday Psychological Society in the autumn of 1902 – attended by Stekel, Kahane, Reitler, Adler and Rank, among others – the assembled luminaries discussed the question of 'the psychological impact of smoking'. Finally, of course, Freud developed jaw and throat cancer as a direct consequence of his habit and, after a series of excruciatingly painful operations, was forced to wear a prosthesis for his last years. Interestingly enough, and despite the pain from his operations, Freud consistently refused to touch the opiates that would have provided him with relief. The rest of this chapter will attempt to provide a context for this notable refusal.

Most interpretations of Freud's 'addiction' have, naturally enough, tended to elaborate themselves in Freudian terms. However, if, as Forrester confirms, 'we all know that Freud spent his working life sucking penises', we also all know that sometimes a cigar is just a cigar (but what *is* a cigar?). Whilst this cigar-addiction is undoubtedly the most familiar and pronounced example of substance-abuse in Freud's life and work, he not only consistently enjoyed other drugs – notably alcohol and caffeine – but, during the period from around 1884 to 1895, he regularly ingested cocaine, a drug whose availability and popularity was on the rise in Europe at that time.

In fact, cocaine seems to have served quite a variety of interconnected functions in Freud's life. Ronald Clark relates an anecdote from 1886, after Freud had gone to Paris to study with Charcot:

> Once it was decided that he should translate Charcot's two volumes of papers, Freud was quietly brought into a new social circle by way of the splendid Tuesday evening receptions held for the smart world of Paris at Charcot's home on the Boulevard Saint-Germain. As he prepared for the first of these ordeals, he was nervous enough to fortify himself with cocaine.[17]

Writing to his fiancée, Martha, regarding his *dressage* on that first night, Freud jokingly bragged that 'I looked very fine and made a favourable impression on myself'. He not only drank beer and coffee along with everyone else, but, as he further confesses, 'smoked like a chimney, and felt very much at ease without the slightest mishap occurring . . . These

[16] Cited in LT, p. 170.
[17] R. Clark, *Freud: The Man and the Cause* (London: Jonathan Cape, 1980), p. 75. Hereafter referred to as 'MC'.

were my achievements (or rather the achievements of cocaine) which left me very satisfied.'[18]

Freud, indeed, was so struck by the supernatural powers of cocaine that he quickly found himself compelled to impose it on his friends and colleagues, prescribe it to his patients, and run a battery of rather unscientific tests on its possible uses, effects and affects. He thus participated in cocaine-use (and drug-use more generally) in a number of characteristic ways: for aesthetic pleasure; as a personality-supplement; as an enhancer of physical and mental performance; as a dubious medical treatment for various physical ailments; and as a crucial element in the formation and maintenance of social community – although, interestingly, he did not explicitly affirm its value as a speculative 'operator of infinity'. For the pre-psychoanalytic Freud, then, cocaine not only healed the sick and almost raised the dead, it also provided surplus pleasure, social confidence and physical and mental strength without demanding anything in return.

Despite this familiar diversity of uses, what is specifically of interest here is Freud's attempt to link his professional status and reputation – hence his name – with the magical properties of this particular substance.[19] Furthermore, the white magic of this foreign substance resided, for Freud, not only in its supposed uniquely beneficial effects on human physiology, but, more surprisingly, in its power to interrupt the deleterious compulsions to which other similar but implicitly more dangerous drugs subject their users. For Freud would also recommend cocaine as the royal road to a successful cure for morphine-addiction, a recommendation that quickly (and unsurprisingly) ended in his abject failure and public humiliation.[20] I will examine the details of this failure in the following section, but before doing so I want to re-mark a number of points that are of major import for any account of the relation of psychoanalysis to addiction.

First, the period during which Freud is loudly singing the praises of cocaine is immediately prior to the development of psychoanalysis;

---

[18] Cited in MC, p. 75.

[19] 'Magic' is Freud's own word for cocaine's efficacy. As he writes in a letter to Martha, dated 2 June 1884, 'Woe to you, my Princess, when I come. I will kiss you quite red and feed you till you are plump. And if you are forward you shall see who is the stronger, a gentle little girl who doesn't eat enough or a big wild man who has cocaine in his body. In my last severe depression I took coca again and a small dose lifted me to the heights in a wonderful fashion. I am just now busy collecting the literature for a song of praise to this *magical substance*' (my emphasis); cited in E. Jones, *Sigmund Freud: Life and Work. Volume One: The Young Freud 1856–1900* (London: The Hogarth Press, 1956), p. 93. Hereafter referred to as 'LW'.

[20] As Ronell puts it, Freud, 'for the sake of some unplumbable purpose, staked his early career entirely on cocaine and on the essays devoted to cocaine. As a result . . . Freud was publicly reprimanded and privately assailed'; CW, p. 52.

as James Bakalar and Lester Grinspoon point out, 'Freud continued to prescribe cocaine until at least 1895, the year of his self-analysis, for topical application to the nasal mucous membranes, and he used it himself for sinusitis.'[21] In less than a year, then, Freud abandons cocaine at the very moment that he is inventing a rather less substantial, if more significant, cure of his own. This apparently merely empirical supersession of one magical cure by another nonetheless had a deep and lasting effect on psychoanalytic theory.

Second, in spite of Freud's initial enthusiasm, psychoanalysis thereafter engages in no extended discussion of cocaine-use, or indeed of its fraught relationship to the question of addiction in general (as we shall see, and for a variety of reasons, Freud constantly elides or confuses the differences between the acceptable *use* and the toxic *ab-use* of this drug). Certainly, the question of drugs does not disappear altogether; as Forrester writes,

> Freud recognizes the fundamental service intoxicants render to human beings in their pursuit of happiness. And he classed them with humour and mystical states of consciousness as possessing a fundamental human dignity. We might conclude that intoxicants are as distinctive a part of human life as our gift for creative sexual perversion. There is, in addition, Freud's hilarious but utterly serious observation that humans are better suited to fidelity to their intoxicants than they are to their sexual objects; a marriage to a Burgundy is always more constant and satisfying than a marriage to a Blonde.[22]

Nevertheless, Freud would also, as aforementioned, later come to denounce the use of drugs in psychiatric treatments, claiming, somewhat contradictorily, that their effects – like those of hypnosis – were at once purely cosmetic, unreliable and a toxic assault on the patient's will.[23]

Furthermore, Freud's acknowledgement of the genuine role played by intoxicants in an 'aesthetics of profane illumination'[24] is a long way from anything resembling addiction. Indeed, if psychoanalysis speaks of addiction at all, it is often anxiously, uncomprehendingly, and in passing – and in order to exclude it from psychoanalysis's legitimate field of operations.[25] Certainly, Freud would consider that addicts

[21] J. Bakalar and L. Grinspoon, *Cocaine: A Drug and Its Social Evolution* (New York: Basic Books, 1976), p. 35. Hereafter referred to as 'BG'.
[22] Forrester, 'Lessons from the Freud Wars'.
[23] See, for instance, the 1917 essay 'Analytic Theory', in S. Freud, *The Complete Introductory Lectures on Psychoanalysis*, trans. J. Strachey (Cambridge: The Belknap Press, 1971), p. 449.
[24] The phrase is derived from Walter Benjamin's essay on 'Surrealism', in *Reflections: Essays, Aphorisms, Autobiographical Writings*, ed. with intro. by P. Demetz, trans. E. Jephcott (New York: Schocken Books, 1986), pp. 177–92.
[25] In Reuben Fine's *A History of Psychoanalysis* (New York: Columbia University Press, 1979), there is a third of a page dedicated to the question of 'Alcoholism and Addiction' (p. 409). Not a bad result, really, after 100 years and over 686 pages!

share 'the charm of cats and birds of prey in their inaccessibility, their apparent libidinal autonomy',[26] but it is precisely this very 'charm' that verifies that they are inappropriate candidates for psychoanalysis. As Freud writes of addicts in a 1916 letter to Ferenczi, 'it is too easy for them to cling to the security of their drug'.[27] This is a judgement that could only be repeated later by Lacan: 'Addiction opens a field where none of the subject's utterances are reliable, and he escapes analysis.'[28] However, it is also necessary to add that this exclusion of addiction from psychotherapeutic practice is founded on the prejudice that addiction's aetiology is nevertheless, in principle, eminently explicable at the level of theory (even if this step is never de facto taken). In this regard, it is truly symptomatic that cocaine (and/or addiction) remains for the most part unmentioned in almost every account of the Freudian corpus and concepts, other than the biographical. And none of these biographies are quite sure what to do with it – typically, they note its importance and obvious continuing influence on Freud (without dealing adequately with the details of such an 'influence'), and yet simultaneously try to limit its significance, as in, for example, Jones's restriction of the 'cocaine episode' to 1884–7.[29] I have already mentioned that the articles Freud published on cocaine were not reprinted in the *Standard Edition*, notwithstanding the inclusion of any number of juvenile or occasional writings in these volumes.

Third, this exclusion of addiction links it, first, with the analogous problems posed for psychoanalysis by the liminal non-figures that are paranoids and psychotics, and, second, with any number of the famous speculative concepts later adumbrated by Freud: acting-out, melancholia, mania, repetition-compulsion, death-drive. But addiction thereby

[26] B. Geraud, cited in P. Spiriot, 'Psychanalyse, drogue: le malentendu', in Spiriot (ed.), *Sigmund Freud et la drogue* (Monaco: Éditions du Rocher, 1987), p. 16.

[27] Cited in L. Albrand, 'Freud et le panegyrique de la cocaïne', in Spiriot (ed.), *Sigmund Freud et la drogue*, p. 43. In an essay mainly dedicated to the case of the little-known Brunswick siblings, Paul Roazen writes, 'It turned out that a central reason for literary reticence about Ruth Brunswick was the extent to which, under Freud's care, she had become addicted to drugs; at one point in Vienna she even put herself in a sanatorium to help overcome her dependency . . . Addicts, like perverts, were in principle deemed to be outside the scope of neurosis, and therefore inaccessible to psychoanalytic influence'; 'Freud's Patients: First-Person Accounts', in T. Gelfand and J. Kerr (eds), *Freud and the History of Psychoanalysis* (London: The Analytic Press, 1992), pp. 297–8.

[28] See J. Lacan, *Écrits*, trans. B. Fink et al. (New York: W. W. Norton & Co., 2006). Revealingly, despite Deleuze and Guattari's affirmation of the figure of the 'schizophrenic' in *Anti-Oedipus* and *A Thousand Plateaus* against the 'neurotic' of psychoanalysis, they nevertheless denounce the drug-addict as 'botching the BwO'. See G. Deleuze and F. Guattari, *A Thousand Plateaus: Capitalism and Schizophrenia*, trans. and foreword by B. Massumi (Minneapolis: University of Minnesota Press, 1987), esp. p. 163.

[29] Indeed, a recent biography of Freud in English simply rehashes the most minimal and familiar details. See L. Breger, *Freud: Darkness in the Midst of Vision* (New York: John Wiley, 2000).

also communicates with other psychoanalytic categories, procedures and practices that may at first seem utterly unrelated to any of these – for example, transference-love, or, perhaps rather more obscurely, the problem that the nose always posed for Freud. As I will want to ask, perhaps bizarrely: why is there no nasal phase in psychoanalysis? But before I examine these points further, it is necessary to look more closely at the details of what Ernest Jones, perhaps a little too flippantly, names Freud's 'cocaine episode'.

THE THIRD SCOURGE, OR 'AN EXCELLENT THING FOR A LONG WALK'

In 1884, a young and ambitious Sigmund Freud completed his medical studies and became an assistant at the Laboratory of Experimental Medicine at the University of Vienna. Freud, indeed, was notoriously ambitious: as Jones relates, 'during the three hospital years Freud was constantly occupied with the endeavour to make a name for himself by discovering something important in either clinical or pathological medicine'.[30] And it was in the course of what Freud himself sardonically called this 'chase after money, position, and reputation' that he first became interested in cocaine.[31] This interest was not especially unusual for the period. Despite the ubiquitous public hysteria today regarding cocaine's production, distribution and supposed abuse; its links to contemporary imperialism, organised crime and military interventions; and the moral, medical and legal prohibitions and exhortations that ensure that cocaine will remain a banned and demonic substance for the foreseeable future, it was not subjected to any governmental regulation anywhere until the US Pure Food and Drug Act of 1906, which restricted the importation of coca leaf and required all medicines containing cocaine or opium to be properly labelled. So it was certainly not the law of the state that got Freud into big trouble; indeed, it was barely a law at all. I have already flagged Freud's own personal use of the drug, but it was the public declarations that he made in its favour that precipitated a rather unpleasant response.

According to Ernest Jones, Freud first mentions cocaine in a letter of 21 April 1884, in which he writes,

> I have been reading about cocaine, the essential constituent of coca leaves which some Indian tribes chew to enable them to resist privations and hardships . . . I am procuring some myself and will try it with cases of heart

---

[30] LW, p. 86.
[31] Cited in LT, p. 44.

disease and also of nervous exhaustion, particularly in the miserable condition after the withdrawal of morphium (Dr. Fleischl). Perhaps others are working at it; perhaps nothing will come of it. But I shall certainly try it, and you know that when one perseveres sooner or later one succeeds. We do not need more than one such lucky hit for us to be able to think of setting up house.[32]

Impressed by Theodor Aschenbrandt's studies of the effects of cocaine on the human body, and by US reports of its efficacity in the treatment of morphine-addiction, Freud proceeded to acquire a gram of cocaine, at unexpected expense, from the Merck chemical factory. After running a number of dubious 'experiments' (of which more below), he published a first essay on the substance, 'Über Coca', in the *Centralblatt für die gesammte Therapie* of July 1884.[33] In this text he lists a number of its benefits for health, as observed by himself and by other authorities, praises its varied effects (the abolition of fatigue, feelings of euphoria, suppression of appetite, its aphrodisiac properties, etc.), and outlines a number of its possible medical uses – as a physical and mental stimulant, as a psychiatric drug (in the treatment of hysteria, hypochondria, melancholic inhibition, stupor, etc.), and as a treatment for digestive disorders, for cachexia (anaemia, phthisis), and even for asthma and syphilis.[34] Furthermore, as he writes in a passage that was scientifically and ethically suspect even then:

> It seems probable, in the light of reports which I shall refer to later, that coca, if used protractedly but in moderation, is not detrimental to the body. Von Anrep treated animals for thirty days with moderate doses of cocaine and detected no detrimental effects on their bodily functions. It seems to me noteworthy – and I discovered this in myself and in other observers who were capable of judging such things – that a first dose or even repeated doses of coca produce no compulsive desire to use the stimulant further; on the contrary, one feels a certain unmotivated aversion to the substance.[35]

But it was the following sections of Freud's paper that ultimately caused the biggest problems: coca in the treatment of morphine- and alcohol-addiction. Drawing on American research published in such reputable journals as the *Detroit Therapeutic Gazette* and *Louisville Medical News*, Freud claims that 'there are some sixteen reports of cases in which the patient has been successfully cured of addiction; in

---

[32] Cited in LW, p. 88.
[33] LW, p. 90.
[34] For example: 'Among the person [*sic*] to whom I have given coca, three reported violent sexual excitement which they unhesitatingly attributed to the coca'; S. Freud, 'Coca', in J. Miller and R. Koral (eds), *White Rabbit: A Psychedelic Reader* (San Francisco: Chronicle Books, 1995), p. 173. Hereafter referred to as 'UC'.
[35] UC, p. 161.

only one instance is there a report of failure of coca to alleviate morphine addiction.'[36] He continues: 'the treatment of morphine addiction
with coca does not, therefore, result merely in the exchange of one kind
of addiction for another – it does not turn the morphine addict into
a *coquero*; the use of coca is only temporary.'[37] Furthermore, Freud
would also recommend the use of injections in the administration of
cocaine.

Following Jean Hyppolite, Lacan notes that, whereas Freud's anatomical researches were successful, his physiological ones (i.e. his
cocaine trials) were extremely weak.[38] At the same time, as Robert
Byck remarks, 'When first I read the papers, I at once realized that they
establish Sigmund Freud as one of the founders of psychopharmacology' (p. xvii). Freud remains so problematic for histories of sexuality,
drugs, psychology and so on, precisely because he grafts imbricated but
incommensurable institutions onto each other: is he a scientist or a lit-
térateur? Is he a great discoverer or a cunning huckster? Such questions
aside, other commentators note that, although Freud was very attentive
to the aesthetic uses of cocaine, he ignored – strangely enough – its
anaesthetic possibilities, for instance, in surgery.

This is a crucial point. Freud completed his article, mentioned his
interest in the drug to a friend, Leopold Konigstein, then decided to
visit his fiancée, Martha Bernays. By the time he'd got back from his
trip, it was all over: an associate of his and Konigstein's, Carl Koller,
had shown how cocaine could function as an effective anaesthetic in
eye surgery. Freud was incredibly bitter about Koller's triumph – he
even later wrote 'it was my fiancée's fault if I did not become famous
in those early years' – but his disappointment did not stop him from
taking cocaine himself for such things as stomach upsets, nose infections, exhaustion, or to make himself 'feel more like a man', and it
didn't stop him prescribing it for others. Unfortunately, he also recommended it to his friend Ernst von Fleischl-Marxow, who had become

---

[36] UC, p. 170.

[37] UC, p. 171.

[38] 'Hyppolite alludes to the fact that the anatomical works of Freud could be considered as
successes, and have been sanctioned as such. In contrast, when he works on the physiological level, he seems to have shown a certain disinterest. This is one of the reasons why he
had not plumbed the import of the discovery of cocain. His physiological investigation was
weak, because it remained too close to therapeutics. Freud busied himself with the use of
cocaine as an analgesic, and left aside its anaesthetic value'; J. Lacan, *Le Séminaire: livre
I: Les écrits techniques de Freud* (Paris: Éditions du Seuil, 1975), p. 34. Yet, as Siegfried
Bernfeld has noted in 'Freud's Studies on Cocaine', reproduced in *Cocaine Papers*, 'In spite
of his poor experimental technique he discovered a fact of basic importance unknown
at that time, namely the existence of two independent variables in the curve of muscular
strength'; Freud, *Cocaine Papers*, p. 338 (first published in *Journal of the American
Psychoanalytic Association*, 4:1 (October 1953).

addicted to morphine as a painkiller following the amputation of one of his thumbs; within a few days Ernst couldn't stop using the substance, and he eventually died as Europe's first official cocaine addict.

Freud's recommendation of cocaine injections is extremely important for a number of reasons: it was this hypodermic recommendation which got him into especial trouble when cocaine rapidly started getting a bad name as the 'third scourge of humanity' (after alcohol and morphine).[39] This phrase was popularised by Albrecht Erlenmeyer, one of the most influential psychiatrists of the era, and was quickly taken up, not only by a number of other physicians working on morphine and alcohol abuse, but also by the popular press. It thus marks the moment of the crystallisation and consolidation of a recognisably contemporary discourse of addiction; it is also the beginning of the enthusiastic social daemonisation of so-called addictive substances, that is, those whose supposed harm derives from nothing more than this very potentiality.

All in all, then, the 'cocaine episode' proved 'the most sombre of [Freud's] life'.[40] His research had been exposed as outrageously unscientific, his most admired friend was addicted and paranoiac (due, in part, to Freud's intervention), his marriage plans had to be delayed, a rival had become world-famous for the development of cocaine anaesthesia in surgery, and the Viennese medical establishment heaped opprobrium upon Freud's name and work. In one stroke, Freud had managed to fail scientifically, reputationally, economically, professionally and personally.

And yet, as always, such public controversy had ambivalent effects. For if, as Ronald Clark points out, 'when [Freud] set up practice in 1886 he at first tended to be remembered in some medical circles not as the doctor who had discovered the anesthetizing value of cocaine but as the man who had let loose the third scourge',[41] it is also the case that 'the first patient who came to [Freud] on his own and not through the recommendations of a colleague had been attracted by the writings on cocaine'.[42] It is also worth mentioning the interest taken by big drug companies in Freud's research, an interest which foreshadows the

---

[39] Very quickly, there came a number of attacks in the medical press. Indeed, for some time there had been a simmering controversy regarding the use of those newly synthesised substances, following Dr E. Levinstein's publication of *Die Morphiumsucht nach Eigenen Beobachtungen* (translated into English in 1878 as *Morbid Craving for Morphia*): 'Levinstein's book was based on his own experiences in the institutional treatment of addiction in Berlin, and was instrumental in defining "morphinism" as a separate condition or disease'; V. Berridge and G. Edwards, *Opium and the People: Opiate Use in Nineteenth-Century England* (New York: Allen Lane/St. Martin's Press, 1981), p. 142.

[40] Cited in Albrand, 'Freud et le panegyrique de la cocaine', p. 39.

[41] MC, p. 62.

[42] BG, p. 34.

crucial links between multinational pharmaceutical companies and the medical institution today. For example, it was in response to Freud's and Fleischl-Marxow's writings on cocaine that the Parke Davis company put out a pamphlet, 'Coca Erythroxylon and Its Derivatives', which declared 'If these [Freud's and Fleischl-Marxow's] claims are Substantiated ... [cocaine] will indeed be the most important therapeutic discovery of the age, the benefit of which to humanity will be incalculable',[43] and the Merck chemical firm invited Freud to 'road-test' their new alkaloid ecgnonin, derived from cocaine, and sent him one hundred complimentary grams.

STICKING YOUR NOSE WHERE IT'S NOT WANTED

Not only does the cocaine catastrophe affect all registers of Freud's life and work in the 1880s and 1890s, but it also overlaps with and imposes itself on the development and structure of psychoanalysis itself. Strangely enough, the privileged conduit for this massively complicated and overdetermined transmission seems to be, of all things, the nose. There are three reasons of particular importance here.

First, the rather confused associations between the nose and the male genitals that remain a staple not only of contemporary popular culture but of scientific discourse as well, and had been so for centuries.[44] For example, as William Acton, one of the most influential British medical practitioners in the third quarter of the nineteenth century and a major figure in the implementation of the notorious Contagious Disease Acts, writes in his *Functions and Diseases of the Reproductive Organs* (by which he means the penis), 'During my researches, I have occasionally been struck with the inaccuracy of the school-boy doggerel, "*Nosciture e labris quantum sit virginis antrum, Nosciture naso quanta sit hasta viro*", and when I have noticed a man with a large organ, I have often looked to see if he had a prominent nose. I feel confident that the

---

[43] Cited in BG, p. 22.

[44] This association is more than simply folkloric. In Sandor Gilman's words, 'The idea that the nasal cavities were anatomically parallel to the genitalia grew out of the study of human embryology during the nineteenth century. As early as G. Valentin's 1835 handbook of human development, the parallels in the development of soft-tissue areas and cavities of the fetus had been noted. By the time of the publication of the standard atlas of human embryological development by Wilhelm His in 1885, the assumption of such parallels was at the center of European embryology ... embryology also proved that the formation of the nasal passages and the incipient genitalia happened very early in the development of the fetus'; Gilman, *Disease and Representation: Images of Illness from Madness to AIDS* (Ithaca: Cornell University Press, 1988), p. 188. Hereafter referred to as 'DR'. A contemporary scientific variant of this scientific association focuses on the apparently profound physiological similarities between orgasms and sneezing.

proverb involves a vulgar error.'[45] If Acton's researches bizarrely meant that he would look first at the genitals and only secondly at the face of their nominal possessor, it was probably more common to see the one and not the other, and only then to speculate knowingly on the basis of the visible facial evidence as to the relative masculinity and potency connoted by the unseen organ. What is also suggestive in such formulations is the semiotic confusion that the nose seems to provoke. In the terms of the philosopher C. S. Peirce's tripartite division of signs – between the index, the icon and the symbol[46] – the nose, in its own way, seems to be all three: as index, it points towards the unseen genitals with which it is causally linked; as icon, it supposedly resembles the aforementioned genitalia; as symbol, it connotes virility. So there are already a number of noteworthy aspects: the nose is acknowledged primarily in terms of visible size, and that only because of what it somewhat obscenely points to. Its function as an organ – what it can *do* – is thereby immediately subordinated to what it looks like.

Which brings me to my second point. For virility is not all a large nose comes to symbolise, and especially not in *fin de siècle* Vienna. The problem here is that if a large nose immediately connotes abundant masculinity, this is not such a good look: (1) if you're a woman; and (2) given its widespread association with a certain pariah race, the Jews. As Sandor Gilman puts it:

> The association between the Jewish nose and the circumcised penis was made in the crudest and most revolting manner during the 1880s. In the streets of Berlin and Vienna, in penny-papers or on the newly installed 'Litfassaulen', or advertising columns, caricatures of Jews could be seen. These extraordinary caricatures stressed one central aspect of the physiognomy of the Jewish male, his nose, which represented that hidden sign of his sexual difference, his circumcised penis. For the Jews' sign of sexual difference, their sexual selectiveness, as an indicator of their identity was, as Friedrich Nietzsche strikingly observed in *Beyond Good and Evil*, the focus of the Germans' fear of the superficiality of their recently created national identity. This fear was represented in caricatures by the elongated nose.[47]

Hence, of course, the theme of 'The Jew's Two Noses'. I have adapted this from a phrase of Ben Hecht's – who was, incidentally, one of the screenwriters for *Gone with the Wind* – who published something called *A Guide for the Bedevilled* in 1945. It is basically an angry account of

[45] W. Acton, *The Functions and Disorders of the Reproductive Organs in Youth, in Adult Age, and in Advanced Life Considered in their Physiological, Social, and Psychological Relations*, 2nd edn (London: John Churchill, 1858), p. 30.
[46] C. S. Peirce, *Philosophical Writings of Peirce*, ed. J. Buchler (New York: Dover Publications, 1955), p. 102.
[47] DR, p. 189.

the abiding and virulent anti-semitism of American culture, motivated by America's reluctance to declare war on the Nazis. At one moment Hecht rather enigmatically introduces into his text the weird lament, 'Ah, this extra nose that the Jew carries! It is an organ out of which he gets little delight and much inconvenience.'[48] In any case, this phrase can function to summarise a number of interconnected themes: the lineaments of social practices based on the primacy of vision, an implicit supposition that 'the bigger's the better-worst', and an entire unconscious complex whereby the penis, the phallus, sexual hierarchy, popular physiognomy, racial difference and social hegemony find themselves irremediably enmeshed.[49]

And, finally, my third reason here: the abiding links between cocaine and the nose, a relation reflected in contemporary slang – for example, 'nose-candy' or, in the Hispanic *perrico*, 'parrot' (presumably because you shove it up your beak, and it makes you squawk like a parrot) – and in the development of certain interesting contemporary surgical techniques (gold septums). This is also a fact which bears crucially on Freud's own fraught relationship with these assorted rhinologies (remember, he recommended nasal, oral *and* subcutaneous application).

But what knotted these three aspects together for Freud was a friendship. At the time of his self-analysis in the 1890s, Freud's best friend was a Jewish ear, nose and throat doctor named Wilhelm Fliess, whose own theories on the nose have most often been judged by subsequent commentators as the work of a demented quack.[50] As Peter Gay puts it, 'Fliess singled out the nose as the dominant organ, which spreads

---

[48] B. Hecht, *A Guide for the Bedevilled* (New York: Garden City Publishing Co., 1945), p. 21.

[49] As a historico-philosophical curio, Hegel's section denouncing physiognomy and phrenology in *The Phenomenology of Spirit*, trans. A. V. Miller, foreword by J. N. Findlay (Oxford: Oxford University Press, 1977), is of some interest here, on at least two points: (1) 'It may be said of the Jewish people that it is precisely because they stand before the portal of salvation that they are, and have been, the most reprobate and rejected: what that people should be in and for it self, this essential nature of its own self, is not explicitly present to it' (p. 206); (2) 'The *depth* which Spirit brings forth from within – but only as far as its picture-thinking consciousness where it lets it remain – and the *ignorance* of this consciousness about what it really is saying, are the same conjunction of the high and the low which, in the living being, Nature naively expresses when it combines the organ of its highest fulfilment, the organ of generation, with the organ of urination' (p. 210). In Hegel's speculative anthropology, 'the Jewish people' are thus placed in a threshold position that is strictly analagous to the position of the penis – as at once the highest and lowest expressions of theologico-natural naivety.

[50] Charles Bernheimer, for instance, calls Fliess 'something of a theoretical madman' and speaks of his 'wild ideas'; C. Bernheimer, 'Introduction: Part One', in Bernheimer and C. Kahane (eds), *In Dora's Case: Freud, Hysteria, Feminism* (London: Virago, 1985), pp. 15–16. Or, as Gay says, 'Fliess is now regarded as a crank and pathological numerologist'; LT, p. 56. Gilman, however, argues that Fliess's ideas about the links between male menstruation, the genitalia and the nose, far from being the fantasies of a lunatic or quack, are inherited from a well-sedimented Christian discourse, dating from the thirteenth century, in which male Jews do, in fact, menstruate. See DR, pp. 190–1.

its influence over all human health and sickness. He was, moreover, enslaved to a scheme of biorhythmic cycles of 23 and 28 days, to which males and females were seen to be subject and which, he believed, would permit the physician to diagnose all sorts of conditions and ailments.'[51] For instance, the evidence for male periodicity included periodic nose bleeds; this evidence would ultimately, at least for Fliess, found a surgical practice capable of altering 'the pathology of the genitalia by operating on the nose'.[52] Indeed, it seems that both he and Freud were only too ready and willing to operate.

PUS IN BOOTS

If there is a canonical text for psychoanalytic dream interpretation, it is Freud's so-called 'specimen dream', otherwise known as the dream of 'Irma's injection', in which the foundational Freudian principle that 'a dream is the fulfilment of a wish' is broached for the first time.[53] It is not only, as Lacan says, psychoanalysis's 'dream of dreams', but constitutes, in Lisa Appignanesi and John Forrester's words, 'the primal scene of psychoanalysis'.[54] Unfortunately, I do not have the time to do a detailed reading of the dream here, and will only list a few pertinent details. Freud's own 'preamble' to the dream runs as follows:

> During the summer of 1895 I had been giving psychoanalytic treatment to a young lady who was on very friendly terms with me and my family . . . This treatment had ended in a partial success; the patient was relieved of her hysterical anxiety but did not lose all her somatic symptoms. At that time I was not yet clear in my mind as to the criteria indicating that a hysterical case history was finally closed, and I proposed a solution to the patient which she seemed unwilling to accept . . . One day I had a visit from a junior colleague, one of my oldest friends, who had been staying with my patient, Irma, and her family at their country resort. I asked him how he had found her and he answered: 'She's better, but not quite well.' . . . The same evening I wrote out Irma's case history, with the idea of giving it to Dr M., in order to justify myself. That night (or more probably the next morning) I had the following dream, which I noted down immediately after waking.[55]

Before proceeding with an analysis of Freud's analysis of his own dream, it is necessary to emphasise a few points about the 'real' incident

[51] LT, p. 46.
[52] DR, p. 189.
[53] S. Freud, *The Interpretation of Dreams*, trans. J. Strachey (Harmondsworth: Penguin, 1985), pp. 169–99. Hereafter referred to as 'ID'. In a footnote added in 1914, Freud notes that 'This is the first dream which I submitted to a detailed interpretation'; p. 181.
[54] L. Appignanesi and J. Forrester, *Freud's Women* (London: Weidenfeld and Nicolson, 1992), p. 119.
[55] ID, pp. 180–1.

which it purportedly reconstitutes. As Appignanesi and Forrester retell it, returning to Irma her real name, Emma Eckstein[56]:

> Emma started receiving treatment from Freud sometime in the early 1890s. We do not know what her symptoms were, but she became a special patient ... The crucial period of her treatment extended from 1895 to 1897, overlapping with Freud's espousal of the seduction theory and his discovery of the meaning of dreams.
>
> In December 1894, Fliess visited Freud in Vienna, examined Emma and recommended that he operate on her nose, in order to alleviate certain of her symptoms, ones possibly connected, in the doctor's view, with masturbation. Fliess returned to Vienna in early February, operated on Emma and left. Freud reported on her post-operative progress on 4 March: the patient was not doing well. She had excessive secretion of pus, a bone chip had been expelled and a rather noxious smell emanated from her nose. Four days later, on 8 March, Freud gave Fliess the sudden upsetting news that Emma's condition had worsened.[57]

Freud called in another ear, nose and throat specialist, Dr Rosanes, to take another look. To continue the story in Freud's own words, a letter to Fliess dated 8 March 1895 reveals:

> Rosanes cleaned the area surrounding the opening, removed some sticky blood clots, and suddenly pulled at something like a thread, kept on pulling. Before either of us had time to think, at least half a meter of gauze had been removed from the cavity. The next moment came a flood of blood. The patient turned white, her eyes bulged, and she had no pulse. Immediately thereafter, however, he again packed the cavity with fresh iodoform gauze and the hemorrhage stopped. It lasted about half a minute, but this was enough to make the poor creature, whom by then we had lying flat, unrecognizable. In the meantime – that is, afterward – something else happened. At the moment the foreign body came out and everything became clear to me – and I immediately afterward was confronted by the sight of the patient – I felt sick ... I do not believe it was the blood that overwhelmed me – at that moment strong emotions were welling up in me. So we had done her an injustice; she was not at all abnormal, rather, a piece of iodoform gauze had gotten torn off as you were removing it and stayed in for fourteen days, preventing healing; at the end it tore off and provoked the bleeding.[58]

This suggests a number of points, some empirical, some speculative, which bear on the interrelations between noses, cocaine (among other drugs), injections and the psychoanalytic text, all of which become irremediably commingled as a result of Freud's own procedures.

---

[56] However, this attribution has been disputed (as has much else) by Jeffrey Masson, *The Assault on Truth: Freud's Suppression of the Seduction Theory* (Harmondsworth: Penguin, 1985), p. 57.

[57] Appignanesi and Forrester, *Freud's Women*, p. 119.

[58] S. Freud, *The Complete Letters of Sigmund Freud to Wilhelm Fliess, 1887–1904*, ed. J. Masson (Cambridge: The Belknap Press, 1985), pp. 116–17. Hereafter referred to as 'CL'.

First, Irma's 'true' identity was not known until the 1960s. However, in the section of Freud's interpretation in which he deals with 'propionic acid', he speaks of this acid as reminding him of a foul-smelling pineapple liqueur named 'Ananas', to which he provides an enigmatic footnote: 'I must add that the sound of the word "Ananas" bears a remarkable resemblance to that of my patient Irma's family name.'[59] Now, 'Eckstein' hardly resembles, remarkably or otherwise, 'Ananas', but, as Maria Torok points out, 'the connection to this patient becomes obvious if we think of Emma's nose operation. *Ananas* is quite similar to the drawling Viennese pronunciation of *eine Nase* (a nose).'[60] Furthermore, Freud himself remarks of the image of the scabby, curly structures in the throat that the:

> scabs on the turbinal bones recalled a worry about my own state of health. I was making frequent use of cocaine at that time to reduce some troublesome nasal swellings, and I had heard a few days earlier that one of my women patients who had followed my example had developed an extensive necrosis of the nasal mucous membrane. I had been the first to recommend the use of cocaine, in 1885, and this recommendation had brought serious reproaches down on me. The misuse of that drug had hastened the death of a dear friend of mine.[61]

This admission or confession is hardly a simple one. In this re-presentation cocaine functions much like Plato's *pharmakon*: though a certain remedy for his own nasal problems, it is yet the probable cause of another's; a legitimate medical treatment he was first to identify (for which he therefore deserves the credit), it yet killed a friend and provoked 'reproaches' (for which he therefore must take responsibility), and so on. The passage thus confusedly identifies cocaine as the divided cause of professional and sexual death-health. And there is another famous Freudian slip here: he had first endorsed cocaine in 1884, and not 1885 at all. This slip is all the more notable inasmuch as, as Jones points out, 'it was of course in 1884 when he recommended the use of cocaine, but it was in 1885 that he recommended the use of the (dangerous) injections'.[62]

Hence my second point; as Avital Ronell remarks, the dream constitutes 'the story of Irma's infection which Freud, however, calls Irma's injection'.[63] As the text of the dream itself has it, 'injections of that sort

---

[59] ID, p. 187.

[60] M. Torok, 'A Remembrance of Things Deleted: Between Sigmund Freud and Emmy von. N', in N. Abraham and Torok, *The Shell and the Kernel, Vol. 1*, trans. and intro. by N. Rand (Chicago: University of Chicago Press, 1994), p. 242.

[61] ID, p. 187.

[62] LW, p. 106.

[63] A. Ronell, *Dictations: On Haunted Writing* (Lincoln: University of Nebraska Press, 1986), p. 48.

ought not to be made so thoughtlessly'.[64] Or, again, as Freud phrases one of the latent wishes expressed in the dream: 'Irma's pains had been caused by Otto giving her an incautious injection of an unsuitable drug – a thing *I* should never have done.'[65] Once more: Freud's sanctioning of subcutaneous injections had not only proved a central issue in the cocaine scandal, but had also been principally responsible for the death of Fleischl (as he admits).[66] Freud himself directly associated the recurrent 'threes' in the dream to the threesome that he, Fliess and Emma literally and manifestly formed, but it is also tempting to refer these triads to Freud's preconscious recollections of cocaine as 'the third scourge' which he had been held to have unleashed.[67] And yet these unfortunate occurrences now come to provide one of the principal supports for Freud's central hypothesis that even the apparently self-recriminatory aspects of dreams are nevertheless self-dissimulating wish-fulfilments. Thus when he dreams 'I thought to myself that after all I must be missing some organic trouble', the truth of this dream-thought runs something like this: 'the patient was not a hysteric at all; I simply overlooked some physical condition; my diagnostic failure was entirely due to my desire that my theories of hysteria be true; therefore, to the extent that I had missed some organic trouble precisely due to this desire, my theories are still true.' But in order to demonstrate the contradictory coherence of his own kettle-logic here, Freud must 'confess' to his cocaine error. It is thus symptomatic that he errs symptomatically in this ambivalently self-aggrandising confession of error.

Third, at the time of the operation, Freud was himself still using and pre-

---

[64] ID, p. 182.

[65] ID, p. 197.

[66] Freud's unconscious doubling of Fleischl and Fliess is obviously also of importance. As Ronell points out, 'Freud was first, as usual; to draw attention to the jarring compatibility of the names of his most vital friends: Fluss, Fleischl, Fliess. Before there was Fliess there was Fluss, and before Fluss (also 'river') dissolved into Fliess (also 'flowing', 'secretion'), there was Fleischl (also 'flesh', 'meat')'; *Dictations*, p. 40.

[67] Freud may indeed be alluding to this when he writes, 'Certain other themes played a part in the dream, which were not so obviously connected with my exculpation from Irma's illness: my daughter's illness and that of my patient who bore the same name, the injurious effect of cocaine'; *The Interpretation of Dreams*, p. 197. The covert numericity of Freud's procedure here seems to consist of a kind of countdown, from three (Freud, Fliess, Emma), to two (Freud and Fliess, the only two who really matter), to one (Freud himself, the true double of Fliess's double, hence in Fliess more than himself). It should go without saying that Freud's numerology is, even by his own lights, utterly unsustainable. But see also Derrida's remarks on the *square of women* who resist Freud's dreams: 'we must recall that everything here is *concentrated* and at the same time *dissolved* in a solution (*Lösung*), a chemical solution but also ... the solution of a problem (it is the same word, *Lösung*), an analytic solution. An analytic solution untangles, resolves, even absolves; it undoes the symptomatic or etiological knot. The same word (solution, analytic resolution, *Lösung*) is valid for the drug and for the end of the analysis. And the reason Freud reproaches Irma in the course of the dream, the reason he reproaches Irma's resistance, is that she has not accepted *his solution*'; *Resistances of Psychoanalysis*, trans. P. Kamuf et al. (Stanford: Stanford University Press, 1998), p. 7.

scribing cocaine for topical application to the nasal mucous membranes. On a related minor note, the dream occurred after he had just taken up smoking again. Freud had been suffering from heart arrhythmia, migraines and nose infections, which Fliess had diagnosed as smoking-related, and he had induced Freud to stop in 1894.[68] It is the details of this third point that, paradoxically, turn the sequence of biographical events into something more than a merely empirical situation. For this scene of appalling surgical malpractice – although absolutely 'real' (even if the details were until relatively recently masked by the analytic text which claimed to unveil them) – is consistently doubled by still another scene, even less legible because so blatantly manifest, and perhaps just as unpleasant. It concerns, above all, a fantasy of pedagogical reproduction.

In his letters to Fliess, Freud describes in graphic detail the effects of the botched operation on Emma: although dosed to the eyeballs on morphine, she is prostrate, in excruciating pain, and blood and pus are running constantly from her mutilated nose, which has the 'fetid odour' of rotting flesh. Throughout this trying time, a confused, even terrified Freud has been constantly dosing himself with cocaine; his own nose – like Emma's – is spurting pus, but of a very different quality.[69] Indeed, he has been writing to Fliess for some time as to the beneficial quality of his own secretions:

> In the last few days I have felt quite unbelievably well, as though everything had been erased . . . Last time I wrote you, after a good period which immediately succeeded the reaction, that a few viciously bad days had followed during which a cocainization of the left nostril had helped me to an amazing extent . . . The next day I kept the nose under cocaine, which one should not really do; that is, I repeatedly painted it to prevent the renewed occurrence of swelling; during this time I discharged what in my experience is a copious amount of thick pus; and since then I have felt wonderful.[70]

---

[68] 'Freud continued to prescribe cocaine until at least 1895, the year of his self-analysis, for topical application to the nasal mucous membranes, and he used it himself for sinusitis. He suffered not only from nasal infections but from migraine and, after an attack of influenza in 1889, heart arrhythmia . . . Fliess induced him to give up smoking in 1894, and a short while afterward he suffered a severe cardiac condition with racing and irregular heart, tension, hot pain in the left arm, and respiratory difficulties. Fliess, who had previously diagnosed Freud's heart troubles as being of nasal origin, now attributed them to nicotine poisoning. Although Freud doubted the diagnosis, he managed to stop smoking for 14 months, until he could no longer tolerate abstinence. By this time Fliess had again decided that the heart condition was of nasal origin, and this conclusion was apparently supported by the improvement that followed an operation and the use of cocaine nose drops. Jones believes that the heart troubles, the migraine, and the nasal infections were all neurotic, although slightly aggravated by the effects of nicotine'; BG, p. 35.

[69] Freud also refers to his own nasal pussing as 'a private Etna'; *The Complete Letters*, p. 116.

[70] Letter dated 24 January 1895, Freud, *The Complete Letters*, p. 106. And, in another letter dated 20 April 1895, following Emma's recovery, 'Today I can write because I have more hope; I pulled myself out of a miserable attack with a cocaine application'; p. 126. Freud was also concurrently taking another drug, strophantus, for his physical complaints.

At this point, everyone's pussing. Fortunately, in Freud's case it is a promising sign of recovery and not at all of dissolution and decay. Furthermore, he's still erect, standing, evidently a man, and therefore his nasal pus – given Freud and Fliess's own theories of the time – is undoubtedly also spermatic fluid (which he is literally measuring out in cups), thick and rich. All thanks to the magic of cocaine. And he and Fliess are thus more than ready to teach the world the lesson of the nose and its links to the genitalia, a lesson which is to be endlessly repeated, verified and transmitted to the world through the only-too-physical, active surgical implantation of their autogenerative, in-corporeal seed in the welcoming nasal-uteruses of hysterical women.[71] A true 'double penetration', then, in a number of senses of that phrase: appearing as both real and fantasmatic figures in Freud's own text, Freud and Fliess aim to penetrate and impregnate the world through im-pustulating Emma's nose, all the while efficiently penetrating and mingling indiscernibly with each other.

This situation is almost explicitly confessed to by Freud the following year, when he writes to Fliess of his desire to 'blend our contributions to the point where our individual property is no longer recognizable'.[72] As it happens, Emma is so badly mutilated by the operation that it is she who is rendered 'barely recognizable'. Unfortunately, in Emma's case, the friends' attempts at procreation are miserably bungled. Her nose will not stop bleeding, 'menstruating', and hence there has been no conception; into the bargain, the pus-sperm of our odd couple is still leaking from her nose, having completely failed to take.[73] Freud has stuffed everything up once more, and already again this failure is personal, professional, reputational, scientific and so on. He will have to keep dreaming if he is ever to make something of himself.

CONCLUSION: SNIVILISATION AND ITS DISCONTENTS

Freud's failure to make his reputation by way of cocaine was a crucial impetus in his turn from neurology to psychology, from explanations that presume that pathologies have a material, organic basis to explanations based on the primacy of 'sex' as available through interlocution.

---

[71] For a very different reading of this scene, see W. Koestenbaum, *Double Talk: The Erotics of Male Literary Collaboration* (New York: Routledge, 1989), esp. chapter one, 'Privileging the Anus: Anna O. and the Collaborative Origin of Psychoanalysis'.

[72] CL, p. 215.

[73] As Ronell remarks, 'it all comes down to the discharge of the male organ contaminated with properties of the female organ ... And it is Irma ... [who] will act as midwife and wet nurse to the dream of dreams, the story of the semen that did not follow'; *Dictations*, p. 53. Ronell also notes that 'Emma' spelt backwards reads 'Amme', 'midwife'!

He made this transition from a neurological approach to a psycho-analytic one precisely because his dream drug had been judged by his culture to be addictive and mortificatory. Again, this is more than a merely empirical event: as I have shown, Freud cannot help but return to this event in the text that is the central document of psychoanalytic dream interpretation. Irma's dream is the place where Freud invokes his failure to support the truth of his new solution. Yet he still can't get his story straight: in his attempt to come clean, he confuses dates, persons, their orifices, treatments and pathologies in a way which bespeaks – in psychoanalytic terms – the continuing activity of an unconscious trauma.

On the other hand, it is also possible to read Freud's cocaine troubles in a way that perturbs the contemporary discourses of addiction: 'addic-tion', for instance, is by no means a well-defined scientific concept, but names a structure that integrally conceals and confuses a number of non-scientific determinations (for example, cultural interdictions, pro-fessional and economic rivalry, obscene psycho-sexual desires, covert racism and so on).

Because of the overdetermined ways in which the cocaine-event con-ditions Freud's transition between very different 'scientific' domains, it is tempting to suggest that this event thereafter regulates an almost indiscernible but insistent series of interruptions of the psychoanalytic corpus. For the specific reasons I have already outlined, we might expect that the psychoanalytic question of the nose continued to bear the traces of this inauguratory event. As I have suggested, the supple-mentary nose is, certainly, the Jew's circumcised penis, but also – and more confusingly in Freud's case – his own nose, Fliess's nose, Irma's nose, the uterine tract, the phallus, Freud's future social and profes-sional reputation and, ultimately, the nose-phallus-uterus of civilisation itself.

It is therefore probable that the foundational problematic I have been sketching will return with the nose – and, indeed, this is precisely what happens in a number of major Freudian texts.[74] But perhaps the most famous return to the nose is in the course of a long footnote to *Civilization and its Discontents*, where Freud writes:

---

[74] In his speculations that Dora was a childhood masturbator, Freud remarks: 'It is well known that gastric pains occur especially often in those who masturbate. According to a personal communication made to me by Wilhelm Fliess, it is precisely gastralgias of this character which can be interrupted by an application of cocaine to the "gastric spot" dis-covered by him in the nose, and which can be cured by the cauterization of the same spot'; *Case Histories I: 'Dora' and 'Little Hans'*, trans. A. and J. Strachey (Harmondsworth: Penguin, 1977), p. 115.

> The diminution of the olfactory stimuli seems itself to be a consequence of man's raising himself from the ground, of his assumption of an upright gait; this made his genitals, which were previously concealed, visible and in need of protection, and so provoked feelings of shame in him.[75]

Thus it is not simply that there is no nasal phase in psychoanalysis. If Freud, under the pressure of his drug-bust, sometimes seems too rapidly to assimilate the nose to the oral cavity, the nose (identified here with the sense of smell) returns here at the very origin of civilisation itself. But if 'ontogeny recapitulates phylogeny', why is there then no definite nasal phase in childhood? Precisely because the nose is the pre-history of the historical erection of the erection, the nose cannot become a phase because it designates the ambivalent residue of an immemorial transition. The nose constitutes the visible remains of the inhuman in humanity, when there was neither civilisation nor shame. But we can speculate that the nose also constitutes the visible remains of neurology in psychoanalysis, when there was neither addiction nor sexuality. This speculation further suggests a fundamental historico-cultural hypothesis, and implicates domains apparently very distant from the psychoanalytical: sexuality is what arises when drugs become addictive.

The introduction established the general lineaments for my central claim that psychoanalysis is an antiphilosophy. Psychoanalysis founds itself as an impossible practice, and does so by essaying to inject literary elements into the methods of science, without subsumption or reduction of one to the other, in order to catch something that would otherwise be indiscernible – the infinite and singular complexities of human language-use as it bears upon psychopathology. As Freud later confirms in 'An Outline of Psycho-Analysis', criticising every attempt to reduce mind to brain:

> We know two kinds of things about what we call our psyche (or mental life): firstly, its bodily organ and scene of action, the brain (or nervous system) and, on the other hand, our acts of consciousness, which are immediate data and cannot be further explained by any sort of description. Everything that lies between is unknown to us, and the data do not include any direct relation between these two terminal points of our knowledge. If it existed, it would at the most afford an exact localization of the processes of consciousness and would give us no help towards understanding them.[76]

---

[75] S. Freud, *Civilization and its Discontents*, trans. J. Riviere, rev. J. Strachey (London: The Hogarth Press, 1963), p. 36.

[76] S. Freud, 'An Outline of Psycho-Analysis', in *The Standard Edition of the Complete Psychological Works of Sigmund Freud*, Vol. XXIII (1937–1939), ed. J. Strachey et al. (London: The Hogarth Press, 1964), pp. 144–5.

The entire method of psychoanalysis is dedicated to creating ever-renovated means of non-violent isolation of a subject's relation to their own speech, and then inventing new ways to enable the subject to transform that relationship through speech itself. That this project is, strictly speaking, 'impossible' by no means vitiates its pertinence or force. But it does raise questions about the emergence, institutionalisation and continuation of psychoanalysis.

This chapter has enabled us to say a number of unusual things about psychoanalysis. First, psychoanalysis is *post-* (not *pre-*) pharmacological, and Freud himself ought to be considered a key figure in the development of modern psychopharmacology, in his failures as much as in his success. Second, it is with regard to this drug-failure that Freud comes upon the functions of sexual-failure: that psychic disorder is entirely bound up with social functions whose operations are not entirely biochemically given. Third, the matrix and medium of these operations is given and can be thought as an obscene assemblage of bodies and words: the nose, Judaism, pus, sperm and cocaine form a deranging cocktail of drug-signs whose effects don't stop continuing not quite expressing themselves. Fourth, the relationship between addiction and sexuality is one of incomplete yet absolute differentiation, and this relationship can also be figured as the servitude-of-physical-pleasure's-diminishing-returns versus the alienation-of-pleasure-in-the-other. Fifth, the attempt to figure or configure this relationship requires a recourse to literary works, to the 'listening' required by literature to the unsaid and unsayable. Slavery-addiction and sexuality-alienation as antagonistic complicities discernible only by crossing science with literature: it is to a further psychoanalytic elaboration of this situation that we now turn, under the rubric of love.

2. Love as Ontology; or, Psychoanalysis against Philosophy

We are of the opinion, then, that language has carried out an entirely justifi-
able piece of unification in creating the word 'love' with its numerous uses,
and that we cannot do better than take it as the basis of our scientific discussions and expositions as well. By coming to this decision, psycho-analysis
has let loose a storm of indignation, as though it had been guilty of an act of
outrageous innovation. Yet it has done nothing original in taking love in this
'wider' sense. In its origin, function, and relation to sexual love, the 'Eros'
of the philosopher Plato coincides exactly with the love-force, the libido of
psycho-analysis.

Sigmund Freud[1]

Love is not a feeling. Love is put to the test, pain not.

Ludwig Wittgenstein[2]

Dance me to the end of love.

Leonard Cohen[3]

THE INDIFFERENCE OF PSYCHOANALYSIS TO PHILOSOPHICAL ONTOLOGIES

Because it is an antiphilosophy, psychoanalysis has, from its beginnings, remained indifferent or suspicious towards that most philosophical of themes: ontology. One can see this indifference operating at a
number of levels. The practice of psychoanalysis has not necessitated
that clinical psychoanalysts intervene directly in ontological question-

---

[1] S. Freud, *Group Psychology and the Analysis of the Ego*, in *The Standard Edition of the Complete Psychological Works of Sigmund Freud*, Vol. XVIII (1920–1922), ed. J. Strachey et al. (London: The Hogarth Press, 1955), pp. 90–1.
[2] L. Wittgenstein, *Zettel*, ed. G. E. M. Anscombe and G. H. von Wright (Berkeley: University of California Press, 1967), remark 504, p. 88.
[3] L. Cohen, *Various Positions* (Passport Records, 1984).

ing, whether implicitly or explicitly. Even in the most volatile moments of its struggles to sustain itself as a singular practice, psychoanalysis has remained relatively unmoved in the face of the counter-claims, concepts and criticisms coming from philosophy – and, a fortiori, from philosophical ontologies. Indeed, the reverse is more the case: it is philosophers who have felt themselves constrained to respond, with some urgency, to the challenges offered by psychoanalysis. However different they may otherwise be, both Ludwig Wittgenstein and Martin Heidegger showed themselves to be irritated and occasionally uncomprehending in the face of psychoanalytic claims, particularly around those inquiries into problems of language, the subject and ethics, which impinged upon philosophy's traditional domains.

This irritation, notably, tended to take the form of imputations of a covert or unexamined ontology. As Jacques Bouveresse comments, 'What Wittgenstein refuses to acknowledge in psychoanalysis, as in set theory, is nothing less than its ontology.'[4] And if Heidegger could denominate the regime of modern science as that of 'enframing', it is not entirely clear that – even if one accepts his account – psychoanalysis can be adequately encompassed by this delimitation.[5] This situation is all the more fraught given that Wittgenstein and Heidegger were themselves attempting to find an exit from classical ontologies. One can suspect a kind of kettle-logic at work: psychoanalysis isn't philosophy, so we don't need to touch it; psychoanalysis is already philosophy, and so succumbs to our own critiques of philosophy; psychoanalysis pretends to philosophy, and so we must punish it. In a word, the relationship between psychoanalysis and philosophy, such that it is, has been asymmetrical: psychoanalysis generates propositions that integrally affect philosophy; philosophy does not generate propositions that integrally affect psychoanalysis.

This has not, of course, been the case for scientific critiques. Precisely because, from Freud to Fonagy, every major psychoanalytic orientation has insisted on some kind of essential relationship to science, psychoanalysis is recurrently interrupted by a damning negative judgement: 'not scientific!'. This judgement can inspire both new exits and new entrances: psychoanalysis has recourse to animal ethology, attachment theory and neuroscience, on the one hand; linguistics, literature and other cultural resources, on the other. In this context, the results are anything but clear. As many 'scientific' psychological

4 J. Bouveresse, *Wittgenstein Reads Freud: The Myth of the Unconscious*, trans. C. Cosman, foreword by V. Descombes (Princeton: Princeton University Press, 1995), p. xvii.
5 See M. Heidegger, *The Question Concerning Technology and Other Essays*, trans. with intro. by W. Lovitt (New York: Harper and Row, 1977).

treatments still considered viable today were developed by those who had trained as psychoanalysts (John Bowlby, for example, or Aaron Beck), the scientific status of psychoanalysis remains a topic of intense dispute, continuing in contemporary debates around neuropsychoanalysis.[6] As a general rule, psychoanalysis is supposed to stand or fall as a clinical discipline on the validity of its scientific methodology. If psychoanalysis is not a science, then it can be consigned to the hell of pre- or non-scientific practices, like alchemy, shamanism or hermeneutics. And if it is not a science, then none of its claims can have any scientific value, not even as a goad, guide or inspiration for scientific work. Because psychoanalysis clearly has something to do with science, it must continue to engage with the ongoing discoveries emanating from various fields of science, from biology to physics. But because it is not clearly a science, its place cannot be simply fixed by such an identification. When psychoanalysis tries to become a 'real' science, it has always given way on its central hypotheses and procedures; when it resorts to more humanistic methods, it has dissolved into just another competing interpretative method. If this state of affairs continues to prove problematic for psychoanalysis, it remains even more of a problem for philosophy in its attempted critiques of psychoanalysis.

This can lead to hilarious polemics. As David Corfield notes of the dispute between Karl Popper and Adolf Grünbaum, 'Each accused the other's principles of being so weak that they allowed even psychoanalysis to be called a science, when their own of course did not.'[7] Moreover, such approaches tend to treat philosophy as auxiliary to the sciences, reduced to pointing out science's contradictions and errors, delineating its limits, and justifying its epistemological priority over other disciplines. Perhaps the minimal form of scientific injunction that should be put to psychoanalysis is the following: ensure that the methodologies of psychoanalysis are not incompatible with the methodologies of contemporaneous science. This situation does not at all prevent us from asking questions as to the ontology of psychoanalysis, but it does introduce a necessary complication: one cannot plausibly explore

---

[6] See in this regard the work of theorists such as Mark Solms and Jim Hopkins, such as M. Solms, 'Freud Returns', *Scientific American*, May 2004, pp. 82–8; J. Hopkins, 'Psychoanalysis, Representation and Neuroscience', in A. Fotopoulou et al. (eds), *From the Couch to the Lab: Trends in Psychodynamic Neuroscience* (Oxford: Oxford University Press, 2012), pp. 230–65; H. A. Berlin and C. Koch, 'Neuroscience Meets Psychoanalysis', *Scientific American Mind*, April/May 2009, pp. 16–19.

[7] D. Corfield, 'From Mathematics to Psychology: Lacan's Missed Encounters', in J. Glynos and Y. Stavrakakis (eds), *Lacan & Science* (London: Karnac, 2002), pp. 179–206 (p. 190). See also the other essays in this indispensable collection. See also J.-C. Milner, *Les Noms indistincts* (Paris: Éditions du Seuil, 1983), pp. 92–3, n. 3.

the ontology of psychoanalysis without taking into account the fraught relation of psychoanalysis to science.[8]

I will take a different tack here. Having identified the themes of slavery, alienation and torture as the key foci of psychoanalysis, which it treats by means of a disjunctive synthesis of science and literature, I want now to propose – following the indications of philosophers as different as Alain Badiou and Jonathan Lear[9] – that it is the new theorisation of love offered by psychoanalysis which binds all this together. Why? Because, finally, we can never forget that psychoanalysis is a therapeutic treatment. This treatment, this therapy, is above all a praxis. Psychoanalysis is not just a theory or a hermeneutic, it does not just provide an account of human desires and drives, nor is it simply a management programme for sexual or traumatic disorders. It is a work of love. Within psychoanalysis itself, love has been primarily understood under the heading of 'transference', thereby simultaneously implicating the clinical and the conceptual, the ongoing vicissitudes of a treatment and the metapsychological theorisation of psychic events. What further complicates this picture is that psychoanalysis – in contradistinction to common belief – comes not to praise, but to bury love. I will argue that this erotic interment procedure provides psychoanalysis with its peculiar 'ontology'.[10] In other words, and despite its ultimate indifference to ontological questioning, there comes a time when psychoanalysis cannot avoid such issues. Let us first turn to Freud and then to Lacan to verify this in detail.

---

[8] In this context, one of the most interesting contemporary philosophical commentators on psychoanalysis, European philosophy and science is Catherine Malabou. See, inter alia, *The New Wounded: From Neurosis to Brain Damage* (New York: Fordham University Press, 2012).

[9] See A. Badiou, 'What is Love?', in *Conditions*, trans. S. Corcoran (London: Continuum, 2008), pp. 179–98; J. Lear, *Love and Its Place in Nature: A Philosophical Interpretation of Freudian Psychoanalysis* (New York: Farrar, Strauss, and Giroux, 1990).

[10] J.-L. Nancy and P. Lacoue-Labarthe, *The Title of the Letter: A Reading of Lacan*, trans. F. Raffoul and D. Pettigrew (Albany: State University of New York Press, 1992), remains the *locus classicus* for such claims, if in a negative key. As is well known, Lacan himself found it expedient to praise and bury this book in *Seminar XX: Encore: The Seminar of Jacques Lacan, Book XX: On Feminine Sexuality: The Limits of Love and Knowledge 1972–1973*, ed. J.-A. Miller, trans. with notes by B. Fink (New York: W. W. Norton & Co., 1998), esp. p. 65. See also J. Derrida's extensive struggle with Lacan, in such works as *Given Time: I Counterfeit Money*, trans. P. Kamuf (Chicago: University of Chicago Press, 1992), *Positions*, trans. A. Bass (Chicago: University of Chicago Press, 1987), *Resistances of Psychoanalysis*, trans. P. Kamuf et al. (Stanford: Stanford University Press, 1998), and elsewhere. For post-Lacanian responses to Derrida, see the rather nasty spat in which Badiou and Derrida get themselves enmeshed, in N. Avtonomova et al. (eds), *Lacan avec les philosophes* (Paris: Albin Michel, 1991), esp. the appendix of letters to that volume (and Badiou's own contribution is of interest too, pp. 135–54), as well as J.-A. Miller's recent coming to terms with Derrida in the 'Annexes' to J. Lacan, *Le Séminaire, livre XXIII: Le sinthome, 1975–1976* (Paris: Éditions du Seuil, 2005), pp. 232–6.

FROM THE SYMPTOM TO THE TRANSFERENCE

Freud was always suspicious of the accusation that psychoanalysis had drawn substantially from philosophy. This position did not simply derive from ignorance or hostility; on the contrary, it was precisely Freud's restrained enthusiasm for philosophy that fuelled his suspicions. Early on, he had been a disciple of Franz Brentano (with whom he later broke), and he had once intended to enrol in a double doctorate in zoology and philosophy.[11] His early adherence to the Brücke-Helmholtz doctrine of science – which held that only physical and chemical forces were operative within an organism – itself clearly entails a kind of (unsophisticated) ontology. And Freud alludes to philosophical ontologies throughout his work, for example in a famous passage from *Beyond the Pleasure Principle*, in which he admits, apropos of his new dualism of life and death instincts, 'We have unwittingly steered our course into the harbour of Schopenhauer's philosophy.'[12] But such references smack more of erudite *politesse* than genuine influence. Even at the moment of Freud's most counter-intuitive explorations of the consequences of his self-confessedly speculative drive hypothesis, with its overtones of Empedocles, he never entirely abandons his dream that psychological functions might eventually be given a biochemical foundation.

In other words, to the extent that Freud expresses any concern for ontology at all, it is tangential, opportunistic or diffident. Ontology is what philosophers do or discuss; it is not a psychoanalytic concern. However – and this needs to be underlined – to the extent that psychoanalysis is part of the modern scientific dispensation, it must have some empirical basis. What, in Freud's opinion, differentiates science from other disciplines is its empiricism, its resolute and ascetic commitment to the reality principle. For Freud, then, psychoanalysis doesn't need an ontology of its own; it can remain happily parasitic on that of contemporary science. It is possible that Freud remains too happily naive, even pre-Kantian, in his understanding of the empirical nature of science.

Yet the problem of what counts as empirical evidence for psychoanalysis cannot be so easily avoided. As previously mentioned, psychoanalysis has always experienced difficulties making itself stick as a science. Freud himself often fixed on an analogy with astronomy as an

---

[11] See E. Zaretsky, *Secrets of the Soul: A Social and Cultural History of Psychoanalysis* (New York: Knopf, 2004), pp. 26–7.

[12] S. Freud, *Beyond the Pleasure Principle*, in *The Standard Edition of the Complete Psychological Works of Sigmund Freud*, Vol. XVIII (1920–1922), ed. J. Strachey et al. (London: The Hogarth Press, 1955), pp. 49–50.

observational science. As he writes in the *New Introductory Lectures on Psycho-Analysis*, a work throughout which the troubled relationship to science insists as a problem:

> Only quite a short while ago the medical faculty in an American University refused to allow psycho-analysis the status of a science, on the ground that it did not admit of any experimental proof. They might have raised the same objection to astronomy; indeed, experimentation with the heavenly bodies is particularly difficult. There one has to fall back on observation.[13]

The cosmology of everyday life, indeed.

Still, Freud's assertion then begs the question: what, exactly, does psychoanalysis observe? If the obvious answer is 'the unconscious', this can't quite be the case. The unconscious is by definition unobservable in any direct fashion. If one wanted to pursue Freud's astronomical reference, one would have to say that the unconscious is not a stellar body like the sun or planets, but something like a black hole, discernible only through the otherwise inexplicable anomalies it introduces into the movements of other, perceivable bodies. So if the unconscious itself remains unobservable (if not 'untestable') by standard psychological means, there is one observable phenomenon that psychoanalysis takes as its own: transference-love.

The peculiar nature of the transference emerges at the beginning of psychoanalysis. At the conclusion of Breuer and Freud's *Studies in Hysteria*, Freud, in the course of a discussion of the way in which patients treat their physician, notes that '[t]ransference on to the physician takes place through a *false connection*'.[14] Not only is such a connection false, patently false, but the patient – who in some way knows very well how artificial, how fictional, this connection is – finds herself 'deceived afresh every time this is repeated'.[15] Such self-deception has very real effects: Breuer seems to have found himself in hot water with regard to at least one of his patients, Anna O. (real name Bertha Pappenheim).[16] Anna O. is the person who famously denominated the unorthodox treatment she helped to invent, 'the talking cure'.

It is worth pausing a moment given the subsequent popularity of this characterisation in psychoanalytic history. Why the talking cure?

[13] S. Freud, *The Standard Edition of the Complete Psychological Works of Sigmund Freud*, Vol. XXII (1932–1936), ed. J. Strachey et al. (London: The Hogarth Press, 1964), p. 22.

[14] J. Breuer and S. Freud, *Studies in Hysteria*, in *The Standard Edition of the Complete Psychological Works of Sigmund Freud*, Vol. II (1893–1895), ed. J. Strachey et al. (London: The Hogarth Press, 1955), p. 302.

[15] Breuer and Freud, *Studies in Hysteria*, p. 303.

[16] See M. Borch-Jacobsen's very detailed and damning account of this case in *Remembering Anna O.: A Century of Mystification*, trans. K. Olson with X. Callahan and the author (New York: Routledge, 1996).

Who is talking? To whom is such talk addressed? What is the significance of talk anyway? The answers psychoanalysis gives to these questions require it to depart from all previous accounts of language-use, not to mention biological explanation. The talk is addressed to shadowy figures who, though failing to exist, nonetheless organise the subject's relationship to reality. Who talks? Something completely other than the person apparently talking. Why these words? Because there is something rotten in the state of the mind which inexorably distorts the utterance, binding it to odd physical symptoms with no discernible physiological basis. Anna O. also spoke of her treatment as 'chimney-sweeping': words can function as a chimney-brush, although the soot sifted ultimately turns out to be made of dirty lost words as well.

What are the ontological consequences of such a phenomenon? That the traces of a past that has no existence but in residues of unconscious infantile decisions continue to shape the physics of the present in ways that do not have any relationship with empirical, social or biological actualities. Into the bargain, the entire comportment of subjects towards their reality is bound up with something they cannot know, but whose effects they evince as ciphers. The transference is not just evidence of the return of these fictions in reality, but is itself emblematic of the work of these fictions: the disorder of subjects is the symptom of a disorder of love. This love has no respect for empirical realities or specific differences.

The effects of the transference are such that, by the time of the notorious case-study of Dora, Freud is forced (as Lacan notes in a context to which we will return) to reconsider the transference not merely as a local or sporadic phenomenon, but as an obstacle of global import for psychoanalysis. In his postscript to this case-study, Freud has recourse to a publishing metaphor to illuminate the ruses of the transference:

> What are transferences? They are *new editions or facsimiles* of the tendencies and phantasies which are aroused and made conscious during the progress of the analysis; but they have this peculiarity, which is characteristic for their species, that they replace some earlier person by the person of the physician. To put it another way: *a whole series of psychological experiences* are revived, not as belonging to the past, but as applying to the person of the physician in the present moment. Some of these transferences have a content which differs from their model in no respect whatever except for the substitution. These, then – to keep to the same metaphor – are merely *new impressions or reprints*. Others are more ingeniously constructed: their content has been subjected to a moderating influence – to *sublimation*, as I call it – and they may even become conscious, by cleverly taking advantage of some real peculiarity in the physician's person or circumstances and

attaching themselves to that. These then will no longer be a new impression, but *revised editions*.[17]

From this time on, the difficulties of the transference will move to the very centre of psychoanalytic treatment, having serious consequences for the theory itself.[18] The transference is found to have a number of disturbing features, to the extent that Freud will suggest the only really serious difficulties of psychoanalytic treatment 'lie in the management of the transference'. First, transference is automatic in the analytic situation. Second, it functions there as a resistance to cure, whereas outside such a situation (in the 'real world', so to speak) it would be a therapeutic force. Third, there is no essential difference between transference and other kinds of love.[19] As such, transference is to be understood as an automatic fictional reprint that works to sustain repression through self-deception; as it does so, it produces the singular world of the subject as something in which that subject is out of joint. But, by the same token, it is also a medium of world transformation, the very medium within which psychoanalysis works and flourishes.

This brings us to a fourth point: the analyst is irremediably implicated in the situation in which he or she is intervening. Hence the problem of 'observing observations' – of second-order phenomena – is injected directly into the heart of the analytic experience. It is no longer enough for the analyst to rely on the classical 'formations of the unconscious' (dreams, slips, symptoms, jokes); rather, we have (apologies for the shop-worn metaphor) something analogous to the paradoxes of particle physics, Freud's transference as Heisenberg's uncertainty principle. The observer transforms the situation simply through observing; such observing, in principle, precludes total knowledge of that situation; such an epistemological gap gives onto an ontological abyss. One hardly needs to add that this aspect of the transference continues to horrify every critic of psychoanalysis, from Grünbaum to the adherents of CBT. By the same token, it continues to horrify every adherent of psychoanalysis too.

This theory of love finds itself further ramped up in Freud's confrontation with the death-drive. As Jonathan Lear remarks, 'In 1920 Freud fundamentally changed his theory of the drives. In particular, he substituted love for sexuality. To this day it remains unclear what this

[17] S. Freud, *Fragment of an Analysis of a Case of Hysteria*, in *The Standard Edition of the Complete Psychological Works of Sigmund Freud*, Vol. VII (1901–1905), ed. J. Strachey et al. (London: The Hogarth Press, 1953), p. 116.

[18] See the papers on technique, including 'The Dynamics of Transference' and 'Observations on Transference-Love', in *The Standard Edition of the Complete Psychological Works of Sigmund Freud*, Vol. XII (1911–1913), ed. J. Strachey et al. (London: The Hogarth Press, 1958).

[19] Freud, *Standard Edition*, Vol. XII, p. 168.

change means.'[20] Lear continues: 'The overwhelming consensus is that the change means very little.' Perhaps Lear is right about such a consensus. If so, it can be read as the index of a resistance of psychoanalysis to itself. (I will return to this below.) But Lear also makes the point that the transference must be understood for Freud as a world-making operation, of worlding or worldliness. Thus:

> Phenomena show up in the world, the world itself is not another phenomenon. Nor is worldliness. So if transference is worldliness itself, then 'it' is not a phenomenon in the world. Rather, it is more like the structuring condition in which phenomena show up for us.[21]

If the transference, then, is something that one 'works through' in the analytic situation, the problem is that one can never overcome transferential relations altogether.[22] To live is to transfer; to transfer is to implicate residues of prior transferences.[23] No world is total, but each is composed of the residues of other worlds – without those worlds ever being able to be absolutely destroyed or normed according to any 'objective' criteria (even the criteria of the hard sciences).[24] Lear goes so far as to identify 'three distinct species of transference':

1. transference of meaning from a significant figure in the analysand's world onto the analyst;
2. transference as an idiosyncratic world coming into view;
3. transference as the active disruption of the capacity to carry out transference in either of the first two senses.[25]

What Lear finds here is a war at the heart of love. Meaning for a subject derives from its indifference to particularity, from the fact that the subject is a repetition machine for whom deranging affects emerge in its trafficking of unconscious investments. In the illegal displacement that is

---

[20] J. Lear, *Therapeutic Action: An Earnest Plea for Irony* (New York: The Other Press, 2003), p. 157.

[21] Lear, *Therapeutic Action*, p. 196. As Lear elsewhere notes, 'There is no content to the idea of a world that is not a possible world for us. And a world that is not lovable (by beings like us) is not a possible world'; *Love and Its Place in Nature*, p. 142.

[22] See S. Freud, 'Remembering, Repeating and Working-Through', in *Standard Edition*, Vol. XII, p. 155.

[23] As Lear adds, 'This is an aspect of transference that is often overlooked: the figures are not only coming from the past, they are coming from an earlier type of world-formation'; *Therapeutic Action*, p. 206.

[24] See Freud's superb deconstruction of the aporias of love, at the centre of *Civilization and its Discontents*, *The Standard Edition of the Complete Psychological Works of Sigmund Freud*, Volume XXI (1927–1931), ed. J. Strachey et al. (London: The Hogarth Press, 1961), pp. 57–146.

[25] J. Lear, *Freud* (New York and London: Routledge, 2005), p. 129. The entire chapter is highly relevant in this context.

transference, an entirely singular subjective world becomes discernible, only to break down again under the conditions of analysis. 'Being' arises as the consequence of an operation of sense, but founders as it does so, undermined by its own operations. Yet there is no way out of these operations: the transference implicates the analyst as much as the analysand.

One can also see in this tripartite division all the difficulties commentators have experienced in identifying Freud's ontology. Is Freud a monist or a dualist? After all, on close scrutiny, his apparent oppositions of 'pleasure' and 'reality' principles or of 'life' and 'death' drives turn out not to be simply opposed, but interruptive modifications of each other (e.g. 'reality' as a deferral or calculating emissary of pleasure, etc.). Moreover these principles/drives proceed at a diagonal to the ways in which philosophers have traditionally considered ontology. Pushing it a little, one might even detect a pastiche of the Hegelian 'science of logic' at work here: the operation of meaning-making posits being, only to find both meaning and being are undone in and by that very positing. This paradoxical situation renders the problem of the psychoanalytic cure very fraught. What, exactly, could a 'cure' be under the conditions of the transference? As we know, Freud himself ended his working life – or rather failed to end it – by canvassing the possibility that an analysis might be 'interminable'.

So the transference introduces a genuinely irreducible division into the field of psychoanalysis. If psychoanalysis is to be a materialism, on what material does psychoanalysis operate? Is it a materialism of the organism or a materialism of discourse? This can be put differently: is language a technology? The transference is precisely something which gives a negative answer to this question and, in doing so, unleashes psychoanalysis both from science and from philosophy. What is most crucial to underline in this context is a reference to something that Freud himself returns to again and again: the practice of psychoanalysis is an experiment and experience of the implications of where the body intersects with language, the former becoming a signifying machine alienated from its own biochemistry, the latter becoming saturated with the alienated affects of the bodies which bear it. As Freud notoriously writes of the 'drive' (*Trieb*): it is 'a concept on the frontier between the mental and the somatic . . . the psychical representative of the stimuli originating from within the organism and reaching the mind'.[26] But all

---

[26] S. Freud, 'Instincts and their Vicissitudes', in *The Standard Edition of the Complete Psychological Works of Sigmund Freud*, Vol. XIV (1914–1916), ed. J. Strachey et al. (London: The Hogarth Press, 1957), pp. 121–2. The entire editorial preface to this work is of extreme interest in this context, as it tracks the variations in this formula throughout Freud's work.

of Freud's concepts ultimately turn out to be located precisely on this frontier.

It is this unrelenting examination of the crossing-site between body and language that is crucial for psychoanalysis – and it is immediately evident why both science and literature would be necessary for such a project. As we have seen, however, problems remain with Freud's conception of the transference. It is part of Lacan's originality to have returned to this conception, in order to clarify and further extend its field of operations. In this clarification, the role of psychoanalysis as a little apocalyptic praxis moves to the fore.

'WHAT IS YOUR ONTOLOGY?'

Where Freud was diffident, Lacan came to be virulent. As a committed antiphilosopher, he consistently insisted on the ruptures from philosophical ontologies that psychoanalysis had effected. As I will discuss further in Chapter 3, Lacan was also far more clearly, directly and intensely interested in philosophy than Freud himself; indeed, there is no other psychoanalytic text so imbricated with philosophical motifs or with the key philosophical debates of its time. Even a cursory glance at Lacan's *Seminars* or *Écrits* would reveal his deeply antagonistic commitment to philosophy. In these pages, we find an extraordinary attention to the pre-Socratics, Socrates, Plato, Aristotle, the Cynics, the Stoics, the Sceptics, the Epicureans, the Scholastics, Descartes, Spinoza, Kant, Hegel, Bentham, Kierkegaard, Nietzsche, Heidegger, Russell – that is, the entire Western tradition – as well as traces of his own highly ambivalent exchanges over more than thirty years with such diverse contemporaries as Alexandre Koyré, Alexandre Kojève, Jean Hyppolite, Paul Ricoeur, Maurice Merleau-Ponty and Jacques Derrida, among others. Yet, as I have noted, this confrontation with philosophy leads to the conclusion that it, coming before or misunderstanding the epoch of modern science, remains absolutely inadequate to the true nature of desire.

Perhaps Lacan's most celebrated declaration in this context arises in response to the young Jacques-Alain Miller in *Seminar XI*. Lacan replies to Miller's demand 'what is your ontology?' with an elusive double statement. On the one hand, the unconscious does serve 'an ontological function'; on the other, '[t]he gap of the unconscious may be said to be *pre-ontological*'.[27] From this Lacanian perspective, the

---

[27] J. Lacan, *Seminar XI: The Four Fundamental Concepts of Psychoanalysis*, trans. A. Sheridan, intro. by D. Macey (London: Penguin, 1994), p. 29. Lacan continues: 'what truly belongs to the order of the unconscious, is that it is neither being, nor non-being, but the unrealised'; p. 30.

entire regime of ontology is the tributary of a poorly posed question, itself dependent upon an incompetent comprehension of language.[28] The unconscious inspires an ethics, not an ontology; indeed, the very ex-sistence of the unconscious acts as a universal caustic, corroding all traditional ontologies. Rather than an ontology, Lacan proposes an 'hontology', that is, discourse about the shame-being of the subject.[29] In the light of this hostility, one might still attempt – as has been done – to throw the dispute onto another level in order to make such concepts as 'the Real' or *jouissance* function as a kind of de facto if disavowed ontology. In my opinion, such attempts fail for at least two reasons: first, because speaking like this is to succumb to the *jouissance* of the idiot', insisting on recuperating what is in question; second, because the *jouissance* of the idiot fails the challenges of science.

This is precisely where the problem of science arises in Lacan: not only the science of linguistics as he adapts it from Ferdinand de Saussure, Roman Jakobson and Claude Lévi-Strauss, but the sciences of animal ethology, cybernetics and genetics. Commentators sometimes fail to note how often references to Pavlov, Norbert Wiener, John von Neumann and Gregory Bateson appear in Lacan's work, showing him to be *au fait* with contemporaneous developments. Moreover, and perhaps better known, Lacan was highly attuned to the problem of the formalisation of psychoanalytic results; for this, unlike Freud, he turned to new developments in mathematical formalisation (notably Bourbaki and topology) as a guide. Among the central outcomes of this interest are the mathemes, allegedly crystallising a specifically psychoanalytic knowledge. Given the (often ludicrous) controversies that surround these little diagrams, it is worth reiterating that they were explicitly presented as fragments of inductive analytic experience and to be deployed as pedagogical devices. As Lacan asserts: 'Mathematical formalization is our goal, our ideal. Why? Because it alone is matheme, in other words, it alone is capable of being integrally transmitted.'[30]

---

[28] Judith Butler has offered a succinct summation of this general tendency in Lacan: 'Lacan disputes the primacy given to ontology within the terms of Western metaphysics and insists upon the subordination of the question "What is/has being?" to the prior question "How is 'being' instituted and allocated through the signifying practices of the paternal economy?"'; *Gender Trouble* (New York: Routledge, 1989), p. 43.

[29] See J. Lacan, *Seminar XVII: The Other Side of Psychoanalysis*, trans. R. Grigg (New York: W. W. Norton & Co., 2007).

[30] Lacan, *Seminar XX*, p. 119. See also B. Burgoyne, 'From the Letter to the Matheme: Lacan's Scientific Methods', in J.-M. Rabaté (ed.), *The Cambridge Companion to Lacan* (Cambridge: Cambridge University Press, 2003), pp. 69–85; A. Cutrofello, 'The Ontological Status of Lacan's Mathematical Paradigms', in S. Barnard and B. Fink (eds), *Reading Seminar XX: Lacan's Major Work on Love, Knowledge, and Feminine Sexuality* (Albany: State University of New York Press, 2002), pp. 141–70; and J. Clemens, 'Letters as the Condition of Conditions for Alain Badiou', *Communication and Cognition*, 36:1–2 (2003), pp. 73–102.

Integral transmission: the matheme is, among other things, an attempt to answer the problem of transference in the institution of psychoanalysis, a materialist way to transmit knowledge beyond meaning or interpretation. Here, one can see the antiphilosophy of Lacan at its starkest. Psychoanalysis is positioned between science and literature, insofar as the *mathematisation* of the former binds knowledge to the *stabilisation* of literality, whereas the latter concerns the *reinvention* of letters.

J.-C. Milner has, moreover, suggested that Lacan thereby affirms the following propositions: '1) that psychoanalysis operates on a subject (and not for example on an ego); 2) that there is a subject of science; 3) that these two subjects are one and the same.'[31] Psychoanalysis and modern science share a subject – which does not mean that psychoanalysis is a science for Lacan. But psychoanalysis, at least, takes that subject as *its* subject.

Descartes proves the touchstone. For Lacan, the Cartesian approach

> is directed essentially not towards science, but towards its own certainty. It is at the heart of something that is not science in the sense in which, since Plato and before him, it has been the object of the meditation of philosophers, but Science itself [*La science*]. The science in which we are caught up, which forms the context of the action of all of us in the time in which we are living, and which the psycho-analyst himself cannot escape, because it forms part of his conditions too, is Science itself.
>
> It is in relation to this second science, Science itself, that we must situate psycho-analysis. We can do so only by articulating upon the phenomenon of the unconscious the revision that we have made of the foundation of the Cartesian subject.[32]

This is where science and psychoanalysis are placed in a particular relation by Lacan: this relation is, as can immediately be seen, different from the relation of science and psychoanalysis maintained by Freud. What Lacan's revision demands is that a subject be the pure support of the signifier (I will come back to this). This sketch also suggests some of the difficulties in discussing Lacan's take on 'ontology'. Not only is Lacan's development complicated and overdetermined, but, as Gilbert Chaitin remarks, he sees the transference 'as the source of a permanent

---

[31] J.-C. Milner, 'The Doctrine of Science', *Umbr(a)* (2000), p. 33. See also 'Lacan and the Ideal of Science', in A. Leupin (ed.), *Lacan and the Human Sciences* (Lincoln and London: University of Nebraska Press, 1991), pp. 27–42. These articles are extracted from Milner's extraordinary book, *L'Oeuvre claire: Lacan, la science, la philosophie* (Paris: Éditions du Seuil, 1995). Milner even identifies two independent, non-trivial and constructive 'doctrines of science' in Lacan, whose subtleties cannot be investigated here.

[32] Lacan, *Seminar XI*, p. 231. See also J.-A. Miller, 'Elements of Epistemology', in Glynos and Stavrakakis (eds), *Lacan & Science*, pp. 147–65.

crisis in psychoanalysis, and repeatedly terms it a paradox'.[33] It remains true, in other words, that for Lacan, as for Freud, the paradox of love is central to whatever he could be said to offer to ontology.[34]

In an early paper entitled 'Presentation on Transference' (1951), Lacan – as will be further examined in Chapter 3 – betrays his demurring indebtedness to Kojève's Hegel, at least in his terms: '*psychoanalysis is a dialectical experience*, and this notion ought to prevail when one poses the question of the nature of the transference.'[35] Returning to the case of Dora, Lacan shows how a development of truth emerges in a series of dialectical reversals, regulated by the transference. First, Freud responds to Dora's complaints by confronting her with her own complicity in the situation of which she complains. Second, the supposed object of Dora's jealousy (her identification with her father) masks another interest. Third, Dora's fascination with Mme K. is not due to the latter's ineffable individuality (i.e. 'the ravishing whiteness of her body'), but derives from the enigma for Dora of her own corporeal femininity. Transference, for Lacan, is thus not only the motor of the emergence of truth in a situation through a series of reversals that involve the negation of the subject's being, but also implicates an asymmetrical doublet of the subject: the analyst who, to be an analyst at all, has already submitted him- or herself to precisely the same procedure and passed through to the other side. The analyst's role here becomes that of 'a positive non-acting', the necessity to make interventions that are not those of an authority, exemplar, teacher, friend or guide.[36]

The relation of the transference to ontology is opened in *Seminar I* (1953–4), by way of a discussion of Freud's case-study of the 'Wolf Man'. Discriminating the transference from resistance as he discriminates *Verdrängung* ('repression') from *Verwerfung* ('foreclosure'), Lacan draws the conclusion that there is something beyond repression that, as its kernel, 'is literally as if it did not exist'. He continues: 'this is the very essence of the Freudian discovery.'[37] This non-existent kernel turns out to be nothing other than the place of the Other itself, that which supports, in Lacan's notorious formulation, the 'unconscious structured like a language'. So as this kernel of non-existence is unveiled at the eccentric heart of the subject by the transference, the transference

---

[33] G. D. Chaitin, *Rhetoric and Culture in Lacan* (Cambridge: Cambridge University Press, 1996), p. 151.

[34] For a different account of this relation, see S. Tomsic, 'The Invention of New Love in Psychoanalysis', *Filozofski Vestnik*, 31:2 (2010), pp. 189–204.

[35] J. Lacan, *Écrits*, trans. B. Fink et al. (New York: W. W. Norton & Co., 2006), p. 177.

[36] Lacan, *Écrits*, pp. 489–542.

[37] J. Lacan, *Le Séminaire, livre I: Les écrits techniques de Freud* (Paris: Éditions du Seuil, 1975), p. 54.

reveals itself as the kernel of love. For if Eros in the later Freud is 'the universal presence of a power of bonding between subjects', the trans- ference is more specifically a 'love-passion, such as it concretely lived by the subject as a sort of psychological catastrophe'.[38] Lacan will even proceed to remark, in response to a comment by Hyppolite, that 'love is a form of suicide'.[39] And if love certainly deploys its effects across the three Lacanian registers – the imaginary, symbolic and real – it primarily operates at an imaginary level.[40] Narcissism and aggression are coeval and inseparable for Lacan, the self and its objects repeat- ing indefinitely across a smeary hall of mirrors. However, and this is crucial, Lacan also always considers love in excess of a pure narcissistic demand. That is, transference ≠ suggestion, although the line between them is irreducibly ambiguous.[41] Bound up with this distinction is Lacan's consistent refusal of another, that is, his critique of the very concept of 'counter-transference'. Transference for Lacan is an open field, not a simple projection of one individual onto another.

If this is not the place to examine Lacan's major technical innova- tions in adequate detail, we can still underline the crucial role that love plays as his premier nut-cracking tool: the paradoxes of transference- love are precisely what Lacan relies on to illuminate every aspect of psy- choanalysis, from very specific clinical issues to large-scale structural concerns. If we run briefly through a few of the published seminars, this immediately becomes very clear. In *Seminar III* (1955–6), Lacan underlines that the transference is resistance not on the patient's part – but on the analyst's. He takes recourse to the mediaevals to illumi- nate the 'question of the subject's relation to the absolute Other'.[42] In *Seminar IV* (1956–7), returning to the ruses of courtly love (as he will continue to do throughout his career), Lacan shows how love separates humans from their biological needs, introducing a permanent dimen- sion of desiring non-satisfaction into life. Love and the gift of love aim at something radically Other than the needs of the organism, that is, they aim at the lack at the heart of being. With love – another famous Lacanian slogan – we find 'there is no greater gift possible, no greater

---

[38] Lacan, *Le Séminaire, livre I*, p. 130.

[39] Lacan, *Le Séminaire, livre I*, p. 172.

[40] Indeed, this is a point common to many if not most psychoanalytic orientations, e.g. 'my patient is a narcissist, like any other person grandiosely surmounting all others by falling in love'; E. Young-Bruehl, *Where Do We Fall When We Fall in Love?* (New York: Other Press, 2003), p. 16.

[41] See, for example, Lacan, *Le Séminaire, livre V: Les formations de l'inconscient, 1957–1958* (Paris: Éditions du Seuil, 1998), p. 429.

[42] J. Lacan, *Seminar III: The Psychoses: The Seminar of Jacques Lacan Book III, 1955–1956*, trans. R. Grigg (London: Routledge, 1993), p. 253.

sign of love, than the gift of what one doesn't have'.[43] Yet love, insofar as it is imaginary, must find its point of support in an object; in doing so, love separates itself from the desire that it wishes to know nothing about, that is, that desire is precisely attached to the lack, the nothing beyond being. This is where the transference remains so crucial, and where Lacan ties the operations of the void back to clinical experience and practice:

> For if love is giving what you don't have, it is certainly true that the subject can wait to be given it, since the psychoanalyst has nothing else to give him. But he does not even give him this nothing, and it is better that way – which is why he is paid for this nothing, preferably well paid, in order to show that otherwise it would not be worth much.[44]

Love is at once tied firmly to the void of the signifier at the very moment that it betrays this void with the demand for the glitter of an unattainable object. By *Seminar VII* (1959–60), love comes to function as a retreat from the enjoyment of the other, yet, as sublimation, works as a kind of barrier against the intolerable emptiness of the Thing, now located beyond the signifier.[45] The following year's seminar is even more apropos: *Seminar VIII* (1960–1), entitled, precisely, 'The Transference', opens with an extended reading of Plato's *Symposium*, in which the role of the *agalma* in love is unveiled. This *agalma*, which Alcibiades discerns in Socrates, is 'the good object that Socrates has in his belly', of which Socrates is no more than the physical envelope.[46]

So if Lacan clearly retains from Freud the automatic, fictional, lawless, passionate, narcissistic, revelatory powers of the transference (it is a world-making illness that can be leveraged through psychoanalytic treatment into a world-unmaking act), he exacerbates its link to an original double, the two of an encounter. For a long time, and despite Lacan's incessant theoretical revisions, this encounter continues to be conceived as a metaphor, that is, as a symptom which at once interrupts and veils the unconscious of which it is precisely the evidence. Hence, in *Seminar XI* (1964), we find that the 'transference is the enactment of the reality of the unconscious' and 'the means by which the communication of the unconscious is interrupted, by which the unconscious

[43] J. Lacan, *Le Séminaire, livre IV: La relation d'objet* (Paris: Éditions du Seuil, 1994), p. 140.

[44] Lacan, *Écrits*, p. 516. As Lacan also says in this essay, 'From this point of view, transference becomes the analyst's security, and the subject's relation to the real becomes the terrain on which the outcome of the battle is determined'; p. 498, p. 596. Translation slightly modified.

[45] See J. Lacan, *Seminar VII: The Ethics of Psychoanalysis (1959–1960)*, trans. D. Porter (London: Routledge, 1992).

[46] J. Lacan, *Le Séminaire, livre VIII: Le transfert* (Paris: Éditions du Seuil, 2001), p. 213.

closes up again'.[47] As one of the 'four fundamental concepts of psychoanalysis' (along with repetition, the unconscious and the drive), transference-love is also an affirmation of a (non) relation, between the desire of the analyst and the desire of the patient.

This 'non-relation' or encounter is never conceived of in any straightforward sense. It is 'odd', excentric to any intersubjective relation qua set of egos. As Lacan notes in *Seminar VII*, 'It's odd that in almost all languages happiness offers itself in terms of a meeting – *tuché*.'[48] But psychoanalysis is suspicious of happiness (in Freud's famous dictum, its job is to turn neurotic misery into ordinary unhappiness), and so this meeting never quite takes place: it is an irrevocably missed encounter. If there is happiness in psychoanalysis, it is, as Lacan will joke in *Seminar XVII*, the happiness of the phallus. Love also, as we all know, doesn't lead to happiness except in fairy-tales, whose too-abrupt endings imply that 'you don't want to know anything more about that', a kind of censorship of the aftermath. Love remains the narcissistic apparition of a symptom.

Which is also why Lacan denounces the notion of an epistemophiliac drive, a *Wisstrieb*. Rather than such a drive, the 'three fundamental passions' are love, hate and ignorance. No one wants to know of his or her own accord. So when Lacan declares 'All true love turns to hate', he is affirming: that knowledge is affective; that a shift in affect is a condition for the production of knowledge; that such knowledge doesn't bring power or pleasure or happiness. In this Lacan's position remains classically Freudian. In 'Instincts and their Vicissitudes' (1915), Freud had declared that 'love' and 'hate' were not symmetrical, and that they arose from different sources. If love begins as the auto-erotic capacity of ego to satisfy its drives before it passes to objects, it turns out that '[h]ate, as a relation to objects, is older than love'.[49] If then there is the appearance of a drive to know, this must be due to something extra, a kind of surplus bound to love. Whence Lacan's doctrine of 'the subject supposed to know': 'As soon as the subject who is supposed to know exists somewhere . . . there is transference.'[50] And, again, in his 'Introduction to the German Edition of the *Écrits*' (1973), Lacan puts it bluntly: 'it is love that addresses itself to knowledge. Not desire.'[51] Desire wants to know nothing about it.[52]

---

[47] Lacan, *Seminar XI*, p. 146, p. 130.
[48] Lacan, *Seminar VII*, p. 13.
[49] Freud, 'Instincts and their Vicissitudes', p. 139.
[50] Lacan, *Seminar XI*, p. 232.
[51] J. Lacan, *Autres Écrits* (Paris: Éditions du Seuil, 2001), p. 558.
[52] 'Hysterics give us the example that we would rather love than know, and that is the value of transference as obstacle: love, instead of knowledge. And it is on this point that Lacan

But the knowledge accessible through love is not 'truth' – for Lacan, famously, the truth can only ever be 'half-said' anyway – and it is more precisely a kind of non-knowledge, given, first, that it consists of a *semblance* of knowledge, and, second, that it emerges as a *consequence* of the psychoanalytic treatment, as a contingent, meaningless signifier: 'In so far as the primary signifier is pure non-sense, it becomes the bearer of the infinitization of the value of the subject, not open to all meanings, but abolishing them all, which is different.'[53] So if love is, on the one hand, a response to a missed encounter in the real, love can also be turned against itself through the clinic of analysis, love against love until the subject confronts the apparition of the master to which he or she is subject. As I discuss in Chapter 7, Lacan ultimately reformulates this master as S_1, the master-signifier.[54] As Slavoj Žižek declares:

> If the symptom in this radical dimension is unbound, it means literally 'the end of the world' – the only alternative to the symptom is nothing: pure autism, a psychic suicide, surrender to the death drive even to the total destruction of the symbolic universe. That is why the final Lacanian definition of the end of the psychoanalytic process is identification with the symptom. The analysis achieves its end when the patient is able to recognize, in the Real of his symptom, the only support of his being.[55]

So if love builds a world, psychoanalysis is a praxis of world-destruction through love. A non-apocalyptic apocalypse: the traversal of the fantasy, the negative limning of the S_1, and the simultaneous suspension of any sense of existence. This is why Lacan could be so astringent in his account of the relationship between love and suicide in such an act: in not giving way on your desire, you lead yourself to a space between-two-deaths, or subjective destitution. This space is 'beyond good and evil', as Lacan underlines:

> The question of the Sovereign Good is one that man has asked himself since time immemorial, but the analyst knows that it is a question that is closed. Not only doesn't he have that Sovereign Good that is asked of him, but he also knows there isn't any. To have carried an analysis through to its end is no more nor less to have encountered that limit in which the problematic of desire is raised.[56]

---

differs from Freud. There is no desire to know. It is love, not the desire to know, that is directed toward knowledge'; J.-A. Miller, 'The Analytic Experience', in M. Bracher and E. Ragland-Sullivan (eds), *Lacan and the Subject of Language* (New York and London: Routledge, 1991), p. 91.
[53] Lacan, *Seminar XI*, p. 252.
[54] This is probably as good a moment as any to acknowledge those whose work on love has been crucial for this chapter. What is a little bizarre is that three of them are literally masters, *domini*: Dominiek Hoens, Dominic Pettman and Dominique Hecq. The fourth, Sigi Jöttkandt, shares the letters of her *Vorname* with the founder of psychoanalysis.
[55] S. Žižek, *The Sublime Object of Ideology* (London: Verso, 1989).
[56] Lacan, *Seminar VII*, p. 300.

The praxis that is psychoanalysis is the transferential working-through of (the lack of) the world until the foundations of that world emerge in a kind of dispensing with the last judgement. Where the loving wannabe was, there an evacuated knowledge becomes – at the cost of the subject itself. This is precisely the 'erotic interment procedure' of which I spoke above.

But this love-burial of the subject opens, in turn, further questions. Is it an experience, a logical moment, or a real act?[57] How does it arise in the praxis of the clinic? Can its processes be generalised beyond a strictly clinical situation? Is it in fact tantamount to a 'cure'? Or is it a false exit? Should not rather the subject be treated to 'partner' their *sinthome*? What sort of being is at stake here? Is it not the case that such interment is the price of any rebirth?[58] These questions take us beyond the scope of this chapter and this book, and into the Bermuda Triangle of contemporary psychoanalytic disputations. But we will follow one of the lines opened here into a peculiarly Lacanian obsession: that the psychoanalytical subject is essentially a slave as a consequence of the encounter between bodies and languages – and not just a slave to love.

---

[57] Again, one might disagree with Žižek's claims here that identification with the symptom is the 'final' Lacanian position on the end of analysis; in fact, the situation is far less clear than such claims might suggest. See, for example, Lacan speaking of Joyce in *Le Séminaire, livre XXIII: Le sinthome, 1975–1976* (Paris: Éditions du Seuil, 2005). On the question of the act as a logical moment, see D. Hoens and E. Pluth, 'What If the Other is Stupid? Badiou and Lacan on "Logical Time"', in P. Hallward (ed.), *Think Again: Alain Badiou and the Future of Philosophy* (London: Continuum, 2004), pp. 182–90.

[58] Hence, as Lear brilliantly puts it, 'patients get better *after the treatment is over*'; *Therapeutic Action*, p. 190. Or, as Žižek likes to put it: the ethical act involves not only giving up your object of love out of love itself, but of giving up love as well.

3. Revolution or Subversion? Jacques Lacan on Slavery

It is claimed that self-interest will prevent excessive cruelty; as if self-interest protected our domestic animals, which are far less likely than degraded slaves, to stir up the rage of their savage masters.

Charles Darwin[1]

The specific hue which nobility had in the ancient world is absent in ours because the ancient slave is absent from our sensibility ... The Greek philosopher went through life feeling secretly that there were far more slaves than one might think – namely, that everyone who was not a philosopher was a slave; his pride overflowed when he considered that even the mightiest men on earth might be his slaves.

Friedrich Nietzsche[2]

The previous chapters pinpointed a new form of the ancient relationship between 'slavery' and 'alienation' emerging at the origins of psychoanalysis in the form of the relationship between drug-addiction and sexuality. The first chapter also showed how this emergence was coterminous with Freud's forced transition from scientific experimentation to linguistic interlocution; that is, it entailed Freud's departure from a strictly scientific field and directed him into situations that, while never abandoning a guiding ideal of science, required supplementation by the extra-scientific armature derived from a form of attentiveness to 'literature'. In terms of the 'therapy' offered by psychoanalysis, this required – as the subsequent history of psychoanalysis testifies – a shift from the pharmacological dosing of patients by state-ratified medical experts to the free associations of lay analysis. What the present chapter outlines is how this triple relationship – between slavery and

---

[1] C. R. Darwin, *Journal of researches into the natural history and geology of the countries visited during the voyage of H.M.S. Beagle round the world, under the command of Capt. Fitz Roy R.N.* (London: John Murray, 1860), p. 500.

[2] F. Nietzsche, *The Gay Science*, ed. B. Williams, trans. J. Nauckhoff (Cambridge: Cambridge University Press, 2001), p. 42.

alienation at the level of experience, between science and literature at the level of theory, and between dispensing and listening at the level of therapeutic intervention – is formalised by Jacques Lacan as at the heart of the psychoanalytic programme. In doing so, this chapter further justifies the specific ways in which psychoanalysis ought to be considered an antiphilosophy. If, as I have shown, a new theory and practice of love became central to this practice, it is because the problem of love is integrally bound up with the relation of language to a living body as founding the primal form of human servitude. This realisation led Lacan to reformulate a peculiarly psychoanalytic form of ethics.

The red thread I follow in this chapter is the fact that the figure of the slave is integral to Lacanian psychoanalysis from first to last. This claim is both simple and unoriginal. Its pertinence derives from the concerted incapacity of commentators, both pro- and hostile to Lacan, to sustain this integral status. One symptomatic index of this incapacity can be located in the indices to nominally Lacanian texts, in which any entry for 'the slave' regularly fails to appear. If it does appear, it is always insofar as it is a correlate or subheading for 'the master' or 'master-signifier' and, at least as often, insofar as it is referred to Lacan's uptake of the 'master-slave dialectic' of Hegel. Not only does this constitute a severe misunderstanding of the stakes of Lacanian psychoanalysis, but it necessarily involves falsifying the stakes of Lacan's relationship to philosophy (not to mention much else). If there is only the space here to give the most minimal indications of the status of the slave – I will for the most part restrict my comments to published evidence found in the *Écrits* – it is nonetheless worth beginning with a grimly quantitative rhetorical question. Is there a single *Seminar* of Lacan's in which the problem of the slave, of slavery, does not occupy a key position, whether overtly or not? This is not just a metaphor for Lacan, as we shall see, but places the biopolitical problem of the genesis of irreparable inequality at the centre of the psychoanalytic project.

The dominant interpretation sees this interest as deriving primarily from Lacan's encounter with Alexandre Kojève's interpretation of G. W. F. Hegel's 'master-slave dialectic'. Lacan and Kojève were friends, and at one stage even planned to write an article together in 1936 on the differences between Freud's and Hegel's theories of desire. Through painstaking archival research, Elisabeth Roudinesco has shown that 'Lacan's specific reading of Freud arose out of his attendance at Kojève's seminar on *The Phenomenology of Spirit* and follows directly from questions asked in the review *Recherches philosophiques*.[3] Lacan was clearly very attentive to philosophy, even if he sometimes professed to despise it, and profuse references to the philosophical tradition are essential in his work. Finally, Lacan develops concepts that are, at the very least, compatible with philosophical thinking, and which can be taken up, contested, extended and applied by philosophy in its own way.

I think, however, that almost everything about this picture is insufficient – if not downright misleading and pernicious. If Lacan was indeed 'influenced' by Kojève's interpretation, the word 'influence' remains an *asylum ignorantiae* if not examined further. I would prefer to say: Lacan treats philosophy as an enemy to be combated, right from the start; precisely because of this, he attacks it, just as Lenin recommended as the best practice for revolutionaries, 'at its strongest point'. Hegel is that 'strongest point'. And Hegel is so because in his work the ideal of total, absolute knowledge is rigorously and relentlessly pursued by discerning, affirming and then absorbing ('sublating') the vicissitudes of negativity.[4] This also accounts for why Lacan is so intimately polemical towards philosophy. Because philosophy, in Lacan's opinion, and Hegelian philosophy a fortiori, is the paradigm of any attempt to establish a knowing-knowing-itself-knowing, a total knowledge. Insofar as total knowledge seeks to bind and reconcile being and becoming, theory and practice, it also seeks to enable any division – for instance, between thought and action – to be bridged by technique (even if 'negative'). To this extent, 'philosophy' is a term used by Lacan to designate all such attempts at cognitive totalisation, and includes the tendencies in psychiatry, psychology and psychoanalysis itself that presume or seek to achieve such totalisation. Lacan's antiphilosophy is thus also, as I noted in the introduction, an antipsychiatry. Because he is also a psychoanalyst, however, Lacan's attack cannot be a head-on attack. As he

[3] E. Roudinesco, 'The Mirror Stage: An Obliterated Archive', in J.-M. Rabaté (ed.), *The Cambridge Companion to Lacan* (Cambridge: Cambridge University Press, 2003), p. 27.

[4] This sort of account of Hegel has of course been brilliantly disputed by Slavoj Žižek throughout his career, from *Tarrying with the Negative: Kant, Hegel, and the Critique of Ideology* (Durham, NC: Duke University Press, 1993) to his latest fat volume, *Less Than Nothing: Hegel and the Shadow of Dialectical Materialism* (London: Verso, 2012). For Žižek, the key is that 'Lacan is fundamentally Hegelian, but without knowing it', and that 'reciprocally, a reading of Hegel in the light of Lacan provides us with a radically different image from that, commonly assumed, of the "panlogicist" Hegel. It would make visible a Hegel of the logic of the signifier, of a self-referential process articulated as the repetitive positivization of a void'; *Interrogating the Real*, ed. R. Butler and S. Stephens (London and New York: Continuum, 2006), p. 28. If Žižek is certainly right to write against the commonplaces, and indeed has illuminated through his montage of Lacan and Hegel unexpected dialectical inversions, his interpretation remains contestable with respect to the letter and spirit of the Hegelian text.

reminds his interlocutors in *Seminar XX*, there is never any point in 'convincing' anybody.[5]

Lacan's 'attack' is therefore rather of the following kind. Philosophy orients us towards the proper objects and terms of study, but does so in a way that falsifies their import and, in doing so, functions to exacerbate misunderstandings. Psychoanalysis needs to 'subvert' – a crucial term in the Lacanian armature – philosophy's operations, since psychoanalysis, in line with its own affirmation of the powers of discourse, has no standing nor authorisation in the public world. Nor can it gain such a standing, except at the cost of its own self-betrayal. What psychoanalysis might do, though, is, from a position of irremediable weakness, exacerbate the routines of philosophy to the point at which the latter literally shows itself in its operations and aims; that is, shows itself as something other than the alibis of truth, knowledge and friendship would allow. Moreover, this also paradoxically means that psychoanalysis can and must lose its public struggle against philosophy, if it is not to lose itself. In its failure, however, psychoanalysis works to sustain modes of 'speaking' (or 'writing' or 'gesture' – there is nothing in these distinctions here) that engage further inventions of freedom within discourse. As such, psychoanalysis is above all a praxis, a praxis whose ethics are those of 'free association'. From *Seminar I*, Lacan could not be more emphatic regarding the singularity of psychoanalysis as a science of singularity, one, moreover, that is perpetually open to revision in its constitutional refusal of philosophical system. In opening this seminar by invoking the blows of the Zen master in response to the questionings of students, Lacan asserts: 'This teaching is a rejection of all system.'[6]

Lacan was always very clear about this, and also very clear that this clarity would inevitably be occluded as a matter of course. For psychoanalysis, the subject is 'split', that is, constitutively inconsistent, and therefore constitutionally foreign to any form of philosophical mastery. People think they think. They even think they think they think. They think they think what they think. And they think they know why they think what they think. Psychoanalysis thinks this too, but thinks it subversively. People do think like this, precisely because they – we, I – can't think any differently. We can't think differently, because what it means to think is thought for us by the signifiers that deploy us. Philosophy,

---

[5] J. Lacan, *Seminar XX: Encore: The Seminar of Jacques Lacan, Book XX: On Feminine Sexuality: The Limits of Love and Knowledge 1972–1973*, ed. J.-A. Miller, trans. with notes by B. Fink (New York: W. W. Norton & Co., 1998).

[6] J. Lacan, *Le Séminaire, livre I: Les écrits techniques de Freud* (Paris: Éditions du Seuil, 1975), p. 7.

to the extent that it has managed to inscribe its ontological obsessions within language, will always essay to effect a recapture of what evades, subverts or evacuates philosophical conceptuality. Yet Lacan throughout his career ceaselessly develops and refines his position on just what this recapture might mean. If it is impossible to provide a full account of the mutations to which Lacan submits his rethinking of the problem of the master, in this chapter I will identify a few of his fateful steps.

Why does Lacan designate the master-signifier the *master*-signifier? What does it mean to be a 'master' of this kind? A 'master' can be opposed to a slave, a serf, a student, an apprentice or even an actor. On the other hand, a master can be allied with or differentiated from a father, a leader, a lord or a sovereign – quite a ragtag collection of putative rulers. A master also implies a certain relation to self. If Lacan's use of the word 'master' displaces a number of these distinctions, its significance shifts quite radically over the course of his work. First, its crucial correlate is the slave, not the student. To be a master for Lacan is not just to be a schoolmaster; it means, first and foremost, being a slave-master, a master of slaves. Law, politics and economics are all enshrined in this structure, whose logic is ultimately established and delivered by the structure of signification. Second, the emergence of the thought of this opposition between master and slave lies in philosophy, specifically Hegelian philosophy, and, vis-à-vis Lacan himself, in his own initial encounter with Hegel by means of Kojève's notorious seminars on *The Phenomenology of Spirit* in 1930s Paris. Third, Lacan himself will use the term 'master' as a way finally to differentiate himself, not only from Freud's account, but from his own. The master-signifier ultimately comes to supplant those of the father, phallus or leader, for reasons that are complex and overdetermined but which hinge on the issue of the consistency of psychoanalysis in a new media age. These three points need to be taken together. None of them would be particularly novel to card-carrying Lacanians, but I would like to emphasise something about the master that remains under-examined, despite being crucial throughout Lacan's career: his analysis of slavery, which insists from first to last, even though it undergoes certain highly significant shifts.

As far as I have been able to ascertain, the word 'slave' (*esclave*) appears twenty times in the *Écrits*, and the word 'slavery' (*esclavage*) once.[7] Unsurprisingly, the word 'master' (*maître*), by contrast,

---

[7] J. Lacan, *Écrits* (Paris: Éditions du Seuil, 1966). Other than n. 8 below, all further reference will be to J. Lacan, *Écrits*, trans. B. Fink et al. (New York: W. W. Norton & Co., 2006), including page references to this English edition.

appears far more frequently in the *Écrits*; 'mastery' (*maîtrise*) eighteen times, *maîtresse* eight times, most often as an adjective (e.g. *les lignes maîtresses*), and 'to master' (*maîtriser*) once.[8] If it's worth at least pointing to this rather disproportionate distribution, this shouldn't prevent us from examining Lacan's uses of the slave further.

In 'Aggressiveness in Psychoanalysis' (1948), Lacan writes:

> A child who beats another child says that he himself was beaten; a child who sees another child fall, cries. Similarly, it is by identifying with the other that he experiences the whole range of bearing and display reactions – whose structural ambivalence is clearly revealed in his behaviours, the slave identifying with the despot, the actor with the spectator, the seduced with the seducer.[9]

> Before Darwin, however, Hegel had provided the definitive theory of the specific function of aggressiveness in human ontology, seeming to prophesy the iron law of our own time. From the conflict between Master and Slave, he deduced the entire subjective and objective progress of our history, revealing in its crises the syntheses represented by the highest forms of the status of the person in the West, from the Stoic to the Christian, and even to the future citizen of the Universal State. Here the natural individual is regarded as nil, since the human subject is nothing, in effect, before the absolute Master that death is for him. The satisfaction of human desire is possible only when mediated by the other's desire and labour. While it is the recognition of man by man that is at stake in the conflict between Master and Slave, this recognition is based on a radical negation of natural values, whether expressed in the master's sterile tyranny or in work's productive tyranny. The support this profound doctrine lent to the slave's constructive Spartacism, recreated by the barbarity of the Darwinian century, is well known.[10]

> The question is whether the conflict between Master and Slave will find its solution in the service of the machine, for which a psychotechnics, that is already yielding a rich harvest of ever more precise applications, will strive to provide race-car drivers and guards for regulating power stations.[11]

There are therefore two major senses in which Lacan is mobilising the resources of the signifier 'slave' in these presentations: (1) as exemplifying a law of projective reversal, of projection as dissimulated reversal: I experience what I do to you as if you had done it to me or vice versa; (2) as a Hegelian *philosopheme*, as marking the origin of human ontology in a struggle, but, notably in a struggle for 'recognition' or

---

[8] The term *maître* appears on the following pages of the French *Écrits*: 21, 32–3, 38, 65, 121–3, 127, 152, 162, 168, 179, 181, 241, 244, 249, 292–4, 304, 313–16, 320, 330, 345, 348–9, 351, 356, 371, 379, 396, 419, 424, 432, 452, 475, 477, 486, 536, 588, 634, 699, 754, 757, 807, 810–11, 824 and 826, most often in connection with the themes of teaching, ancient politics and the Hegelian dialectic.
[9] Lacan, *Écrits*, p. 92.
[10] Lacan, *Écrits*, pp. 98–9.
[11] Lacan, *Écrits*, p. 99.

'prestige', founded on a 'radical negation of natural values'. A particular phenomenon of *mis*recognition, in other words, regulates both senses of the slave. The truth of intersubjective relations inverts itself as part of its integral operations; this inversion is the medium of an irreducible antagonism; technology is a symptom of this antagonism. The problem of technology is raised integrally in the question of the slave, a category which for the ancients seems to have been essentially a technological one; by comparison, our 'objectifying' world demands a 'psychotechnics' (perhaps what is now dominant as cognitive behavioural therapy and psychopharmacology?) as a correlate. Finally, one cannot miss that, at least in this account of Lacan's, Hegel's philosophy mis-speaks of the *imaginary* functions of the self. If Hegel is right to identify the master-slave dialectic as crucial, some of its routines (the irreducible narcissistic-aggressiveness it marks), and its essentially anti-natural character, his analysis takes place at the cost of mistaking the relationship between philosophy and the world. Philosophy at once pinpoints something essential but miscomprehends it, not least because it ultimately seeks to suture truth to knowledge in a totalising system. Paradoxically, as Lorenzo Chiesa points out, 'from this standpoint, an anti-philosopher is ultimately more "scientific" than a philosopher', insofar as the latter is unable to bear incompleteness.[12]

This early position of Lacan's derives, as I have said, from his encounter with Kojève. Kojève, who was Alexandre Koyré's brother-in-law and Wassily Kandinsky's nephew, had studied under Karl Jaspers, before ending up in Paris. His central work in this context is not really a book at all; it is basically an assemblage of texts and lecture-notes taken by the great French writer Raymond Queneau, at Kojève's seminar at the École des Hautes Études. The seminar was attended by Raymond Aron, Georges Bataille, Maurice Merleau-Ponty, Eric Weil, Aron Gurwitsch, André Breton and Lacan, among others. In a superb twist of contingency, the lectures were only given in the first place because Koyré was off to Egypt for a couple of years and had invited Kojève to take his seminar for him. Kojève, then, proceeded on his reading of Hegel with extreme violence. As Michael Roth comments, 'it would be a complete mistake to try to understand or evaluate Kojève's work on the basis of its faithfulness to Hegel'.[13] What, then, was crucial about this seminar? It:

---

[12] L. Chiesa, *Subjectivity and Otherness: A Philosophical Reading of Lacan* (Cambridge: MIT, 2007), p. 4.

[13] See M. S. Roth, 'A Problem of Recognition: Alexandre Kojève and the End of History', *History and Theory*, 24:3 (1985), p. 295.

1. identified Hegel as the crucial philosopher of modernity;
2. identified the anthropological elements as crucial to Hegel's philosophy;
3. identified temporality as crucial to this anthropology;
4. identified the master-slave dialectic as crucial to this temporality;
5. identified the struggle for recognition as crucial to the master-slave dialectic;
6. identified the epitome of this struggle in the self-seizure of self-consciousness as such;
7. identified self-consciousness as such as finalised at the 'end of history'.

These identifications – despite their obvious failings as a reading of Hegel – are nonetheless compelling in the detail given them by Kojève.[14] Human being only properly begins when humans are willing to risk their animal, biological existence in a fight to the death for pure prestige, that is, recognition by the other; the winner, who becomes master, is the one willing and able to stare death, the absolute master, full in the face, and, in this total risk of life, dominates the other, who, fearful, has decided it would be better to live at any price than die; the master, however, is then condemned to enjoyment. For not only does he not get the recognition that he craved, except as recognition by an inferior (which is no real recognition at all), but his reward is enjoyment, the enjoyment of the fruits of the slave's labour, without truth; the slave, on the other hand, forced to toil at matter, comes, in the course of his enforced labours, to transform the world really, and, in this transformation, comes to know the truth of matter.[15] Note that 'recognition' here is not recognition of/by something real, but of a nothingness, of the desire of the other, a desire directed towards another desire. Note, too, that here we have a pre-existing philosophical version of the origins of the dialectical development between slavery and sexuality – *from* slavery *to* sexuality – that, as I showed in the first chapter of this book, emerged spontaneously in the early Freud as a dehiscence between bio-chemical addiction and the self-alienation of the symptom. I will return to this doubling and difference towards the end of this chapter.

[14] Badiou himself notes the abiding impact of Kojève's intervention in a 1977 piece reprinted in Badiou et al., *The Rational Kernel of the Hegelian Dialectic: Translations, Introductions and Commentary on a Text by Zhang Shiying*, trans. T. Tho (Melbourne: re.press, 2011), pp. 11–15.

[15] In truth, Kojève's discussion is more complex than this sketch will allow. See E. Kleinberg, *Generation Existential: Heidegger's Philosophy in France, 1927–1961* (New York: Cornell University Press, 2007), where he summarises Kojève's extension of the master-slave dialectic into the 'Pagan', 'Christian' and 'Bourgeois' state, pp. 75–9.

'The End of History' is a controversial thesis, to say the least. In the second edition of the commentary on Hegel, Kojève notes that:

> If Man becomes an animal again, his arts, his loves, and his play must also become purely 'natural' again ... But one cannot then say that all this 'makes Man *happy*.' One would have to say that post-historical animals of the species *Homo sapiens* (which will live amidst abundance and complete security) will be *content* as a result of their artistic, erotic, and playful behaviour, inasmuch as, by definition, they will be contented with it. But there is 'more.' 'The *definitive annihilation of* Man *properly so-called*' also means the definitive disappearance of human Discourse (*Logos*) in the strict sense.[16]

For Kojève, then, the 'end of history' does not mean that things don't continue to happen. What it means, however, is that, in accordance with a reading of Hegel that sees the dialectic of knowledge concluding with an immanentisation of all relations in the absolution of Spirit, that is, absolute as no longer articulated with any contradictions whose dynamic leads to irreversible developments, we see a paradoxical reconciliation of humanity with its natural animality. As such, language (*logos*, reason) will no longer project ideals that drive man forward through false starts and illusions, but will be resolved back into the pleasures of the body itself as forms of purposiveness-without-purpose. An unending aesthetics of post-philosophical snobbery is on the discursive cards, accompanied by an endless post-historical economics exemplified by the European Union.

It is against this philosophical sense of an end to man's becoming that Lacan develops his own position. As such, the properly 'structuralist' Lacan remains locked in a struggle with Hegel regarding ends. In Charles Shepherdson's words:

> Lacan's early seminars (1953–5) are marked by a prolonged encounter with Hegel, who had a substantial and abiding effect not only on his account of the imaginary and the relation to the other (jealousy and love, intersubjective rivalry and narcissism), but also on his understanding of negation and desire while leading to the logic of the signifier.[17]

Again, this is true as far as it goes. Take the important *écrit* 'The Subversion of the Subject and the Dialectic of Desire' (delivered

[16] A. Kojève, *Introduction to the Reading of Hegel*, ed. A. Bloom, trans. J. H. Nichols (New York and London: Basic Books, 1969), pp. 159–60.
[17] C. Shepherdson, 'Lacan and Philosophy', in Rabaté, *Cambridge Companion*, p. 116. See also T. Huson, 'Truth and Contradiction: Reading Hegel with Lacan', in S. Žižek (ed.), *Lacan: The Silent Partners* (London: Verso, 2006), pp. 56–78.

1960, but first published 1966), which opens with a reference to *The Phenomenology of Spirit*. First presented at a conference entitled 'La Dialectique', organised by Jean Wahl, the paper proceeds to distinguish psychoanalysis from philosophy, and both from science. Psychoanalysis properly speaking subverts the nature of the subject as it is delivered by philosophy. For Lacan, 'we expect from Hegel's phenomenology' the 'marking out [of] an ideal solution – one that involves a permanent revisionism, so to speak, in which what is disturbing about truth is constantly being reabsorbed, truth being in itself but what is lacking in the realization of knowledge'.[18] But scientific theories 'do not, in any way, fit together according to the thesis/antithesis/synthesis dialectic';[19] rather, science abolishes the subject altogether. Freud emerges in the non-space of this deadlock:

> In Hegel's work it is desire (*Begierde*) that is given responsibility for the minimal link the subject must retain to Antiquity's knowledge if truth is to be immanent in the realization of knowledge. The 'cunning of reason' means that, from the outset and right to the end, the subject knows what he wants.
>
> It is here that Freud reopens the junction between truth and knowledge to the mobility out of which revolutions arise.
>
> In this respect: that desire becomes bound up at that junction with the Other's desire, but that the desire to know lies in this loop.[20]

What goes wrong, in the end, for Lacan with Hegel is not that the latter hasn't touched on a number of fundamental propositions – for example, that language divides man from animal, that 'the word is the murder of the thing', or that the powers of negation cannot be ignored if one is even to begin to take account of singularities – but that 'the reason for Hegel's error lies in his rigour'.[21] What this means is that *Bewusstsein* comes to cover over the split in the *Selbst* produced by the external opacity of the shifter 'I', which no knowledge can contain, precisely because the utterance of any statement is in excess of the statement itself (and vice versa). Thus Hegel fails to note the 'generic prematurity of birth' in humankind (the 'dynamic mainspring of specular capture'), the fact that death is not the absolute master (the subject for Lacan being split between 'two deaths'), and misunderstands entirely the *jouissance* of the slave (that loss itself and not merely recognition is what is at stake in the struggle, insofar as the former is the index of a surplus-pleasure). *Jouissance* for Lacan is what becomes of Freud's problems with addiction; tied to the vicissitudes of the drive,

---

[18] Lacan, *Écrits*, p. 675.
[19] Lacan, *Écrits*, p. 675.
[20] Lacan, *Écrits*, p. 679.
[21] Lacan, *Écrits*, p. 685.

it necessarily founds and recaptures in its gravitational attraction the centrifugal tendencies of alienated desire as delivered by the structures of signification. For Lacan, this relationship is *not* a dialectical one.

Note that the theme of 'the end of history' is immediately subverted by the possibility of an analysis that is 'interminable'. One can see how Lacan implicitly maintains: (1) there is and can be no 'end' to history; (2) 'history' itself is an *ex post facto* reconstitution of events that necessarily effaces the divided operations of self-effacement essential to the subject; (3) 'history' therefore cannot function as any 'determination in the last instance' or as the ultimate place of the taking-place of events. History is always the history of masters, even when allegedly written 'from below'. For the 'unconscious', as Freud insisted, is characterised by its 'untimeliness', and in a number of senses. First, its activity always comes as a shock, whose effects are in excess of their causes, or rather retroactively create a cause which they dissimulate; second, the materials from which the unconscious is composed are not chronologically organised, nor are they even in principle able to be organised thus; third, the unconscious withdraws itself from any possible positive knowledge. Excess, disorganisation, unknowability: rather than history, then, Lacan emphasises the radical 'loopiness' of revolutions (something he will, of course, continue to do in different ways throughout his career), directed by the Freudian revelation that 'truth' and 'knowledge' have to be held apart on the condition of the unconscious. Psychoanalysis affirms the loopiness-without-end of subjectivity, its incessant detotalisation and its a-conceptuality. Indeed, Lacan will at one point formalise the operations of fantasy as $\$ \lozenge a$ (that the subject is correlated with an object-cause of desire), while the unconscious becomes structurally Other, a diacritically defined treasury which is an eccentric locus in which the fundamental signifier (the 'phallus') is always lacking from its place. Yet what Lacan's assault on dialectical teleology also means is this: slavery will always be with us – and it is us.

As ever, and despite the crucial inflection delivered by the Kojèvian-Hegelian encounter, Lacan's reference to the slave is drawn from, relies upon and extends Freud – against Hegel. In *The Future of an Illusion* (1927), his rather bilious tract on religion, Freud comments that 'every civilization must be built up on coercion and renunciation of instinct . . . It is just as impossible to do without control of the mass by a minority as it is to dispense with coercion in the work of civilization', and he goes on to speak of the concomitant necessity for producing an 'identification of the suppressed classes with the class who rules and exploits them'.[22] The enforcement of work and the control of the passions become the two major factors in rendering most members of a civilisation slaves; indeed, as Freud acerbically remarks, every person is in actuality to be treated as an enemy of the very civilisation of which they are a part, each individual being, irrevocably, a potential revolutionary. Hence, too, the necessity for 'illusion' – not error – on the part of the slaves themselves, which is for Freud the literally addictive narcotic that religion provides to the masses.

Yet, for all that, Freud is just as hostile to those allegedly egalitarian attempts to combat such servitude. As he will add a couple of years later in *Civilisation and its Discontents*:

> No matter how much we may shrink with horror from certain situations – of a galley-slave in antiquity, of a peasant during the Thirty Years' War, of a victim of the Holy Inquisition, of a Jew awaiting a pogrom – it is nevertheless impossible for us to feel our way into such people – to divine the changes which original obtuseness of mind, a gradual stupefying process, the cessation of expectations, and cruder or more refined methods of narcotisation have produced upon their receptivity to sensations of pleasure and unpleasure.[23]

Freud's cocaine scandal shows its continuing influence in such remarks: servitude qua addiction is the fated lot of the bulk of humankind, supported by public practices of self-dissimulating self-dosing. Yet there are two further aspects of these passages to underline here. The first is simply that the conscious 'shrinking' (so to speak) one might experience when confronted by the psychological horrors of oppression is itself a trick of perspective: it depends on a false identification, which cannot be ratified by psychoanalysis. On the contrary, psychoanalysis insists that any such identifications are necessarily false, and themselves freight, by occluding, a ferocious enjoyment. Note, moreover, how Freud's list deliberately relies on historically distant characters so as to circumvent the unconscious resistances that would inevitably arise if he had mentioned more recent or current events – although he does permit himself to wonder openly what will happen in the Soviet Union when the new masters finally rid themselves of their bourgeoisie.

The second point, perhaps unexpectedly, once again implicates Freud's own Jewishness, as it reinscribes the transition Freud himself makes from medical science (as care for the body) to antiphilosophy (as affirmation of the irreducibility of literary elements in thinking psycho-

---

[22] S. Freud, *The Standard Edition of the Complete Psychological Works of Sigmund Freud*, Vol. XXI (1927–1931), ed. J. Strachey et al. (London: The Hogarth Press, 1961), p. 7, p. 13.
[23] Freud, *Standard Edition*, Vol. XXI, p. 89.

pathology). The sequence leads directly to *Moses and Monotheism*. As Peter Sloterdijk has put it,

> Read in the context of Freud's speculations, the term 'exodus' now no longer refers to the secession of Judaism from foreign rule by the Egyptians, but to the realization of the most radical Egypticism by Jewish means. From that point on, the history of ideas takes the form of a massive game of displacement in which motifs from Egyptian universalism are acted out by non-Egyptian protagonists.[24]

In other words, Freudianism becomes a form of 'Josephian dream-interpretation', the slave decoding the otherwise-incomprehensible dreams of the Pharaoh in the name of an unknown-knowledge of fate. The deep historical articulation between addiction-servitude and alien-ation-sexuality re-emerges as the crux of the antiphilosophical project with regard to the origins of monotheism itself. Freud is thus himself a slave who transforms his fate by means of an interpretative genius, which takes the circumstances of slavery as its privileged material (I will speak more of this situation in Chapter 5, with regard to the tradition of Aesop's fables).

It is presumably for these eminently Freudian reasons that, at this stage of Lacan's work, the slave – the subject of the signifier – *is not really correlated with the master at all*. This may seem like a preposter-ous remark. Yet what is important here is that the 'mastery' of which Lacan most often speaks is correlated with the ego, that is, with the imaginary. As Lacan says, 'we analysts deal with slaves who think they are masters'.[25] Mastery is thus an imaginary function; slavery is a symbolic one. The subject is a subject insofar as it subsists in a state of servitude, servitude to the signifier. Lacan suggests that, with respect to the Freudian doctrine of the death-drive, a *savoir* is involved without any possible *connaissance*

> in that it is inscribed in a discourse of which the subject – who, like the messenger-slave of Antiquity, carries under his hair the codicil that con-demns him to death – knows neither the meaning nor the text, nor in what language it is written, nor even that it was tattooed on his shaven scalp while he was sleeping.[26]

When he arrives at his destination, the tattoo that the slave bears will be read, and enacted; this slave-messenger will be put to death. The cri-tique of the Hegelian master-slave dialectic is pursued: 'it is not enough to decide the question on the basis of its effect: Death. We need to know

---

[24] P. Sloterdijk, *Derrida, an Egyptian: On the Problem of the Jewish Pyramid*, trans. W. Hoban (Cambridge: Polity, 2009), p. 16.

[25] Lacan, *Écrits*, p. 242.

[26] Lacan, *Écrits*, p. 803.

which death, the one that life brings or the one that brings life.'[27] And this requires a recourse to Freudian doctrine again: Freud's Father is a dead Father, and this is, in Lacan's terms, of course the 'Name-of-the-Father'. For Lacan, 'the Father the neurotic wishes for is clearly the dead Father . . . But he is also a Father who would be the perfect master of his desire.'[28] A fantasy, evidently, a fantasy of mastery whose very form of demand actively works against its satisfaction. The master-slave dialectic is rather a phallus-slave a-dialectic.

So what, finally, has to be emphasised is that it is *sexuality* that returns to give the possibility of subverting the master-slave relationship upon which it is founded. If there is something that Lacan doesn't substantially seem to change his mind about, it is this. We can exemplify it briefly here by recourse to the famous *Seminar VII*, on the 'ethics' of psychoanalysis. The key to this seminar hinges on the central psychoanalytic problematic – and it is indeed problematic, as Lacan underlines – of sublimation. The three major instances that he provides are, not coincidentally, 'literary': the mediaeval troubadours, the Marquis de Sade and Sophocles's *Antigone*.[29] Against the usual understanding of the actions of Antigone herself in the secondary literature as the exemplum of Lacanian ethics (perhaps due to the influence of critics such as Slavoj Žižek and Alenka Zupančič), I maintain something quite different: Antigone is indeed, as Lacan says, an exemplum of the tragic experience of psychoanalysis, but she does not for all that constitute the final word on psychoanalytic ethics. Moreover, she does not provide 'an ethics of the real'.[30] Rather, it is the sallies of courtly love that provide a more elaborate and elaborated model, a 'better enough' model if one can say so.

If, as I am claiming, psychoanalysis is *sui generis* in its formulation and thinking through of the problem of the master-slave, this singularity is not monotony: psychoanalysis is only itself because it was called into being by a certain kind of speech, a hysterical demand for love. It is at this particular juncture that the example of Antigone should be located. The insistence of psychoanalysis, as well as its emergence, is conditioned by the persistence of hysteria. For Lacan, hysteria itself is

[27] Lacan, *Écrits*, p. 686.
[28] Lacan, *Écrits*, p. 698.
[29] See J. Lacan, *Seminar VII: The Ethics of Psychoanalysis (1959–1960)*, trans. D. Porter (London: Routledge, 1992).
[30] For an extended discussion of the issues here, see M. de Kesel, *Eros and Ethics: Reading Lacan's Seminar VII*, trans. S. Jöttkandt (Albany: State University of New York Press, 2009), as well as the relevant chapters in R. Grigg, *Lacan, Language, and Philosophy* (Albany: State University of New York Press, 2008). For more on Žižek, see for instance *Interrogating the Real*; for Zupančič, see above all the stunning account given in *Ethics of the Real: Kant, Lacan* (London: Verso, 2000).

a response to the primary uptake of discourse, that of the servitude of humanity to signification. To some extent, this also mimics a dictum of Hegel's, to the effect that 'woman is the eternal irony of community', as the latter remarks in *The Phenomenology of Spirit* precisely with respect to the character of Antigone. Lacan certainly has this Hegelian remark in his mind when he proposes his own interpretation of Antigone. Lacan's notorious formula is: 'from an analytical point of view, the only thing of which one can be guilty is of having given ground relative to one's desire.'[31] Antigone is the only one who does not give way on her desire and, in her consistent yet inexplicable refusal to conform to familial, legal and sovereign entreaties to do so, she enters into a space of para-existence suspended 'between two deaths'.

Yet, as Lacan will later note of the hysteric: if she is not a slave, she certainly does not want to get rid of the master; rather, she wants a master she can rule over.[32] Yes, hysteria is fundamental to psychoanalysis; yes, it is the basis upon which any ethics must be constructed; yet it cannot be the model for a properly psychoanalytic ethics. Psychoanalysis is not a Camus-type existentialism in which a revolt in being against being proves to be its own justification and reward. Its ethics will be rather an ethics of poetic creation – but a creation of a rather particular kind.

This is where the example of courtly love proves decisive. Lacan begins by outlining several enigmas of the practice: it emerges in a time unpropitious to women; it emerges among such unsavoury characters as Guillaume de Poitiers (essentially, serial-killers and -rapists), who have no evident reason to begin to compose verse in this way, indeed, have every reason not to embark on such a strange endeavour at all; it bears extraordinary resemblances to all sorts of religious poetry from around the world, to which it has no clear or direct connection. Hence the question: how is it that such personages, enjoying every good available to humanity, namely sovereignty, power, reputation, money, land, women and so on, suddenly turn themselves to composing the most refined esoteric verses? As Lacan notes, before Guillaume de Poitiers

> devoted himself to his early poetic activities in the sphere of courtly love poetry, he appears to have been a formidable brigand of the kind that, goodness knows, every right-minded feudal nobleman of the period seems readily to have been . . . he can be seen to have behaved in conformity with

[31] Lacan, *Seminar VII*, p. 319.
[32] J. Lacan, *Seminar XVII: The Other Side of Psychoanalysis*, trans. R. Grigg (New York: W. W. Norton & Co., 2007), p. 129.

the norms of the most barbarous practice of ransom. That was the kind of service one could expect from him.[33]

Mediaeval Occitania thus becomes a kind of laboratory for isolating the routines of sublimation in an exceptionally stark experiment.

Against the backdrop of such an unpropitious milieu, courtly love introduces several new elements regarding the practice of ethics: love and sex no longer appear as just one among many other zones of life to be regulated by a generalised ethics (e.g. the dietary restrictions, religious practices and social obligations familiar from classical philosophy), but as the source and centre of ethics itself; impossibility is explicitly and manifestly celebrated by the poem-songs as the highest form of service; this impossibility is a new way of knowing that knowing is impossible, whether in philosophical, theological or sexual senses, and is essentially non-religious; the *gai saber* is therefore at once a knowing and a 'happy' form of knowing; troubadour versification is an elaboration of self-given, patently artificial restraints in a new mode of free association and free invention. If it begins amongst the nobility, courtly love by no means remains exclusive to them.[34] In its praise of the cruel Lady, troubadour poetry explicitly stages not just the trials and tribulations of the experience of love, but the absolute impossibility of the relationship itself. In doing so, it exemplifies the very work of sublimation which it itself represents – as Lacan defines it at this point in his thought, the raising of an indifferent object to the dignity of the thing. Such sublimation, crucially, must be distinguished from the idealisation with which psychoanalytic theorists have too often confounded it: the songs of courtly love are often of an unparalleled obscenity, beginning with the barbaric cats of Guillaume himself.

Such poetic creation, insofar as it is *ex nihilo*, constitutes a decisive historical experience of the sexual non-relation as central to ethical practice. In doing so, it also provides a key to the abiding Freudian puzzlement over the paradox of *Vorlust*: that foreplay increases tension, and thus unpleasure, in the ultimate service of pleasure itself. What resolves this puzzlement for Lacan is the analysis that the troubadours incised into their song as 'the pleasure of experiencing unpleasure': the key to ethics is not 'well-being', as promulgated by philosophers of all stripes (including your garden-variety psychologists, psychiatrists, pharmacists and phamacologists), but 'well-speaking' (*bien-dire*). In doing so, ethics becomes something other than the 'service of goods'.

---

[33] Lacan, *Seminar VII*, p. 148.

[34] Despite some apparent consonances, Lacan's position is very different from that of Nietzsche; see F. Nietzsche, *The Gay Science*, ed. B. Williams, trans. J. Nauckhoff (Cambridge: Cambridge University Press, 2001).

If Antigone therefore constitutes the paradoxical matricial figure for psychoanalysis, exposing psychoanalysis's own origins and the structure of hysteria as its characteristic experience – the tragic refusal of servitude beyond reason – it is courtly love that exemplifies the possibility for an ethics not founded in the law, in goods or in a sovereign good. So we can now further specify the sense of psychoanalysis as antiphilosophy: we have a fundamental topic (the phallus-slave relation), a theme of subversion (the hysterical subversion of a sexual disorganisation that it thereby reveals), a *différend* (psychoanalysis against philosophy), and a new model of ethics (post-hysterical poetic creation that has reference neither to the law nor to the good).

There are two more issues raised by this relationship to philosophy that I wish to mention before briefly turning to *Seminar XVII*, which constitutes a rupture in the thought of the master-slave relationship for Lacan. The first of these is that, in his long-term efforts to defend Freud's Oedipus against the intra-psychoanalytic critiques proffered by Melanie Klein and others, he couples the hysteric with the Father, the latter reconceived by Lacan as the Name-of-the-Father, and delivered to the place of the Other. One consequence of this is that castration and fatherhood are thereby implicitly confused; another is that the 'signifier' and the 'letter' are thereby not able to be fully separated and, indeed, are used vaguely synonymously until at least the late 1960s. I shall speak more of this later.

Second, Lacan, in pursuing his antiphilosophical animus, recurrently attends to three great philosophers in particular: Plato, Descartes and Hegel. Each has something different, yet essential, to teach psychoanalysis. I have already indicated the centrality of Hegel in this affair. Regarding Plato, the problem is to separate Plato from Socrates, and, in doing so, to produce a renovated account of identification and the transference.[35] This, in accordance with Freud's own remarks regarding the scope of libido in psychoanalysis having a comparable field and function to that of love in 'the divine Plato', projects a new, rigorous genealogy for psychoanalysis (I have dealt with some of these questions in the previous chapter). Descartes, by contrast, involves a consistent reference to be at once sustained and subverted with regard to the decentring of the *cogito*, with the invention of modern science. As Lacan hilariously asserts in *Seminar XI*, regarding Descartes's introduction of algebra:

---

[35] See J. Lacan, *Le Séminaire, livre VIII: Le transfert* (Paris: Éditions du Seuil, 2001). For further commentary, see M. N. Armintor, *Lacan and the Ghosts of Modernity: Masculinity, Tradition, and the Anxiety of Influence* (New York: Peter Lang, 2004), esp. Chapter 1; S. Jöttkandt, *First Love* (Melbourne: re.press, 2010).

he substitutes the small letters, a, b, c, etc., of his algebra for the capital letters. The capital letters, if you will, are the letters of the Hebrew alphabet with which God created the world and to each of which, as you know, there corresponds a number. The difference between Descartes' small letters and the capital letters is that Descartes' small letters do not have a number – they are interchangeable and only the order of the commutations will define their process ... the presence of the Other is already implied in number ... Descartes inaugurates the initial bases of a science in which God has nothing to do. For the characteristic of our science, and its difference with the ancient sciences, is that nobody even dares, without incurring ridicule, to wonder whether God knows anything about it, whether God leafs through modern treatises on mathematics to keep up to date.[36]

The Cartesian decapitation of the letters of Scripture is also a kind of *innumeration*, one which literally reconfigures modern science as a form of godlessness: modern science takes off not simply from the *mathematisation* of the universe, but simultaneously from the *literalisation* of the universe; or, more precisely, by separating the material bases of mathematics from number and line before refinding this material already inscribed in the cosmos.[37] This separation-application also engages the work of the *cogito*, in which Descartes seeks to sustain the subject in its formalised ex-sistence. For Lacan, Descartes's God is no longer a perfect or all-knowing God, but becomes the field of knowledge itself qua infinite being. Psychoanalysis is also involved with this Cartesian subject, but operates by voiding and delocalising it; in doing so, psychoanalysis also founds an ambivalent link with modern science, from which the subject must be excluded.

If part of Lacan's genius, then, is to rip apart the key figures of the philosophical tradition to the benefit of psychoanalysis, and, in doing so, help to formalise essential psychoanalytic operations in avoiding the traps of philosophical consistency, he thereby creates a number of difficulties for himself. Let me list three of these symptoms. First, having separated Plato from Socrates, Lacan not only aligns himself with liberal analytical philosophy – as Badiou has pointed out – but, more pointedly, will thereafter be unable to decide just whether Socrates is an analyst or a philosopher or indeed something else.[38] Second, having subverted the Cartesian subject, Lacan will thereafter be unable to decide just how much modern science (i.e. a form of non-philosophy) continues to owe Descartes (and hence philosophy) and, hence, how

---

[36] J. Lacan, *Seminar XI: The Four Fundamental Concepts of Psychoanalysis*, trans. A. Sheridan, intro. by D. Macey (London: Penguin, 1994), p. 226.

[37] On this point, see the indispensable work of J.-C. Milner, most recently the interview with Ann Banfield and Daniel Heller-Roazen in the journal *S*, 3 (2010), pp. 4–21, where he discusses his theory of modern science as tied to 'literalisation'.

[38] See Lacan, *Le Séminaire, livre VIII, passim*.

much psychoanalysis continues to owe philosophy. Third, despite his critique of Hegel, flecks of Hegel's absolute knowledge start to reappear in unexpected places in Lacan's text.[39] These symptomatic vacillations are structurally irreducible given Lacan's interpretations of these figures in relation to the field of philosophy, and they will eventually lead to a rupture internal to Lacan's work.

This approach is at once consecrated and transformed with *Seminar XVII*. Why? Because there the master returns, as correlated with but differentiated from the slave, and the relation between master, slave and knowledge is at the heart of that seminar. Certainly, a master is always a master of a *mansion*, or what Lacan would call a *dit-mansion*, and hence not only of persons or positions, but of places. The existence of a – or every – master implies a topological determination. Moreover, Lacan will speak here of the master-signifier as well as of the master's discourse, the fundamental structure of signification upon which the human world literally turns:

> S_1 is, to say it briefly, the signifier, the signifier function, that the essence of the master relies upon. From a different angle you may perhaps recall what I emphasized several times last year – that the slave's own field is knowledge, S_2. Reading the testimonies we have about life in Antiquity, in any case discourse about this life – read Aristotle's *Politics* on this – what I am claiming about the slave as being characterized as the one who is the support of knowledge is not in doubt.[40]

What is the master? He is not a person – not simply, anyway – but more fundamentally a signifier. Even more precisely, the signifier function is not quite the master himself, but what the 'essence of the master relies upon'. He is, in what we could call Lacan's post-1968 *mathemations*, an effect of the S_1. How to speak of him, then? After all, the conceptual tools we have to speak about him derive primarily from philosophy, and philosophy itself is a master's discourse – if, as Lacan says, a 'subtle' one. We must avoid philosophy, then, but how? And, furthermore, even if we do, how then do we evade another form of discourse, one that is just as fundamental as the master's, that of the 'university'? For S_1 can only be an S_1 because of S_2, the signifiers of knowledge. The master doesn't know, but addresses himself to those who do. Who are these little S_2s, then? They are slaves, if knowing slaves. A slave is

---

[39] As Mladen Dolar has definitively shown in an unparalleled reading of Lacan's *Seminar XVII*, which, moreover, focuses on precisely the centrality of the master-slave dialectic in Lacan's work, Hegel functions, simultaneously and inconsistently, as an exemplar of the discourses of the university, the master and the hysteric; 'Hegel as the Other Side of Psychoanalysis', in J. Clemens and R. Grigg (eds), *Jacques Lacan and the Other Side of Psychoanalysis* (Durham, NC: Duke University Press, 2006), pp. 129–54.

[40] Lacan, *Seminar XVII*, p. 21.

always a slave of knowledge, in subjective and objective senses of the genitive. If, as we know from the notorious *Seminar XX*, 'there is no sexual relationship', analysis doesn't for that reason deny the existence of all relationships. Indeed, if there are relationships between human beings, if there is indeed any basis for a social bond, they all share a fundamental basis: S_1–S_2, the master and the slave. At the origin of language, there is the pure command without content, to which is correlated a knowledge of dependence. The cost, of course, is that of the splitting of the speaking being, marked by castration and by death. Like 'primitive accumulation' for Marx, the master-slave relationship is at the origins of the subject for Lacan.[41] I will return to this phenomenon in more detail in Chapter 7, where I pick up and re-examine the structure of the S_1.

From the beginning to the end of his career, then, Lacan constantly returns to the problem of the master-slave relation. In a 'Lecture on the Body', delivered by Lacan at Yale University on 25 November 1975, we find the following very clear link drawn between geometry and servitude: 'A slave is defined by the fact that someone has power over his or her body. Geometry is the same thing, it has a lot to do with bodies.' Lacan continues:

> Slaves knew that the master would set a price on their body, they were property, and in itself this protected them. A slave would know that the master wasn't about to carve up his body: small chance his body would end up fragmented. He thereby knew himself to be safe from a good many things.[42]

Power over the body, geometry, property: Lacan's identifications are, if not entirely original, certainly suggestive in his characteristic fashion. In this context, too, they might remind us of a number of crucial Lacanian themes which bear on the singularity of the discourse of psychoanalysis. There are above all two intricated elements to be scored in this context: psychoanalysis as an 'antiphilosophy' and, qua antiphilosophy, a discourse for which the problem of the master-slave relationship is at its heart. Simply put, the ancient slaves – contrary to certain widespread opinions about that status – could at least rely on their bodies being maintained in their integrity by their masters, at least as long as they remained functional in one way or another. Their speech was, of course,

---

[41] As Marx points out, vis-à-vis Adam Smith, 'This primitive accumulation plays approximately the same role in political economy as original sin does in theology'; *Capital*, Vol. 1, trans. B. Fowkes, intro. by E. Mandel (Harmondsworth: Penguin, 1976), Section 8, Chapter 26, p. 873. It is with respect, however, to primitive accumulation that Marx notes that violence and force are integral to its operation, that is, 'extirpation, enslavement and entombment': 'Force is the midwife of every old society which is pregnant with a new one. It is itself an economic power'; Chapter 31, p. 916.

[42] J. Lacan, 'Lecture on the Body', *Scilicet* 6/7 (1976), p. 38.

another matter, given that a slave's speech could only count in antiquity insofar as it had been extorted through torture under legal instruction. (I shall return to these matters in Chapters 5 and 6, regarding the status of torture and slave-speech.) Now we are free today, however, or at least nominally so in the field of speech, one thing we should be able to count on is the laceration, the dismemberment of our bodies, given that no one is prepared to stand as a master over them – not least ourselves.

So the problematic of slavery is there in Lacan from first to last. Ultimately, man is a slave to the signifier. To be a speaking being for Lacan is thus not to be free, but to be enslaved; and the very act of speaking is itself not freedom but evidence of coercion. 'Free association' is therefore literally an impossible affair. This is partially why, in the end, the entire elaborate edifice of Lacanian approaches to philosophy ends up by coming down on the side of the slave against philosophy, or, rather, on psychoanalysis as a non-revolutionary but essentially rebellious discourse that takes the side of the slave revolt against the master. This slave revolt is not Spartacist, but Antigonian, if I can put it like that. The hysteric is the beginning of ethics in this regard: one can never abolish the structures of mastery for Lacan, but one can at least assault in words the law of language as groundless 'NO!'. The hysteric, in other words, is a *condition* of psychoanalytic ethics, not its *model*. So the hysteric is not the end of ethics: rather, this is better characterised in the mode of poetic inventiveness, the 'least stupid', as Lacan says, of all human activities. In regard to sublimation, then, the little scabrous and esoteric songs of courtly love go beyond the experience of tragedy.

4. *Messianism or Melancholia? Giorgio Agamben on Inaction*

Hence loathèd Melancholy
   Of Cerberus, and blackest Midnight born,
In Stygian cave forlorn
   'Mongst horrid shapes, and shrieks, and sights unholy,
Find out some uncouth cell,
   Where brooding Darkness spreads his jealous wings,
And the night-raven sings;
   There under ebon shades, and low-browed rocks,
As ragged as thy locks,
   In dark Cimmerian desert ever dwell.

John Milton, L'Allegro[1]

Hence vain deluding joys,
   The brood of folly without father bred,
How little you bestead,
   Or fill the fixèd mind with all your toys;
Dwell in some idle brain,
   And fancies fond with gaudy shapes possess,
Or likest hovering dreams
   The fickle pensioners of Morpheus' train.
But hail thou goddess, sage and holy,
Hail divinest Melancholy,
Whose saintly visage is too bright
To hit the sense of human sight;
And therefore to our weaker view,
O'erlaid with black staid wisdom's hue.

John Milton, Il Penseroso[2]

---

[1] J. Milton, *The Poems of Milton*, ed. J. Carey and A. Fowler (London: Longmans, 1968), pp. 132–3.
[2] Milton, *Poems*, p. 140.

AGAMBEN'S PASSAGE THROUGH
ANTIPHILOSOPHY

In the preceding chapters, I tried to show how psychoanalysis emerged as an antiphilosophy and, in this emergence, came to establish certain routines as its own: the diagnosis of slavery as the consequence of the encounter between the body and language, a concomitant intrication of sexual protest, the ambivalence of love as at once mediating, obscuring and transforming this relation between slavery and sex, and, finally, the development of an ethics of poetic invention. This chapter, by contrast, turns its attentions to a different kind of thinker: one who begins as a self-nominated 'philosopher', but who, in covertly drawing from the antiphilosophical powers of psychoanalysis, recovers and remarks phenomena that much contemporary philosophy had felt itself able to overlook; these phenomena include the *Muselmann*, the potentiality of poetry, and a practical theorisation of study in which stupefaction and stupidity become avatars of messianism. If this chapter then makes the claim that Giorgio Agamben's mature work is formed as the result of a crucial encounter with psychoanalysis, especially regarding the foundations, extension and destiny of the concept of 'disavowal', this is not intended to claim him as an antiphilosopher, but to illuminate some of the ways in which philosophy can indeed go beyond antiphilosophy – but only if the former takes antiphilosophy with the seriousness that it requires.[3]

These claims may at first seem counter-intuitive, even paradoxical. After all, in the very few places where Agamben mentions psychoanalysis, he tends to be circumscriptive when not directly derisory. And if there is one theme upon which psychoanalysis expatiates interminably, it is the problem of sex; for Agamben, in contrast, sex is only rarely explicitly thematised. Nonetheless, a kind of trans-sexualised eroticism is at the heart of his philosophical project. As for the other claims, 'stupidity' is hardly a familiar category in the history of political thought, except, of course, insofar as it serves as a predicate of the rabble and a justification for their subjection. Its apparition in Agamben's thought is all the more noteworthy for that reason. Not only the symptom of a real failure of a certain kind of modern revolutionary politics, it bears

---

[3] This proposition further suggests (although it cannot be demonstrated here) that the usual contempt with which self-styled 'philosophers' and 'scientists' treat psychoanalysis today is one major means by which philosophy actively fails to live up to the challenges of the times. Rather, the *unthinking* hostility to psychoanalysis – as opposed to a genuinely *thoughtful* hostility, as evidenced by Agamben and Badiou, among others – is, generally speaking, a symptom of a suture to the powers-that-be.

links to a peculiar 'weak messianic' practice whose exemplar is the idiot student. Finally, I want to suggest that this analysis of disavowal and this gesture of stupidity cannot be separated if we are to understand something essential about Agamben's subsequent work, in its punctuated trajectory, in its conceptual details and in the singularity of its presentation.[4]

First, I will briefly discuss Sigmund Freud's classical psychoanalytical account of melancholia, to give a particular context to Agamben's own position in his early work *Stanzas*.[5] Second, this demonstration will simultaneously effect a translation of these accounts into the terms of affect (especially shame, rage and hate), modal categories (necessity, possibility, impossibility and contingency) and potential treatments for melancholy (a question concerning technology). Third, I will link the sexual aspects of psychoanalysis to the political aspects of Agamben's theories, showing, in this demonstration, how and why Agamben can legitimately draw on a limit case of psychoanalytic psychopathology in order to apply it to problems in political philosophy (sovereignty, society of the spectacle, commodity fetishism). In doing so, I want to suggest how this early work of Agamben's also establishes and illuminates certain elements of his later development, from *The Coming Community*, through *Homo Sacer* and beyond – but also why and how he left it behind.[6]

What I would, moreover, like to emphasise in all this is the following: that Agamben has, quite brilliantly, discerned a link between Freudian concepts that have traditionally been considered independent. To give only one instance here, though a crucial one in the context, 'melancholia' has not in the psychoanalytic literature usually been linked to the phenomenon of perversion. This is for a number of connected reasons. First, the manic, hallucinatory and self-persecutory elements of a typical melancholic presentation can immediately seem to share features with

---

[4] This, of course, has not been satisfactorily done in the secondary literature on Agamben to date, which at best invokes Freud and psychoanalysis, without following through the conceptual lineage in a demonstration: see, for example, L. Deladurantaye, *Giorgio Agamben: A Critical Introduction* (Stanford: Stanford University Press, 2009); C. Dickinson, *Agamben and Theology* (London: Continuum, 2011); C. Mills, *The Philosophy of Agamben* (Stocksfield: Acumen, 2008); A. Murray, *Agamben* (London: Routledge, 2010); J. Clemens et al. (eds), *The Work of Giorgio Agamben* (Edinburgh: Edinburgh University Press, 2008); M. Calarco and S. DeCaroli (eds), *Giorgio Agamben: Sovereignty and Life* (Stanford: Stanford University Press, 2007); A. Norris (ed.), *Politics, Metaphysics, and Death: Essays on Giorgio Agamben's Homo Sacer* (Durham, NC: Duke University Press, 2005).

[5] G. Agamben, *Stanzas: Word and Phantasm in Western Culture*, trans. R. L. Martinez (Minneapolis: University of Minnesota Press, 1993).

[6] G. Agamben, *The Coming Community*, trans. M. Hardt (Minneapolis: University of Minnesota Press, 1993); *Homo Sacer: Sovereign Power and Bare Life*, trans. D. Heller-Roazen (Stanford: Stanford University Press, 1998).

those of certain psychoses (paranoia, for instance). Under both descriptive psychiatry and structural psychoanalysis, the tendency has thus historically been to classify melancholia with the psychoses, or, as in early Freud, with the extreme anxiety neuroses. Second, it also has been the case that 'perverts' don't often seek psychiatric treatment or psychoanalytic cures by themselves. Foot-fetishists, for instance, don't tend to feel that they have a painful, life-threatening disorder; on the contrary, they tend to feel that they have quite a sustainable relationship to their desires. Perversion, despite being at the centre of psychoanalysis's developmental theories – not least in the infant's 'polymorphous perversity' – is nonetheless peculiarly subordinate in the field of clinical discussion to the neurotic and, later, the psychotic disorders. Third, the times, places, terminology, concepts and evidence connected to these phenomena develop separately in the literature, from Freud himself onwards.

At the same time, however, I would like also to emphasise that Agamben's own reconstruction of this operation – despite his persuasive demonstration of its continuities with well-sedimented antecedents in mediaeval theological doctrine – could not have been possible without psychoanalysis itself. For it is psychoanalysis that formalised melancholia and fetishism in such a way as to enable the integral connection to be made, and such a connection is, precisely, absolutely unavailable before such a formalisation (and a fortiori for the mediaevals). In other words, Agamben underplays a distinguishing feature of psychoanalysis upon which he nonetheless relies in order to render psychoanalysis continuous with its unexpected ancestors.

This brings up further questions regarding: the problematic of modern science, under whose aegis Freud proceeds, even as he directs it towards experiences that also have an intrinsically linguistic freighting; the problematic of Romanticism, for which such experiences at the limits of language come to figure, in their singular negativity, potentials for humanity in general; the problematic of political action when the only viable subject has become divided, stupid and impotent, unable to be thought of as an agent that actualises a potential; and so on. In any case, it is this psychoanalytic formalisation which I believe gives 'the decisive impetus' to Agamben's own subsequent trajectory. In other words, Agamben is far more reliant on psychoanalysis than is immediately apparent (and in ways he clearly is not quite happy to admit to), and Freud and Lacan are thus esoteric interlocutors whose import for Agamben's work is at least as determining as the more evident influences of Martin Heidegger and Walter Benjamin. It is this conviction that necessitates and guides the following exegesis of Freud's 'Mourning and Melancholia'.

MOURNING AND MELANCHOLIA

Freud's essay 'Mourning and Melancholia' (1917) is widely considered one of the classic essays of psychoanalysis. In it, Freud draws a crucial distinction between 'mourning', a standard process of grieving for a lost object, and 'melancholia', a refusal to give up on the lost object. For Freud, melancholia has many possible triggers, but it essentially revolves around such a loss, with deleterious consequences for its sufferers:

> the distinguishing mental features of melancholia are a profoundly painful dejection, abrogation of interest in the outside world, loss of the capacity to love, inhibition of all activity, and a lowering of the self-regarding feelings to a degree that finds utterance in self-reproaches and self-revilings, and culminates in a delusional expectation of punishment.[7]

We need, then, to underline these symptoms of melancholia: dejection, dereliction of the world, erotic destitution, physical debilitation, expressed self-loathing and delusional guilt. Each of these features receives attention from Freud, who essays to give a systematic metapsychological explanation of the condition.

In mourning, which shares, at least superficially, many features with melancholia, there is at least a conscious recognition of the loss of the object, emblematically a 'love' object. Recognising the loss consciously, the mourning ego struggles to withdraw its libidinal investments from this object. However, this struggle is not easy, and must be accomplished only in stages, bit by bit. This is what Freud refers to as 'the *work* of mourning' (my emphasis); the mourning or grieving person literally works through the pain of their loss in an attempt to come to terms with its necessity, and with their own incapacity to restore the loss in reality. For the mourner, a loss in reality cannot simply be made good, nor ignored, repressed or repudiated, but it may, ultimately, be accommodated, ultimately enabling the cathecting of a new object.

If melancholia can present in a similar fashion to mourning, it differs from mourning in a number of crucial ways. Whereas the lost object is always in part *consciously* recognised as such by the mourner, the melancholic's lost object is finally unknown or unconscious: *the melancholic does not know what he or she has lost.* This unconscious status of the object proves extremely problematic for the sufferer, and in a number of senses. For Freud, the overwhelming, incapacitating sadness

---

[7] S. Freud, 'Mourning and Melancholia', in *The Standard Edition of the Complete Psychological Works of Sigmund Freud*, Vol. XIV (1914–1916), ed. J. Strachey et al. (London: The Hogarth Press, 1957), p. 244.

of melancholia cannot easily be worked through insofar as this object remains unconscious. Furthermore, the psychic energy (or libido) freed by the loss of the object is thereafter withdrawn into the ego itself by a thoroughgoing *identification with the object*, indeed, by an 'incorporation' of the object. In melancholia, this terrible sequence – unknown loss, repression, incorporation – entails that the melancholic person constantly persecutes him- or herself, turning against his or her own ego ambivalence about the loss. As Freud notes, whereas mourning recognises the loss of an object that was 'good' and 'loved', the melancholic's relation to the object is necessarily more ambivalent, that is, a dense complex of love and hate. For Freud, the bitter recriminations that a melancholic typically turns against him- or herself are rather more appropriate to the object itself. He writes:

> Thus the shadow of the object fell upon the ego ... In this way the loss of the object became transferred into a loss in the ego, and the conflict between the ego and the loved person transformed into a cleavage between the criticizing faculty of the ego and the ego as altered by the identification.[8]

Let us briefly note that Freud is already pointing towards a split within the ego as a result of the incorporation of the other. If the 'criticizing faculty of the ego' of which Freud speaks here will soon be formalised as the 'superego' in the 'second topography' introduced in 1923 (id, ego, superego), we might also point to the very final developments of Freud's work in the late 1930s, in which he starts to speak of 'the splitting of the ego in the process of defence'.[9] It is at such a point that the problem of fetishism proves central, as we shall see below. But to return to the fundamental distinction at stake here, this is also why Freud can characterise melancholia as a 'refusal to mourn', insofar as the lost object is incorporated within the sufferer's psyche itself, a self-torturing denial of loss-in-its-preservation. This gives the three major 'conditioning factors' in melancholia as object-loss, ambivalence and the regression of the libido into the ego itself. Hence the return of the division between the ego and its objects inside the ego, eviscerating the melancholic with an inadmissible rage against loss.

Yet there is another point to be made here, regarding the apparent lack of sociability that is one marked aspect of melancholia, the withdrawal, exhaustion and sluggishness of the sufferer. The suspension of any effective relation to the social world is indeed crucial, especially

---

[8] Freud, 'Mourning and Melancholia', p. 249.
[9] S. Freud, 'The Splitting of the Ego in the Process of Defence', in *The Standard Edition of the Complete Psychological Works of Sigmund Freud*, Vol. XXIII (1937–1939), ed. J. Strachey et al. (London: The Hogarth Press, 1964), pp. 271–8.

given the inability of the melancholic to work properly. Such features, indeed, are very often underlined in the vast literature on the subject, dominating personal accounts of melancholic suffering to governmental reports of depression. Freud himself emphasises that the melancholic is prone to all sorts of externalised self-reproaches which are often performed before others – whether those 'others' are family or friends, medical professionals, or even fantasmatic figures. Freud even sardonically remarks that:

> When in his heightened self-criticism he describes himself as petty, egoistic, dishonest, lacking in independence, one whose sole aim has been to hide the weaknesses of his own nature, it may be, so far as we know, that he has come pretty near to understanding himself; we only wonder why a man has to be ill before he can be accessible to a truth of this kind.[10]

That self-knowledge and health may be constitutionally at odds in humans is a standard post-Nietzschean point of view. Truth-telling is an illness characteristic of man, the sick animal *par excellence*. What makes the point more specifically psychoanalytical is Freud's insight that such apparent self-knowledge is nothing of the kind. On the contrary, these ravings are a betrayal of sadistic impulses against the incorporated object, and not really against the ego that seems to be both its source and its target.

More recent commentators have also picked up on this peculiar form of public self-condemnation. As Judith Butler notes, 'the performance of melancholia as the shameless voicing of self-beratement in front of others effects a detour that rejoins melancholia to its lost or withdrawn sociality'.[11] What this means, among other things, is that the melancholic retains a link to the very society from which he or she is withdrawing, by showing, *exposing*, through this singular combination of rupturing shamelessness and indolence, the 'bans' of that society, its fundamental bonds and demands. If shame is one of the fundamental social affects, then there is something about the debilitating enervation of melancholy that suggests an attempted evasion of shame. Melancholics begin to act in ways that they would never countenance when well; or, to put this differently, they act in ways that well persons would never countenance. And because Freud also considers that melancholia is integrally constituted by a rage at other(s) returned upon the self, it is possible to consider melancholia as a peculiarly self-lacerating form of social revolt. Melancholics, says Freud, 'make the greatest

---

[10] Freud, 'Mourning and Melancholia', p. 246.
[11] J. Butler, *The Psychic Life of Power: Theories in Subjection* (Stanford: Stanford University Press, 1997), p. 81.

nuisance of themselves'.[12] For Freud, melancholics can be so shameless because it is not really themselves that they are addressing, but the other encrypted inside. This peculiar relationship between an apparently solitary experience of incomprehensible, inconsolable incapacity and a simultaneous dependence upon others is integral to the ambivalence of melancholy, which proceeds 'from a mental constellation of revolt'.[13]

Before leaving the classical Freudian account, let us emphasise several salient aspects:

1. Melancholia is linked to an unknown loss, a loss that doesn't know itself. The object itself is not known, even knowable;
2. The unknown object is nonetheless now incorporated into the ego itself through a specific form of identification. The difference between self and other has therefore experienced a peculiar collapse;
3. This incorporation is bound to primordial affects, above all, inadmissible erotic rage at the object;
4. This has the consequence of impotence, incapacity, for the sufferer in relationship to the social world as well as his or her own body;
5. This impotence supports a relationship of ambivalent suspension towards the world;
6. This relationship is then compulsively enacted by the sufferer in a mode of non- or counter-performance.

So, unknown loss, collapse of subject and other, primal affect, incapacity, suspension and counter-performance: these features all prove determining – albeit given a striking torsion – for Agamben's own reconstruction of the perverse potentials of melancholia.

STANZAS AS A RESPONSE TO FREUD

Agamben's *Stanzas* (first published in Italian in 1977) both draws on psychoanalytic theories of melancholy and critiques them, at once placing them in a larger historical-geographical context and attempting to show what the topic of melancholia has to offer to theories of human existence more generally. This philological and philosophical distance that Agamben takes from psychoanalysis allows him to refine the conceptual structure and operations of melancholia, but it also entails that – unlike the practising psychoanalysts – he plays down the *sexual*

[12] Freud, 'Mourning and Melancholia', p. 248.
[13] Freud, 'Mourning and Melancholia', p. 248.

aetiology of the condition. Agamben's model for the melancholic is, in fact, the mediaeval monk, and one might suggest that the account he provides of melancholia partially owes its novelty to both this restriction and this historical expansion. Yet an erotic relationship remains crucial in melancholia, one which, as we shall see, is a response to the fundamental sexual differences allegedly established by castration.

Agamben discovers in the European Middle Ages the origins of modern melancholia. Explicating the mediaeval texts on the subject – which occasionally hold acedia, melancholy, to be the most deadly of the seven sins – Agamben writes:

> If, in theological terms, what the slothful lacks is not salvation, but the way that leads to it, in psychological terms the *recessus* of the slothful does not betray an eclipse of desire but, rather, the becoming unobtainable of its object: *it is the perversion of a will that wants the object, but not the way that leads to it, and which simultaneously desires and bars the path to his or her own desire.*[14]

Agamben continues: 'Since its desire remains fixed in that which has rendered itself inaccessible, *acedia* is not only a flight from, but also a flight toward, which communicates with its object in the form of negation and lack.'[15] Agamben explicitly identifies this double flight (both away from and towards its object) with the psychoanalytic concept and operation of disavowal.

In Chapter 6 of *Stanzas*, entitled 'Freud; or The Absent Object', Agamben spends some time explicating this concept. Speaking about 'Fetishism' in a 1927 article of that name, Freud attempts to specify the characteristic operation of the fetishist. For Freud, the exemplary fetishistic primal scene is that of the little boy who, glancing up his mother's skirt, is horrified by her unexpected lack of a penis, and, though somehow acknowledging this lack, simultaneously refuses it as well. The integrity of the phallic mother is thereafter preserved by the fetishist in the form of a metonymic substitution (e.g. for the mother's pubic hair), often as fur, velvet, undergarments or shoes.[16] Leaving aside this preposterous aetiology of the fetishist (which Freud, in any case, doesn't really consider determining), the details of the psychical defence remain of real interest. Jacques Lacan was a master at identifying such operations in Freud, deploying them to provide rigorous foundations for the fundamental nosological categories of psychoanalysis:

---

[14] Agamben, *Stanzas*, p. 6.
[15] Agamben, *Stanzas*, p. 7.
[16] S. Freud, 'Fetishism', in *The Standard Edition of the Complete Psychological Works of Sigmund Freud*, Vol. XXI (1927–1931), ed. J. Strachey et al. (London: The Hogarth Press, 1961), pp. 147–58.

the neurotic's repression (*Verdrängung*), the psychotic's foreclosure (*Verwerfung*) and the pervert's disavowal (*Verleugnung*).[17] Indeed, Freud himself is very careful at this point, noting that, while the word 'repression' can still be used to speak of what becomes of the *affect* of horror, disavowal is an operation performed on the *idea*. Repression is, for Freud, emblematically a flight from an affect; disavowal, by contrast, is simultaneously a retreat from and an assent to an idea. That is, with the fetishist, the idea of castration is denied and accepted simultaneously; in doing so, it produces supplements of the inexistent.

It is in this frame that Agamben brilliantly identifies the double structure of this operation of disavowal with the peculiar double suspension we have already discovered in melancholia:

> the fetish confronts us with the paradox of an unattainable object that satisfies a human need precisely through its being unattainable. Insofar as it is a presence, the fetish object is in fact something concrete and tangible; but insofar as it is the presence of an absence, it is, at the same time, immaterial and intangible, because it alludes continuously beyond itself to something that can never really be possessed.[18]

We will return to one crucial consequence of this operation shortly, that is, the dissolution of the object in the acid-bath of phantasms, and its return as the indefinite proliferation of indifferent substitutes. For the moment, however, we should underline how Agamben uses the concept of disavowal to effect transitions from the deadly sin of acedia to the psychological condition of melancholia, to the operations of fetishism qua generation of pure artifice. Or even, to parody Baudelaire, to fetishism as the exemplum of the *artificial paradise*.

For psychoanalysis, the psychological operation of disavowal is exemplarily perverse: for Freud, the fetishist is a person who simultaneously recognises and denies the fact of sexual difference (emblematically, maternal castration). For one dominant line of psychoanalysis, as exemplified by Freud, Klein and Lacan, hysteria (neurosis) essentially remained the fundamental category of analytic diagnosis and treatment (even allowing for various sophistications and divagations); for antipsychoanalysts like Deleuze and Guattari, a better model for thought would be that of psychosis (especially schizophrenia); for Agamben, it is by means of an exacerbation of the routines of *perversion* that we can find another route through the thickets of contemporary philosophies of the subject. This perverse element will in fact become a principal

---

[17] See, for example, J. Lacan, *Seminar III: The Psychoses: The Seminar of Jacques Lacan Book III, 1955–1956*, trans R. Grigg (London: Routledge, 1993).

[18] Agamben, *Stanzas*, p. 33.

strut of Agamben's demonstration. It is not 'capitalism and schizo-phrenia' that is at stake for him, but 'capitalism and fetishism'. Even in this telegraphic summation, one might discern certain suggestive links between melancholia, heterodox belief and commodity fetishism. In this sense, melancholy is at once the paradigm and the other side of fetishism – whether fetishism is understood in a Freudian or Marxian sense. Despite appearances, then, melancholy would be a necessary stage in the invention of new possibilities for life; it might even, unex-pectedly, provide the indispensable underlining of joy (as the title of Chapter 16 of *Stanzas* has it, 'The "Joy That Never Ends"'). Indeed, Freud speaks of the tendency of melancholics to turn manic; and, as it happens, perverts are usually very happy with their fetishes. Moreover, this illuminates an element that will remain active in Agamben's work for some time after *Stanzas*: part of his politics, scholarly and studi-ous as they are, is to exacerbate the essence of the deleterious logics of the present. Not simply to reject (repress, deny, foreclose) the fetish or commodity fetishism, in other words, as if one could simply detach oneself from the present in order to deliver a devastating critique of it, or change it as a result of knowing it, but to study its prehistory in intense detail (following Aby Warburg's maxim 'Der gute Gott steckt im Detail'), and, in doing so, to try to unleash an unheard-of potential for transformation from the worst aspects of the disaster itself.

Agamben notes that, despite the enormous differences in time, place, language and attitude, the psychoanalytic accounts of melancholy further retain two key features of the mediaeval approach to acedia: (1) the withdrawal of the object; (2) the withdrawal of the libido (or the 'contemplative tendency' in mediaeval terms) back into the subject itself. What makes Agamben's interpretation of interest here is that he argues that it is possible to invert the standard reading of melancholia as a *reaction* to the loss of an object; rather, the melancholic imagina-tively and actively acts *as if* he or she had lost an object that he or she in fact never possessed. To put this another way, the melancholic acts as if it were in his or her power to *prohibit the impossible* – thereby rendering the impossible *possible as absence*. The melancholic struggle is to turn the Thing into an absent Object, all the while not knowing that it is doing nothing of the kind. The unconscious logic would then run something like this: if I have lost the object, then I must at some stage have had it; if I once had the object, then it must exist; if it exists, then it is possible to reacquire it; only, it cannot be reacquired now. Impossibility is thereby turned into *unactualised potential*, necessity into contingency. In other words, the melancholic 'proves' to him- or herself that 'God' (or 'happiness', 'utopia', 'the love object', etc.) really exists and can be grasped precisely because he or she no longer has it:

> If the libido behaves *as if* a loss had occurred although *nothing* has in fact been lost, this is because the libido stages a simulation where what cannot be lost because it has never been possessed appears as lost, and what could never be possessed because it had never perhaps existed may be appropriated insofar as it is lost.[19]

The unknowing simulations of melancholia are thus directed towards the creation of loss in order to summon the non-existent into absence. Or, to put this another way, both the melancholic and the fetishist create, in their disavowed ways, like God, *ex nihilo*.

Agamben wishes to show how this imaginative logic – however bizarre or irrational from the point of view of common sense or scientific rationality – at once is essential to human life and provides in some way the motivation for reimagining and transforming that life. Freud states that there is something of the frustrated social revolutionary in the melancholic temperament, and other, explicitly political writers such as Walter Benjamin and Judith Butler have also been taken with the phenomenon. There is even a similar implication in the work of Melanie Klein, insofar as the infantile depressive position is a crucial developmental reaction to (maternal) loss. One cannot go forward without looking backward, without a creative, retrospective stock-taking of loss. And the return of melancholy in adulthood can be understood, analogously, not only as a terrible moment of deadlock, but as an integral part of seizing and thinking-through an impossibility. As Agamben himself notes, the Western philosophical tradition evinces a marked solidarity on this point. Melancholy and imagination are essentially linked, and, without a touch of melancholy – which in principle interrupts all and any of the received or automatic processes of acting in the world – genuine thought is impossible.

Agamben's contribution is to show how the reacquisition of the allegedly lost object (or, indeed, the dissolution of the libidinal bond with it) is not the ultimate nor even the real goal of the project of melancholia. Because the sufferer of melancholia can no longer live either with the world of objects or with him- or herself, he or she exists in an intermediate zone which might be called (not that fancifully, given the consistency of descriptions offered by heterogeneous authorities) a *placeless place*, a *u-topia*. This utopian zone that the melancholic inhabits is unlivable and intolerable, a 'no man's land' at the very limits of human existence. It is a zone that the melancholic, in Agamben's

---

[19] Agamben, *Stanzas*, p. 20.

view, can only escape by creating and populating it with new objects; emblematically, cultural objects such as art or literature. This is one way in which Agamben reinvigorates the millennia-old link that, from Aristotle to the present, has been drawn between creative artists, lovers and melancholia. And one can also then see why melancholia is so often associated with fantasies of omnipotence: the melancholic who can do and say nothing in reality is paralysed by the (unconscious) conviction that he or she is still with God, has even incorporated God. This is why acedia is also, through a scandalous subterfuge, often understood as the flip-side of another deadly sin, that of pride (*superbia*).

Indeed, the utopia of the melancholic cannot be separated from the dissolution of the category of the object itself. Not only does the melancholic junk any and all of the existent objects of the world – *nota bene* Agamben's interpretation of Dürer's *Melencolia I*, in which the meditating angel sits surrounded by the discarded instruments of the *vita activa* – but the 'object' he or she produces as lost is not, *stricto sensu*, an object at all. Something similar goes for the fetishist, as Agamben suggests. Freud himself underlines that a fetish need not be an object, for example, in regard to the young man whose fetish had undergone a linguistic translation in the passage from English to German, from 'a glance at the nose' to 'a shine on the nose'. Moreover, as Agamben notes:

> However much the fetishist multiplies proofs of its presence and accumulates harems of objects, the fetish will inevitably remain elusive and celebrate, in each of its apparitions, always and only its own mystical phantasmagoria.[20]

Agamben's relating the melancholic's saturnine incorporation to the fetishist's operation of disavowal enables him to draw unexpected continuities: between apparently disparate psychological phenomena (acedia, melancholia, fetishism); between apparently disparate historical periods (mediaeval feudalism and modern capitalism); and between apparently disparate conceptual *dispositifs* (mediaeval theology and poetry, psychoanalysis, structural linguistics).

Because Agamben is a philosopher and not a clinician, he has little interest in practical techniques for curing or alleviating melancholia; rather, he implies that any overcoming of melancholia requires a certain imaginative invention of solutions for and by each particular sufferer. The singularity of each melancholic is thereby underlined. Although Agamben is certainly interested in discerning regularities in the symptomatology and theory of the condition, these regularities by no means

[20] Agamben, *Stanzas*, p. 33.

have the status of biophysical laws. His work suggests that contemporary medical difficulties, in clarifying the fuzziness of the category of melancholy and depression – not to mention the often wildly divergent responses of sufferers to medication and therapy – are absolutely irresolvable. Because melancholy is, for Agamben, an intense affective rejection by the sufferer of his or her inherited technologies and modes of life, the sufferer cannot simply be treated by those very technologies which he or she is (unconsciously) rejecting. Moreover, language necessarily fails in and in talking about melancholia, as symbolic bonds are central among those 'things of the world' which the melancholic suspends. This state of affairs renders many of the supposed 'treatments' for melancholia part of the problem itself. Yet it is also by creating (new) words and images that a way out of enervated suspension might be found by the melancholic sufferer. This creation must be, in the peculiar sense that Agamben gives it, literally a creation *ex nihilo*. The melancholic conjures loss out of nothingness in order to recreate unprecedented forms of life that are necessarily fetishistic – that is, new organisations of substitutable multiplicities.

On Agamben's account, melancholy, to the extent that it is bound up with a loss it does not know yet cannot abandon, is at the same time an unconditional demand for something new. The melancholic is typically obsessed with everything that he or she cannot bear about the world, which suggests also that he or she will not put up with any existing 'solutions' to his or her *Weltschmerz*. In this sense, melancholy is not, paradoxically, a backward-looking phenomenon, but is rather authentically forward-looking, or, more precisely, subsists in a temporality skewed between *already-over* and *not-yet*. Its cure would then be at least partially dependent on the sufferer's ability to reinvigorate both self and world by an imaginative solution (and not just chemical solutions in the manner of the governmental-pharmacological programmes regnant today). Not biology nor society nor economics will ever effectively explain or treat the melancholic: Freud himself confesses that his theory must not be taken to be of 'general validity' and that there remain points of obscurity about the 'economics' of melancholy.

'MEANS WITHOUT END'

Yet any possible solution to the deadlock of melancholy cannot simply involve the creation of new objects, that is, commodities. After all, the melancholic temperament is dedicated to the production of phantasmagoria, in which one fetish is already multiple, and in which that multiple may itself multiply indefinitely, indifferently. To extend

Agamben's argument here along his own lines, the passage beyond melancholia must involve the invention of new *means without end* (objects, goals, etc.). This programme is characteristic of Agamben's work: for instance, he will later speak of this post-melancholic problematic in terms of 'gesture':

> What characterizes gesture is that in it nothing is being produced or acted, but rather something is being endured and supported . . . if producing is a means in view of an end and praxis is an end without means, the gesture then breaks with the false alternative between ends and means that paralyzes morality and presents instead means that, *as such*, evade the orbit of mediality without becoming, for this reason, ends.[21]

'Something is being endured and supported': the gesture itself clearly remains in the ambit of the melancholic limit-experience. Moreover, the melancholic's is a profane belief, a deadly sin. And yet, despite its painfulness, it partakes already in an astringent kind of play.[22] In *Profanations*, Agamben remarks that, 'Just as the *religio* that is played with but no longer observed opens the gate to use, so the powers of economics, law, and politics, deactivated in play, can become the gateways to a new happiness.'[23] The polymorphous perversity of the infant is revivified in limit-experiences of adulthood.

In a section from *The Idea of Prose* entitled 'The Idea of Study', and after reminding us that in the Jewish tradition 'Talmud means study', Agamben gives a brief etymology of the word 'studium':

> It goes back to a st- or sp- root indicating a crash, the shock of impact. Studying and stupefying are in this sense akin: those who study are in the situation of people who have received a shock and are stupefied by what has struck them, unable to grasp it and at the same time powerless to leave hold. The scholar, that is, is always 'stupid.'[24]

The scholar, smacked across the forehead by an unexpected enigma, no longer convinced that he or she knows what he or she is supposed to know, compulsively pursues his or her stupefaction through the texts that he or she may once have thought that they had known, deranged by details which now shift and crawl and become other than they were once known to have been. The scholar is not a productive researcher, insofar as he or she doesn't necessarily come up with well-formulated problems, let alone useful results, but finds knowledge deranged and

[21] G. Agamben, *Means Without End: Notes on Politics*, trans. V. Bineti and C. Casarino (Minneapolis: University of Minnesota Press, 2000), p. 57.

[22] Agamben, *Stanzas*, pp. 25–6.

[23] G. Agamben, *Profanations*, trans. J. Fort (New York: Zone Books, 2007), p. 76.

[24] G. Agamben, *The Idea of Prose*, trans. M. Sullivan and S. Whitsitt (Albany: State University of New York Press, 1995), p. 64.

deranging at the moment it ought to have been established. The scholar does not know where he or she is going, even as he or she stumbles over strange correspondences and unstable esoteric communications, unable to decide even if they have any sense. In exile from his or her proper place, the scholar lingers in the realms of the intransmissible. As Agamben adds, 'This also explains the sadness of the scholar: nothing is bitterer than a long dwelling in potential.'[25] There is not even a method in such a madness, since the scholar's attention to details, which he or she follows forward through texts that simultaneously take him or her backwards (philology), scrambles any a priori methodology, any established routines. This is therefore a crucial fold in Agamben's text, whereby the unworking 'non-method' of scholarly stupefaction finds itself attending to the unworking 'non-methods' of exemplary figures such as the melancholic. This attentiveness is itself a political practice – modest, certainly, but just as certainly not without effects. It is legible in *Stanzas*, not least in the book's anomalous structure – three major divisions whose articulation is not immediately obvious, a stunning introduction, chapters of varying lengths, with different relationships to footnotes and to scholia, the reproduction of a variety of images – and in its brilliant style. Above all, it is by means of this fold that the scholarly text and its melancholic subject coincide in their unknowing reconstruction of the immemorial.

For Agamben, the psychological condition of melancholy is a necessary interruption in the continuity of life, and has an integral if non-standard political significance. If it seems a withdrawal from the realm of the political in its 'unworking', melancholy's ambivalence nevertheless constitutes a revolt against what exists without simply denying its existence or power. Both the self and its objects are unmade in melancholy. Melancholy 'unworks' without clear object, end or principle, implying that the principle must itself be refound and refounded. It cuts itself out from the orders of life without simply trying to flee, without committing suicide, without mythic violence – although it does run the risk of (self-) annihilation. It is neither bare nor qualified life, but a life that is literally *dis*qualifying itself. It is a revolutionary persistence without programme. As such, melancholia certainly harbours lessons for disenchanted political militants. Yet it is more than a merely individual psychological phenomenon, insofar as the crucial operation of recuperative negation that Agamben extracts from his readings in melancholia and fetishism – disavowal – has itself a double destiny in the world of law.

---

[25] Agamben, *The Idea of Prose*, p. 65.

On the one hand, this operation bears a family resemblance to the operation of sovereignty analysed in *Homo Sacer*, in which the law imposes itself most forcefully and insidiously not by violent injunction but by suspension and withdrawal; on the other hand, it bears family resemblances to the creatures like Bartleby, who, as 'a scribe who has stopped writing, [becomes] the extreme figure of the Nothing from which all creation derives; and at the same time, he constitutes the most implacable vindication of this Nothing as pure, absolute potentiality'.[26] (One should recall too that acedia is typically an intellectual's disorder.)

Let me briefly examine one of these examples, that of sovereign power, in more detail. For Agamben, the melancholic does not impose himself directly upon the world, but withdraws from it. Sovereign power does not impose itself directly upon qualified life, but withdraws from it. In his withdrawal, the melancholic creates God as lost to him; in its withdrawal, sovereign power creates bare life as lost to it. The melancholic includes the object as that which is excluded from his grasp. Sovereign power includes bare life as that which is excluded from its grasp. In his creation, the melancholic posits a relation to the absolute. In its creation, sovereign power posits a 'relation with the nonrelational'.[27] The melancholic dwells in potentiality, as does the sovereign ban, which 'corresponds to the structure of potentiality'.[28] In both cases, too, the matrix can be thought of as under the rubric of 'abandonment'. These are more than simple analogies, precisely because what they share is clearly due to Agamben's own obsession – an obsession that he himself is trying to interrupt.

In his own development, then, Agamben passes from this early study of melancholy to more directly political interventions which – in their themes, references, operations and intentions – exceed the melancholic closure. One indication of this is that the 'as if' of the melancholic simulation has now been supplanted by an analysis and affirmation of the 'as not' of Pauline messianism.[29] Yet one can also see how this attentiveness to melancholia has had a decisive import for Agamben's thought more generally. In addition to the operations of sovereign power discussed above, the problems of the affects of melancholia return in *Remnants of Auschwitz* in the analyses of 'shame' and of the

[26] G. Agamben, *Potentialities: Collected Essays in Philosophy*, ed. and trans. with intro. by D. Heller-Roazen (Stanford: Stanford University Press, 1999), pp. 253–4.
[27] Agamben, *Homo Sacer*, p. 29.
[28] Agamben, *Homo Sacer*, p. 46.
[29] See G. Agamben, *The Time That Remains: A Commentary on the Letter to the Romans*, trans. P. Dailey (Stanford: Stanford University Press, 2005).

biopolitical destiny of modal operators;[30] the anticipation of a theory of gesture in *Means Without End* and the messianic advent in *The Time That Remains*; and the use of exemplary figures, such as that of 'Limbo' in *The Coming Community*.[31] What Agamben has essentially done, then, is to isolate the irreducibly paradoxical melancholic operation in order, first, to divide it again, and, second, to discern and reconstruct the vicissitudes of that operation and its consequences in what are usually considered radically heterogeneous situations. If this ultimately leads to a transformation of the details of the operation itself, the vocabulary, references and frames for study, the avatars of melancholia in Agamben's work persist to the present.

One can then see why Agamben himself concludes the opening chapter of *Stanzas*, 'The Noonday Demon', with the following remark: 'As of a mortal illness containing in itself the possibility of its own cure, it can be said of acedia that "the greatest disgrace is never to have had it".'[32] Beyond the repulsive exhortations of contemporary powermongers to health, wealth, happiness, life, the service of goods and the pursuit of pleasure, and beyond the presently unactionable demands for mass revolution and the triumph of the will, there may well be an impotent power worth affirming in the demonic ingenuity of melancholy. But, as we have suggested, Agamben has also glimpsed that the melancholic must be interrupted by the messianic, in an over-coming from below. We can now add that this is precisely the switch-over within Agamben's work from antiphilosophy to philosophy, but in doing so the new account of messianism is doubled, unsurprisingly, by an account of new infernos.

At stake in this characterisation will be a redescription of the relation between the contemporary master and his slaves. The primal figure of these infernos, the *Muselmann*, has already been cited, and we shall return to it and to Agamben in Chapter 6, as it exacerbates and complicates the logics of servitude discussed in Chapter 3. But I first turn to an elaboration of the problematic of slave-speech: how the limit-characters in whom antiphilosophy is interested can come to speak otherwise about their situation; how they can participate in an ethics of 'well-speaking'.

[30] G. Agamben, *Remnants of Auschwitz: The Witness and the Archive*, trans. D. Heller-Roazen (New York: Zone Books, 1999), pp. 104–12, pp. 146–7.
[31] Agamben, *The Coming Community*, p. 5.
[32] Agamben, *Stanzas*, p. 7.

5. The Slave, The Fable

You can speak as openly as you like against ... tyrants, as long as you can be understood differently, because you are not trying to avoid giving offence, only its dangerous repercussions. If danger can be avoided by some ambiguity of expression, everyone will admit its cunning.

Quintilian, Institutes of Oratory[1]

By nature slaves have no share of the laws.

Anonymous Greek tragedian[2]

BACK TO SERVITUDE

Having established slavery as a key antiphilosophical theme – whether considered primarily as an essential possibility of the animal body or as a necessity of the political one – I turn here to one of the extant ancient practices of 'slave-speech', those texts commonly generically recognised as 'Aesopic fables'. I will argue here that 'the Aesopic' is always intimately connected with the problem of slavery, 'real' slavery, slavery in a real political sense. But the Aesopic is not simply the discourse of the slave as such; it is rather a discourse that is at once the expression and evidence of that slavery transfigured, although not entirely abolished. A penumbra of the threat of torture halos the Aesopic. I will also argue that the particular genre that exemplifies Aesopic discourse – 'the fable' – is a peculiarly primordial one in regard to human community, and in a number of closely connected ways. The Aesopic fable presents the enigma of the foundations of politics in a language that hovers ambiguously between 'nature' and 'culture'. If the Aesopic does so, however, it

---

[1] Cited in A. Patterson, *Censorship and Interpretation: The Conditions of Writing and Reading in Early Modern England* (Madison: University of Wisconsin Press, 1984), p. 15.

[2] Cited in M. Gagarin and P. Woodruff (eds), *Early Greek Political Thought from Homer to the Sophists* (Cambridge: Cambridge University Press, 1995), p. 75.

does not do so in a simply historical way. Yes, the Aesopic is irrevocably situational in the sense of always being located in a specific political milieu, and is uttered from a specific position within that milieu, but it is also unhistorical, 'untimely', insofar as it evades the established laws of that situation, addressing itself to something that that situation both exemplifies and occludes, as well as to something that exceeds the situation. In this address, the utterer also becomes other than his or her politico-legal status. This power of the Aesopic can only be a 'weak' or 'impotent' power since it draws solely on the most basic techniques of fabulation for its effects, and not on force, fact, demonstration or argument. But if the Aesopic only ever emerges as already on the verge of disappearing – as servile, childish, pointless, nugatory and so on – this disappearing is itself an integral trait, not a state of affairs that somehow needs to be rectified in the name of 'saving' it from its own marginality. On the contrary, the attempt to save the Aesopic is one of the counter-ruses of the master.

In making this argument, I will draw on a range of secondary materials, from literary and anthropological studies to classic philosophical accounts. What I have to say is not in itself novel, but rather draws out certain insistent features not usually articulated as such in authoritative accounts. This leads me to a perhaps unexpected corollary. The sorts of studies that one might expect to be attentive to the key problematic of slavery in the Aesopic corpus (literary theory, for example) constantly neglect it; the discourse that never seems to forget this problematic is, perhaps surprisingly, philosophy in the grand style. For Plato, Aristotle, Hegel, Marx and Nietzsche (and this is a shortlist) all have an extremely interesting and, indeed, decisive relationship to the Aesopic, as do philosophers much closer to us, including Bernard Williams and Giorgio Agamben. Moreover, all of these philosophers are very careful as to how the question of the relation of the law of the polis to the life of the body is necessarily articulated with the question of – what else? – the articulation of this relation. The key, again, is the problematic of slavery as a fundamental political phenomenon. This does not mean that philosophers 'like' the Aesopic, or praise it; often they are quite dismissive, even antagonistic. But they find themselves forced to respect it in a way that gives it a covertly essential place in their work. The modern discourse, however, that bears the closest relationship to the Aesopic is psychoanalysis, insofar as it also treats the real by means of a symbolic utterance which can never be stated clearly, distinctly or directly. Psychoanalysis is the return of the Aesopic within and against the philosophic.

A SHORTLIST OF OMISSIONS

It is striking how few histories of Greek literature take Aesop with any seriousness. Let me list some omissions. In Suzanne Saïd et al.'s *Histoire de la littérature grecque*, over 700 pages long, there is only one mention of Aesop, about whom nothing substantive is said.[3] In Tim Whitmarsh's *Ancient Greek Literature*, there is no index listing for Aesop.[4] In Christopher Pelling's *Literary Texts and the Greek Historian*, there is no index listing for Aesop.[5] The same author has edited a collection entitled *Characterisation and Individuality in Greek Literature*, in which there is no index listing for Aesop.[6] In Simon Goldhill's *The Invention of Prose*, there is no discussion of Aesop (this is a particularly deleterious omission, for reasons we will come to).[7] In Charles Rowan Beye's *Ancient Greek Literature and Society*, there is no index listing for Aesop.[8] In Maurice Bowra's *Ancient Greek Literature*, there is no index listing for Aesop.[9] In Albin Lesky's *A History of Greek Literature*, there is only the most minimal mention of Aesop.[10] Examples could be multiplied.[11]

Why does Aesop not really count for such accounts? There are a number of immediate possible answers. First of all, there is Aesop's own quasi-mythological status. Did he really exist at all? Did he really invent the fables that have come down to us under his name? Did he really write those fables down? And so on. But it is of course also the case that Aesop's fables do not really seem worthy of the appellation 'literature'; they are, rather, examples of something like 'folk-literature'. Hence a handful of fables are indeed anthologised by Michael Gagarin and Paul Woodruff in their *Early Greek Political Thought from Homer to the Sophists* so long, we understand, that they

[3] S. Saïd, M. Trédé and A. Le Boulluec, *Histoire de la littérature grecque* (Paris: Presses Universitaires de France, 2004).
[4] T. Whitmarsh, *Ancient Greek Literature* (Cambridge: Polity, 2004). When I write 'no index listing', this also means neither could I find any discussion of Aesop in the text.
[5] C. Pelling, *Literary Texts and the Greek Historian* (London and New York: Routledge, 2000).
[6] C. Pelling (ed.), *Characterisation and Individuality in Greek Literature* (Oxford: Clarendon Press, 1990).
[7] S. Goldhill, *The Invention of Prose* (Oxford: Oxford University Press, 2002).
[8] C. R. Beye, *Ancient Greek Literature and Society*, 2nd edn (Ithaca and London: Cornell University Press, 1987).
[9] C. M. Bowra, *Ancient Greek Literature* (London: Oxford University Press, 1964 [1933]).
[10] A. Lesky, *A History of Greek Literature*, trans. J. Wilis and C. de Heer (New York: Thomas Y. Crowell, 1966).
[11] The notable exception is Leslie Kurke's new book which, unfortunately for me, came out after this chapter had been drafted: *Aesopic Conversations: Popular Tradition, Cultural Dialogue, and the Invention of Greek Prose* (Princeton: Princeton University Press, 2011).

appear there merely as a kind of representative of the 'folk-wisdom' of the era.[12] This 'representative status' of those fables attributed to Aesop himself means that, however little attention they get, they actually get more attention than any other. As J. G. M. Van Dijk says, 'Paradoxically, the multitudinous fables that are embedded in Greek and Latin literature have so far received little, if any, scholarly attention. Most of the comparatively few *Fabelforscher* traditionally concentrate on the extant fable collections and on Aesop, the legendary *pater fabulae*.'[13] The whole genre of fable is therefore treated as substandard. Due to the lowliness of their origin, the simplicity of their form and the basic nature of the 'messages' they convey, Aesopic fables are and ought to be nothing more than a minor footnote in such histories.

Yet at the same time it remains true that Aesop himself is far more popular, influential and famous worldwide than Aeschylus and Sophocles and Pindar and the rest. As Michael Finke says, 'The Aesopic fable may be the single most familiar literary genre to us all.'[14] The Aesopic has a popular history that is far deeper and more involved than the classical texts recovered by the great Renaissance humanists. Indeed, in David Marsh's words, the 'history of the Aesopic fable from antiquity to the Renaissance is notoriously complex' precisely because 'unlike other Greek texts, Aesop was not rediscovered by Western humanists during the Italian Renaissance, for there was a continuous Latin tradition of prose compilations'.[15] And this for precisely the same reasons as above. As M. Ellwood Smith puts it,

> owing to its place in the regular school curriculum, its quaint and picturesque allegory, and its epigrammatic appositeness to human affairs, the fable once held a unique position among sources of allusion, and today there are many whose only knowledge of Aesop consists in allusions which still survive in current speech.[16]

The Aesopic fable, in other words, remains a primary pedagogical mode, one which is – in its brief and engaging accounts of its animal characters – eminently fit for children. Invented by a slave, now aimed at children, the Aesopic is on such evidence not for sophisticated tastes.

[12] See Gagarin and Woodruff (eds), *Early Greek Political Thought*.
[13] J. G. M. van Dijk, 'The Function of Fables in Graeco-Roman Romance', *Mnemosyne*, fourth series, 49:5 (1996), p. 513.
[14] M. Finke, 'Puškin, Pugačev, and Aesop', *The Slavic and East European Journal*, 35:2 (1991), p. 179.
[15] D. Marsh, 'Aesop and the Humanist Apologue', *Renaissance Studies*, 17:1 (2003), p. 9.
[16] M. E. Smith, 'Aesop, a Decayed Celebrity: Changing Conception as to Aesop's Personality in English Writers Before Gay', *PMLA*, 46:1 (1931), p. 225.

Yet more acceptable forms of literature are often literally built out of fables insofar as fables provide the background from which the work emerges and are also presented as such in the course of the narration itself.[17]

This peculiar status is not simply a historical accident that has befallen the Aesopic. As it happens, the Aesopic was already degenerate for the ancients themselves. K. S. Rothwell Jr notes, in the course of discussing Aristophanes's own complex take on Aesop, that 'In the more serious genres no Greek of the respectable classes tells a complete animal fable; instead fables were relegated more to comedy and iambos than to epic and tragedy.'[18] The genre, moreover, was popular with peasants and slaves, and slaves are often the tellers and addressees of the fables. At the same time, the discourse of the fable is acknowledged to be more complex than this situation might suggest. As Rothwell remarks in the course of an analysis of one of Hesiod's 'fables', it was 'aimed at a social superior, but in terms meant to be understood by a social equal'.[19] One might add that things are even more complex than this. For fables can surely be told that are at once directed at setting the social superior at ease by means of a flattery of content (e.g. moral: 'don't resist your superiors') and at the same time showing a social equal: look at them thinking we're confirming their superiority, they even think we're dumb and pliable, and so on. I will return to this question of the addressee below.

The colourful (and apocryphal) *Life of Aesop* – itself an anonymous, composite text – is absolutely clear about the meanness of Aesop's origins, to the point that their hyperbolic expression itself can only be received as having an allegorical function. Here, for example, is the opening of the *Life* (in Sir Roger L'Estrange's engaging late-seventeenth-century translation):

> *AESOP* (according to *Planudes, Cameraius* and others) was by Birth, of *Ammorius*, a Town in the *greater Phrygia*; (though some will have him to be a *Thracian*, others a *Samian*) of a mean Condition, and his Person deformed,

---

[17] Indeed, this tends to be demonstrated by specialist studies, which can show the importance of Aesop to later poets and philosophers. See, for example, B. Acosta-Hughes and R. Scodel, 'Aesop *Poeta*: Aesop and the Fable in Callimachus' *Iambi*', in A. Harder, R. F. Regtuit and G. C. Wakker (eds), *Callimachus II* (Leuven: Peeters Publishers, 2002), pp. 1–21. The authors themselves remark how – compared, say, to 'Callimachus' recasting of Hipponax' – 'Aesop, as figure, as authorial voice, and as associative matrix, has received somewhat less emphasis. Yet clearly Aesop, and fable, play an integral role not only in individual poems in the *Iambi* and in the arrangement of the book but also in the authorial statement of the Aetia prologue'; pp. 1–2.

[18] K. S. Rothwell Jr., 'Aristophanes' *Wasps* and the Sociopolitics of Aesop's Fables', *The Classical Journal*, 90:3 (1995), p. 237.

[19] Rothwell, 'Aristophanes' *Wasps*', p. 236.

to the highest degree: Flat-nos'd, hunch-back'd, blobber-lipp'd; a long mis-shapen Head; his Body crooked all over, big-belly'd, badger-legg'd, and his Complexion so swarthy, that he took his very Name from't; for *AEsop* is the same with *Aethiop*. And he was not only unhappy in the most scandalous Figure of a Man, that ever was heard of; but he was in a manner Tongue-ty'd too, by such an Impediment in his Speech, that People could very hardly understand what he said.[20]

The ugliness, deformity, meanness, animality, foreignness, homeless-ness of the man could hardly be emphasised more. He is even foreign at home, both black and white, a slave, with a name that is itself not a patronym, not a real name, but a name that is indexed to his appear-ance itself: Aesop, Aethiop. Notably, his master is a philosopher, Xanthus, whom he mocks in endlessly inventive ways. The *Life* goes into great detail about Aesop's exploits, following his wanderings through different kinds of polities to his end in Delphi. There, falsely accused of stealing a golden cup that the Delphians have themselves planted on him, Aesop is condemned to death. He tells the fable of the 'Frog and the Mouse', which fails to convince the citizens; he flees to an altar, but is given no sanctuary, whereupon he responds with the 'Eagle and the Beetle'; he is then taken to the precipice from which he is to be flung, and relates a final fable, of a countryman who wishes to see the town before he dies but, due to terrible weather, is dragged by the asses that are carrying him into a pit: 'where he had only time to deliver his last Breath with this Exclamation. *Miserable Wretch that I am, to be destroy'd, since die I must, by the basest of Beasts, by Asses.*' While Aesop is still telling this fable, his executioners fling him to his death.[21]

So when studies do turn themselves toward the Aesopic, they cannot but note the meanness, lowness and animality of its mythical progeni-tor as providing essential if duplicitous features of the genre. Indeed, there is a close tie between the inventor of the discourse and the content of the discourse. This tie is constitutively ambivalent. Hence Annabel Patterson, in her *Fables of Power: Aesopian Writing and Political History*, remarks that, for sixteenth- and seventeenth-century readers, 'the stories of the beasts, the birds, the trees and the insects quickly acquired or recovered their function as a medium of political analysis and communication, especially in the form of a communication from

---

[20] This translation is available online at <http://aesopus.web.fc2.com/LIF/Life01.html> (last accessed 19 October 2012).

[21] However, the tradition differs on this denouement: Aesop sometimes flings himself off, and is not pushed. See T. Compton, 'The Trial of the Satirist: Poetic Vitae (Aesop, Archilochus, Homer) as Background for Plato's *Apology*', *The American Journal of Philology*, 111:3 (1990), p. 333, n. 12.

or on behalf of the politically powerless'.[22] The subjugated must code
their utterances, which must nonetheless be authorised (a code-name
of some kind is necessary, such as 'Aesop'); these utterances are themselves allegories of the situation of inequality in which they are uttered;
their very utterance is itself an act of freedom, a demonstration, at the
very least, that if freedom can be found nowhere else, it can be found in
speech. Moreover, the ambivalence of the Aesopic is such that the *Life
of Aesop* can be read, as Keith Hopkins as argued, as a veritable resumé
of ancient masters' anxieties about the treacherous nature of slaves.[23]
What can appear to be an entertaining celebration of low-cultural folk-
protest might rather be better understood as a kind of analysis-therapy-
handbook for the master.[24]

It may be tempting to attempt to reverse or at least lament the injus-
tice of the genre's apparent fate, of the narrow judgements of literary
theorists and historians who spurn or overlook the fundamental nature
of the Aesopic.[25] Hence one can find a countervailing critical tradition

[22] A. Patterson, *Fables of Power: Aesopian Writing and Political History* (Durham, NC: Duke
University Press, 1991), p. 2. See also her *Censorship and Interpretation: The Conditions of
Writing and Reading in Early Modern England* (Madison: University of Wisconsin Press,
1984) and *Reading Between the Lines* (Madison: University of Wisconsin Press, 1993), in
which she asserts that, 'in the early modern period, reading between the lines, which unlike
the last two practices [she has just mentioned psychoanalysis and deconstruction] was
dependent on writing between the lines, was already clearly understood to be a political
strategy with liberating consequences' (1993, p. 7). One could object, however, that psychoanalysis is interested in how the Aesopic precisely confuses the received distinctions between
'reading' and 'writing' between the lines: the unconscious is both a reader (of what Freud
calls 'the day's residues', for instance, that is, in all senses of the phrase, of 'the remains of
the day') and a writer (of 'compromise formations', that is, symptoms such as dreams).

[23] See K. Hopkins, 'Novel Evidence for Roman Slavery', in R. Osborne (ed.), *Studies in
Ancient Greek and Roman Society* (Cambridge: Cambridge University Press, 2004),
pp. 206–25. Hopkins writes: 'The appeal of the story for Romans depended, I think, on its
nightmarish understanding of all that might go wrong in a master's control over his slaves'
(p. 216). The paradox, moreover, is that 'we are asked and expected in a slave society to
side with the slave against the master' (p. 219).

[24] Interestingly, visual art and art-history have had a long and productive engagement with
the Aesopic since the seventeenth century and, it seems, primarily from the point of view
of the masters' enjoyment. Perhaps the most striking example of this would be the labyrinth at Louis XIV's palace at Versailles designed by André Le Nôtre which was, in Craig
Wright's words, 'the most elaborate and expensive horticultural labyrinth ever created': 'At
the entrance stood two statues, one of Cupid and the other of Aesop, allegorical figures of
Love and Wisdom. Along the paths Le Nôtre placed thirty-nine fountains, each of which
contained sculpted creatures that acted out one of Aesop's fables. The gist of each tale
was inscribed in gilded letters on a bronze plaque affixed to the fountain'; C. M. Wright,
The Maze and the Warrior: Symbols in Architecture, Theology and Music (Cambridge:
Harvard University Press, 2001), p. 229. I also cannot resist referencing the following
article, by none other than A. F. Blunt, great art-historian, advisor to Queen Elizabeth
II, and Communist spy, who notes that 'Representations of Aesop's Fables in the visual
arts before the seventeenth century seem to be curiously rare'; A. F. Blunt, 'Poussin and
Aesop', *Journal of the Warburg and Courtauld Institutes*, 29 (1966), p. 437, n. 7. See
also N. Tromans, 'The Iconography of Velázquez's Aesop', *Journal of the Warburg and
Courtauld Institutes*, 59 (1996), pp. 332–7.

[25] Psychoanalysis is again the great exception to these opinions. Leaving aside the great trajec-

that attempts to do just this.[26] Recently, writers such as Patterson, Louis Marin, Michel Serres and Thomas Keenan, among others, have found the genre, in its very simplicity, an extraordinarily complex one.[27] In doing so, they have reread precisely the 'low', 'animal' nature of the fables as of key significance. Marin, above all, is attentive to the reflexively corporeal nature of the Aesopic. For Marin, the narrator of the fable 'is not a voice at all, but a body, a fable-animal. The animal of fable is a devouring-devoured body, but one that, in addition, speaks.'[28] Patterson, referring to Aesop's fable of the body and its members, writes of how ambivalent its formulation has proven historically, being able to be understood both as an apologia for mastery and as a complaint against it. Nonetheless, 'What both formulations shared was the image of the human body and its nutritional needs as a symbol of the distribution of wealth in the body politic.'[29] The belly and the animal, the slave and his ambiguous speech, emerge from below to speak of the polity in the same terms. As such, Marin argues,

> [i]t might well be that the 'fable' in general, the narrative of the weak and of the marginal is – in the element of the discourse itself – a device for the displacing and turning back, by the weakest, of the force of the discourse of the strongest.[30]

But to simply recanonise the fable would be to mistake something that is absolutely essential about the conditions of the Aesopic: one cannot

tory of works from Freud and Jung to Bettelheim, Lacan comments: 'It is to this immense envelopment [of the numinous] and at the same time to a degradation that the genre of the fable bears witness. Ancient fables are full of meanings that remain richly rewarding, but we have trouble realizing that they could have been compatible with something like a faith in the gods, because, whether they are heroic or vulgar, they are shot through with a kind of riotousness, drunkenness, and anarchy born of divine passions'; *Seminar VII: The Ethics of Psychoanalysis (1959–1960)*, trans. D. Porter (London: Routledge, 1992), p. 172. Lacan himself later intriguingly invokes 'not so much of the myth of Sade (the term is inappropriate) but of the fable of Sade'; p. 209.

26 As Marc Redfield notes, 'The fable is an intriguingly contradictory genre. It takes its name from the Latin word for "narration," as though it were a genre of pure story, which is to say, not properly a genre at all. Yet it names a highly encoded sort of narrative, instantly recognisable and often condescended to ... The fable occupies an uncertain place in the literary universe, but it has fascinated narratologists and literary theorists because it raises and complicates questions of exemplarity, rhetoric, and power'; M. Redfield, '*Fables of Responsibility: Aberrations and Predicaments in Ethics and Politics* (review)', *MLQ*, June 1999, p. 288.

27 See L. Marin, 'The "Aesop" Fable-Animal', in M. Blonsky (ed.), *On Signs* (Baltimore: Johns Hopkins University Press, 1985), pp. 334–40; M. Serres, *The Parasite*, trans. L. R. Schehr (Minneapolis: University of Minnesota Press, 2007); T. Keenan, *Fables of Responsibility: Aberrations and Predicaments in Ethics and Politics* (Stanford: Stanford University Press, 1997).

28 Marin, 'The "Aesop" Fable-Animal', p. 334.

29 Patterson, *Fables of Power*, p. 4.

30 Marin, 'The "Aesop" Fable-Animal', p. 339.

speak directly, cannot assert oneself or one's position, precisely because the Aesopic arises under conditions of persecution, of the threat of torture and death. In other words, one cannot simply recover or affirm the Aesopic without thereby showing that one is oneself *not* Aesopic, that one speaks from a position of (often unknowing) exteriority to its situation of constraint. There is no meta-voice for Aesopic voices. If one speaks of the Aesopic, one has already achieved a 'freedom' that the Aesopic itself is directed towards and against. To the extent that this is the case, it is no surprise that the works by these critics about the power of fables tend, even when they recognise the fundamentally corporeal nature of the genre, to overlook how crucial the threat of torture is to its functioning.[31]

TORTURE AS THE GUARANTEE OF THE TRUTH OF THE SLAVE'S SPEECH

The threat is very real.[32] It is not simply due to the fact that being a slave is just not that great. Though slaves in ancient Greece often massively outnumbered their masters, even Athenian democracy showed little interest in protecting the physical and social integrity of slaves. I use the word 'even' here advisedly, given that, as Whitmarsh notes, 'unlike the Homeric *dmos*, the classical *doulos* certainly could be imag-

---

[31] This is presumably why, in his review of Keenan's book, Redfield is induced to remark that 'We gain little sense of why our next stop on the fabular bus line, after Aesop, should be Sade's "Philosophy in the Bedroom," a text with an interesting relation to the fable, but not an obvious one'; *Fables of Responsibility* (review)', pp. 289–90. My argument is that the 'non-obviousness' of this relation is precisely due to Keenan's overlooking the sheer political brutality that is the condition of fable: although he is in some sense right to have done so, Keenan cannot say why he has ordered his sections in this way because his notion of 'ethics and politics' doesn't really want to touch upon their foundations in the juridically supported torments of the speaking body.

[32] See P. duBois, *Torture and Truth* (London: Routledge, 1991) for an extended recent account of the classical uses of torture. In a review of duBois's book, Katherine Callen King gives her own 'more pragmatic interpretations': 'the key term of differentiation in Athens was not "free" but "citizen", an unambiguous category that was for all practical purposes both inalienable and unattainable; second, the most important effect of requiring that slave evidence result from torture is practical: since no slave could be tortured without the master's permission, it decreased slaves' ability to subvert their masters' interests through bribery or promise of freedom; and finally, in the manner of privileging tortured testimony (if indeed it was privileged), the important issue is the relative effectiveness of torture and law for compelling true speech'; K. C. King, '*Torture and Truth* by Page duBois (review)', *Comparative Literature*, 47:3 (1995), p. 262. Perhaps most importantly, 'Freedom from torture is freedom from compulsory self-incrimination'; ibid. p. 262. As Russell Grigg and I have argued, the point of 'freedom of speech' in democracy, both ancient and modern, doesn't mean 'say anything you like, anything at all', but rather *the state cannot torture*. See J. Clemens and R. Grigg, 'A Note on Psychoanalysis and the Crime of Torture', *Australian Feminist Legal Journal*, 24 (2006), pp. 159–76, as well as Chapter 6 of the present book.

ined as properly and naturally a slave, especially in Athens'.[33] Or, as
Bernard Williams summarises the situation:

> The slave was called (as elsewhere) 'boy,' *pais*, and it was a joke that *pais*
> came from *paiein*, 'to beat.' Public slaves, at least, were marked with a
> brand, which, as Xenophon observed, made them harder to steal than
> money. The overwhelming difference between free and slave, Demosthenes
> remarked, was that the slave was answerable with his or her body. Evidence
> from slaves was acceptable on condition that it had been extracted under
> torture. In a speech of Lysias, a man's reluctance to allow his slave concu-
> bine to be tortured is cited as evidence against him.[34]

I would particularly like to underline the centrality of the citizen-slave
relationship even to democracy.[35] This relation is so absolute in that it
speaks a difference between free citizens, that is, those who can speak
in their own name, and slaves, that is, those who have no name of their
own (a slave's name was given by the owner) and who, having no juridical status of their own either, could only utter legitimate speech when
tortured. I do not believe this point can be over-emphasised, especially
since the Greeks themselves recognised there was an essential bond
between politics and human language.[36] The hallmark of this relationship is the asymmetry of torture. As Michel de Certeau puts it, 'torture
is the perfect example of an *initiation* into the reality of social practices.
Its effect is always to demystify discourse. It is the passage from what

---

[33] Whitmarsh, *Ancient Greek Literature*, p. 219.

[34] B. Williams, *Shame and Necessity* (Berkeley: University of California Press, 1993), p. 108.

[35] Nicole Loraux, in her study of 'autochthony and the Athenian imaginary', writes: 'To be
born an Athenian, then, means – by law – to be born of two Athenian parents. The citizen
is thus both an *aner* and a child of two parents. The first stipulation implies that the city
is built on the exclusion of women; the second assumes that all women who reproduce are
already integrated into the city. In the discourse of *andreia*, the ideal condition would be
to forget that women exist, but the reference to parentage must always bring these *andres*
back to reality. The official declaration of autochthonous origin constantly confronts these
two stipulations and all they imply, with all their asymmetries and contradictions'; *The
Children of Athena: Athenian Ideas about Citizenship and the Division Between the Sexes*,
trans. C. Levine (Princeton: Princeton University Press, 1994), p. 17. On the bottom of
the same page, one finds a footnote that alerts us to the exclusions of slavery: 'parentage
is also a norm, both an obligation and a right. The position of the citizen is antithetical
to that of a slave, who is always treated as a unit of work or of exchange and is allowed
to have "relatives," but does not have a right to a recognised lineage. This fact is shown
by the slave market, which deals only with individuals, and never with families;' p. 17,
n. 26.

[36] For a recent study of the consequences of this bond between language, politics and death,
see G. Agamben, *Language and Death: The Place of Negativity*, trans. K. E. Pinkus with
M. Hardt (Minneapolis: University of Minnesota Press, 1991). One might also link the
Aesopic to Christianity as, in Nietzsche's damning terms, the exemplary 'slave religion',
or, in Agamben's much more positive terms: 'in Paul, *doulos* [slave] refers to a profane
juridical condition and at the same time refers to the transformation that this condition
undergoes in its relation to the messianic event'; G. Agamben, *The Time That Remains: A
Commentary on the Letter to the Romans*, trans. P. Dailey (Stanford: Stanford University
Press, 2005), p. 14.

is *said* outside to what is *practised* within.'[37] The slave, whose labour
founds the economy, whose legal exclusion founds the polity, whose
everyday speech has no status other than as a *flatus vocis*, is therefore
nothing more than, as Aristotle put it, 'living property'.[38]

In this context, then, the Aesopic comes to look like a transfiguration
of servitude: the speech of a slave that somehow counts for the masters
even though it has not been extracted by torture, and which, in its very
utterance, shows that the foundations of 'free speech' are erected upon
the enslavement of populations. As such, the Aesopic is constrained
temporal dissimulation. It is constrained: that is, it is a response to
repression whose emblem is the political asymmetry of torture. It is
temporal: that is, even if what it speaks about does not necessarily have
a narrative or temporal structure, it must be presented temporally. It
is dissimulation: it cannot directly speak about what it speaks about;
it pretends to speak of something else, most often the non-human.
Regarding repression or oppression, the Aesopic speaks from the side
of the repressed or oppressed; it is a resource of weakness. Moreover,
this 'weakness' is a consequence of a serious threat, or at least of taking
the threat of the other seriously. The other may not even have to have
offered a direct threat; the other's very existence is a threat in and of
itself. The Aesopic always presumes that there are at least two parties
involved in an encounter, that one is stronger than the other, that this
strength is not a question of speech and that it has torture and death at
its limit.[39] It may even imply that those who have to speak at all are

---

[37] M. de Certeau, *Heterologies: Discourse on the Other*, trans. B. Massumi, foreword by
W. Godzich (Minneapolis and London: University of Minnesota Press, 1986), p. 41.

[38] See Aristotle, *The Politics*, trans. T. A. Sinclair, rev. T. J. Saunders (Harmondsworth:
Penguin, 1986).

[39] It is then suggestive that the political theorist Carl Schmitt brings up the use of animal
fables in precisely the context of an anthropological discussion about whether man is
'good' or 'evil': 'Striking in this context is the political significance of animal fables. Almost
all can be applied to a real political situation: the problem of aggression in the fable of the
wolf and the lamb; the question of guilt for the plague in La Fontaine's fable, a guilt which
of course falls upon the donkey; justice between states in the fables of animal assemblies;
disarmament in Churchill's election speech of October 1928, which depicts how every
animal believes that its teeth, claws, horns are the only instruments for maintaining peace;
the large fish which devour the small ones, etc. This curious analogy can be explained by
the direct connection of political anthropology with what the political philosophers of the
seventeenth century (Hobbes, Spinoza, Pufendorf) called the state of nature'; C. Schmitt,
The Concept of the Political, trans. G. Schwab and J. Harvey Lomax, with L. Strauss's
notes on Schmitt's essay (Chicago: University of Chicago Press, 1996), pp. 58–9. Note,
too, that it is precisely on this point (man as good/evil) that Schmitt is criticised by Strauss
as proposing an ethical, not a properly political distinction (see the latter's text reprinted in
the same volume). I believe the real issue at stake here is somewhat different: not Schmitt's
inconsistency in covertly reinjecting ethics into politics, nor his recourse to the logic of
natural law, but his *covert naturalisation of slavery*. This, to my mind, is the truth of
Schmitt's conservatism, which thus bears strong links to a classical Aristotelian posture:
some men are slaves by nature.

weak, that speech itself is not a power but an impotence, or, at least, at once a betrayal and attempted transubstantiation of an impotence. But even the wolves and lions in the fables sometimes seem to need to justify their power, a superb irony: in Aesopic fable, power at once needs no justification and yet is always looking for more, to be justified in speech, or at least have the appearance of being able to have some kind of justification in speech. Regarding its temporality, the very possibility of telling a fable shows that death has, at least for the time of its presentation, been staved off: in this sense, the Aesopic already implies the explicit frame of *A Thousand and One Nights*. It emerges in and as a time that is limned or haloed by death, a death to which it cannot literally refer, but which it has deferred in its speaking. Regarding dissimulation, the Aesopic is therefore never spoken in a single voice. There are only ever Aesopic voices, plural. The voice of the speaker is illegitimate as such (he is a slave); the fable told seems to be about something else, though no one is confused about its real referent; yet this referent is itself at least doubled, first, because the fable is situational (told in a particular situation to particular people about that situation), and second, because it dissimulates its own relation to this situation in terms that are 'naturalised'. So the Aesopic must always at least *pretend that it is able to be misunderstood*: there must always be some arbitrariness in its play of figures and events; on the other hand, one should also be able to reconstruct what it speaks of from the presentation itself.

COPS AND PHILOSOPHERS

It is therefore of decisive importance that there are at least two types of people who have always been very attentive to the utterances of slaves. The first type is the police, who, not coincidentally in the classical context, were in fact freed slaves. The cop is the slave who upholds the law that upholds slavery. In the field of utterance, we find his avatars in the stool-pigeon and the censor: the former is the one who, while pretending to be with you, reports your speech to the masters; the latter is the one who, in the name of public security, excises allegedly subversive or insurrectionary words. The second type is the philosopher. The philosopher's discourse is neither that of the slave nor that of the cop. The philosopher's is, as Jacques Lacan insisted, 'the discourse of the master'.[40] This is meant in a number of senses: the philosopher works for mastery of self, of knowledge, but, above all, and often

---

[40] See J. Lacan, *Seminar XVII: The Other Side of Psychoanalysis*, trans. R. Grigg (New York: W. W. Norton & Co., 2007).

without knowing it, on behalf of the political masters of the present. Philosophy is that discourse that extracts from the slave's *savoir faire* a disembodied *savoir* that will then be put to work, once again at the slave's expense. Not despite but because of his incessant questioning of all existing verities, the philosopher turns what is enigmatic about the labour of others into propositions that are then able to be systematically deployed in the service of political elites.[41] Whether this last point is in fact the case is dubious, as we shall see; nonetheless, it serves a very useful heuristic function in the current context.

Aesop is neither a cop nor a philosopher. Yet, like Aesop, the philosopher is also a master of coded speech if one is to believe Leo Strauss. In *Persecution and the Art of Writing*, Strauss elaborates a theory of 'reading between the lines' which is justifiably famous: such literature 'is addressed, not to all readers, but to trustworthy and intelligent readers only. It has all the advantages of private communication without having its greatest disadvantage – that it reaches only the writer's acquaintances. It has all the advantages of public communication without having its greatest disadvantage – capital punishment for the author.'[42] We will immediately mark two features of this explicitly political account of philosophy: (1) its coded nature, which gives it a family resemblance to the Aesopic; (2) the closed, elite nature of this coding, which places it in opposition to the Aesopic. It is therefore no surprise that, at the canonical beginning of Western philosophy, we find crucial references to Aesop, and in a directly political frame.

In Plato's *Phaedo*, Phaedo speaks to Echecrates of Socrates's last hours in prison. Socrates brings up the name of Aesop in connection with the peculiar feeling one gets when one is suddenly released from chains, in which pleasure and pain are peculiarly commingled: 'I think that if Aesop had noted this he would have composed a fable that a god wished to reconcile their opposition but could not do so, so he joined their two heads together, and therefore when the man has the one, the other follows later.' Cebes immediately picks up on the reference to Aesop in regard to Evenus the poet. Evenus, it appears, wanted to know why Socrates, 'who had never composed any poetry before', is in prison versifying Aesop and writing a hymn to Apollo. Socrates responds that he has always had dreams telling him he should make music, and that he has always taken this as an encouragement to continue to do what he has already been doing: philosophy, the 'noblest and best of

---

[41] See R. Grigg, *Lacan, Language, and Philosophy* (Albany: State University of New York Press, 2008), p. 136.

[42] L. Strauss, *Persecution and the Art of Writing* (Glencoe: The Free Press, 1952), p. 25.

music'. Just in case, however, the dream was speaking of music in the popular sense of the word, 'I thought it safer not to leave here until I had satisfied my conscience'.[43] As he waits for the hemlock, Socrates sings Aesop. Why?

In an article entitled 'Plato, Aesop, and the Beginnings of Mimetic Prose', Leslie Kurke notes that 'there is almost no scholarly discussion of Aesop as a precursor for Socrates or Aesopic fable as a speech genre that might have contributed to Socratic dialogue'.[44] While it is certainly true that this discussion is lacking in places where one might expect to find it,[45] the lack is perhaps not as extreme as Kurke's claim might suggest; after all, the relations between Socrates and Aesop have indeed been the subject of some concerted attention. Acosta-Hughes and Scodel, Compton, and Patterson, among others, have attended to this problematic, and all of them stress a number of the key 'points of continuity' between Aesop and Socrates.[46] As Compton puts it:

> The points of continuity [of Plato's Socrates] with Aesop are numerous: like Aesop, he is a righteous critic of an unjust populace, led by unjust leaders; when his blame becomes intolerable to the populace and leading citizens, he is brought to trial. Like Aesop, he uses animal parable to accuse and satirise his accusers in his last great speech. Like Aesop and Homer, he prophesies doom for the city after receiving his sentence. Like Aesop, he is imprisoned, and finally, after he has been given the death penalty, complies willingly, dying seemingly voluntarily.[47]

These 'points of continuity', however, are drawn to enforce an unprecedented difference: the difference that is philosophy. What Kurke emphasises is something that she finds in the great German philosopher

---

[43] Plato, *Phaedo*, in *Complete Works*, ed. with intro. and notes by J. M. Cooper (Indianapolis: Hackett, 1997), pp. 52–3 (60c–61b).

[44] L. Kurke, 'Plato, Aesop, and the Beginnings of Mimetic Prose', in *Representations*, 94 (2006), p. 16. See also her more extended discussion in *Aesopic Conversations*, cited above.

[45] Take, for instance, two close readings for which this entire Platonic passage is central: L. Taran, 'Plato, *Phaedo*, 62A', *The American Journal of Philology*, 87:3 (1966), pp. 326–36; and T. Ebert, 'Why is Evenus Called a Philosopher at *Phaedo* 61c?', *The Classical Quarterly*, New Series, 51:2 (2001), pp. 423–34. Note that these articles, which focus on what happens in the text *just after* the Platonic invocation of Aesop, each make one reference to it in passing, and make nothing of it, despite the fact that, as Ebert says, 'the stress put upon the ascetic and otherwordly traits in the picture of the philosopher makes this dialogue unique among Plato's writings'; p. 423. One would think that the way in which Socrates spends his time before dying is not irrelevant to his practice as a philosopher, and if Aesop and Apollo both come up, they therefore might have something to do with this project – even if in an ironic or negative fashion.

[46] See Acosta-Hughes and Scodel, 'Aesop *Poeta*', pp. 4–6 and *passim*; Compton, 'The Trial of the Satirist', pp. 338–43; Patterson, *Fables of Power*, p. 7.

[47] Compton, 'The Trial of the Satirist', p. 340.

G. W. F. Hegel – the historico-theoretical problem of the beginning of prose.[48]

'Im Sklaven fängt die Prosa an' ('prose begins with the slaves'), Hegel says in his section on the fable in his *Aesthetics*, under the precise general heading of 'Development of the Ideal into the Particular Forms of Art', 'Section I. The Symbolic Form of Art', 'Chapter III. Conscious Symbolism of the Comparative Art-Form', in 'A. Comparisons originating from the external object'. There are a number of absolutely crucial features here. For Hegel, this is the moment at which man begins to have a relationship with natural things qua natural, finite things, and not simply as expressions of a divinity. Yet it is not simply a question of pure practical interpretations of nature:

> Here we no longer have the divine will revealing its inwardness to man by natural events and their religious interpretation. Instead there is an entirely commonplace course of natural occurrences; from its detailed representation there can be abstracted, in a way we can understand, an ethical maxim, a warning, a doctrine, a prudential rule, and it is presented for the sake of this reflection and displayed to contemplation.[49]

---

[48] This problematic – that of the historical emergence of prose – is clearly absolutely critical to the fable. So Acosta-Hughes/Scodel and Compton suffer from not being attentive enough to this development: the former simply take the emergence of the fable as itself unproblematic, to explore the uses to which it is put by Callimachus; Compton, on the other hand, too rapidly assimilates prose to poetic utterance in general and, worse still, to Socratic philosophy in particular. Moreover, it is undoubtedly symptomatic that Simon Goldhill's book, precisely on 'the invention of prose', has no listing for Aesop, nor for Hegel, nor for that matter for Thomas De Quincey or Giorgio Agamben or in fact anyone who has written seriously on the topic. Goldhill writes that 'I want to suggest not merely that in the West prose as a written form flourishes for the first time in the fifth century BCE in Greece, but also that prose first takes the stage as a trendy, provocative, modern, and highly intellectualised form of writing' (*The Invention of Prose*, p. 1). I can't help but see in this claim an unconscious academic projection of nobility, which, once again, effaces the foundations of culture in slavery. Goldhill is certainly right when he says that 'the invention of prose involves a *contest of authority*' (ibid. p. 5, his emphasis), but for the wrong reasons: let us remember that what democracy represses is the fact that its free citizens are free precisely *because* others are slaves (and not just non-citizens or barbarians). Goldhill's blindness is most evident when he discusses Plato's *Meno* (82b8–85b7) and its account of the slave boy – making nothing whatsoever of the fact that the demonstration is prosecuted with regard to a figure who is both *slave* and *boy*. As for De Quincey, in his brilliant essay on 'Style', from *Blackwood's Edinburgh Magazine* (serialised from July 1840 to February 1841), he asks, 'What was it that first produced into this world that celebrated thing called *Prose*?', and notes that the Delphic oracle was like 'bad Latin from Oxford' and that prose therefore 'was something of a discovery', being born as a 'function of public haranguing' and addressing 'the public without limitations'; T. De Quincey, 'Style', in *De Quincey as Critic*, ed. J. E. Jordan (London: Routledge and Kegan Paul, 1973), p. 87, p. 88. For a recent philosophical take on the problem of prose, see G. Agamben, *The Idea of Prose*, trans. M. Sullivan and S. Whitsitt (Albany: State University of New York Press, 1995), and A. G. Düttmann, 'Integral Actuality: On Giorgio Agamben's *Idea of Prose*', in J. Clemens et al. (eds), *The Work of Giorgio Agamben* (Edinburgh: Edinburgh University Press, 2008), pp. 28–42. Agamben places the problem of prose at the centre of his work, noting that Plato, on Aristotle's testimony, was aiming at something that was neither poetry nor prose, but their *medium*.

[49] G. W. F. Hegel, *Aesthetics: Lectures on Fine Art*, trans. T. M. Knox (Oxford: Oxford University Press, 1975), p. 384.

For Hegel, 'the most attractive of what are called Aesop's fables are those ... which relate actions – if you like to use that word – or relations and events which a) have animal instinct as their basis, or b) express some other natural relationship, or c) in general, actually occur and are not merely put together by some capricious fancy'.[50] The limitation is for Hegel that all this is, finally, not free, because the fable restricts itself to the quotidian and the bestial, precisely 'because Aesop does not dare to recite his doctrines openly but can only make them understood hidden as it were in a riddle which at the same time is always being solved'.[51] This, for Hegel, is the origin of prose: conscious symbolism, falsely riddling, linked to the everyday and the animal, merely prudential in its import, and yet, also, a step away from the pure eclosion of divinity in a world to be sung with sublime poetry.[52]

Kurke takes up Hegel's philosophical insight from a different political and philological perspective. Unlike most of the other commentators on this point, she is extremely careful to trace the relationship between Socrates and Aesop as not just contingent on the external traits of this identification (they are both ugly, low class, poor, etc.), but to *particular operations of prosaic interaction*. As she puts it, Aesop is the 'precursor for two specific modes of Socratic discourse – *epagoge*, or induction through analogy, and *elenchos*, or the refutation of an interlocutor's position as self-contradictory'.[53] The former of these – induction through analogy – is relatively straightforward and is, as

---

[50] Hegel, *Aesthetics*, p. 385.

[51] Hegel, *Aesthetics*, p. 387.

[52] This is by no means the end of Hegel's tarrying with Aesop. At an absolutely crucial moment, in his preface to his *Philosophy of Right*, Hegel unexpectedly resorts to Aesop's fable of the boasting athlete: 'Philosophy cannot teach the state what it should be, but only how it, the ethical universe, is to be known. Ἰδου Ῥοδος, ιδου χαι το πηδημα. *Hic* Rhodus, *hic* saltus. To apprehend what is, the task of philosophy, because what is, is reason. As for the individual, every one is a son of his time; so philosophy also is its time apprehended in thought. It is just as foolish to fancy that any philosophy can transcend its present world, as that an individual could leap out of his time or jump over Rhodes. If a theory transgresses its time, and builds up a world as it ought to be, it has an existence merely in the unstable element of opinion, which gives room to every wandering fancy. With little change the above saying would read: Here is the rose, here dance'; G. W. F. Hegel, *Reading Hegel: The Introductions*, ed. A. Singh and R. Mohapatra (Melbourne: re.press, 2008), p. 88. This (mis)quotation of Aesop is, moreover, taken up by Marx in 'The Eighteenth Brumaire', where it is further addled in the name of a clearly political translation. In addition to this very complicated and overdetermined invocation-translation of Aesop, I would also link this invocation of the slave to the problematic of the master-slave dialectic in *The Phenomenology of Spirit*, where, in line with the very influential interpretation given it in the twentieth century by Alexandre Kojève, the struggle for recognition ends in the master becoming the master because he is prepared to risk death, whereas the slave becomes the slave precisely because he prefers life at any cost to death. As such, the slave is forced to labour for the master, and, in this bitter exploitation, comes to know a truth of existence that forever eludes the master. See Chapter 2 for further discussion of this question.

[53] Kurke, 'Plato, Aesop, and the Beginnings of Mimetic Prose', p. 23.

we have seen, usually considered a hallmark of the Aesopic (e.g. the discrete tales of animals that lead us to a moral of some kind). But the latter mode is of particular interest in this context, and for a number of reasons, notably because of its situational, dialogic qualities. As Kurke notes, in the *Gorgias* (472b6–c1) Socrates carefully distinguishes his *elenchos* from that of the legal system: rather than a formal process of questioning leading to an assignation of legal guilt, Socrates 'defines the essence of his *elenchos* as compelling one person – one's interlocutor or opponent in argument – to bear witness for one's own position and against himself'.[54] The court process is: formal, legal, localised, agonistic. Socrates's is: informal, in that it can take all sorts of unexpected directions; extra-legal, in that Socrates himself has no power to compel or to judge or to punish; extra-local, in that it can happen anywhere in (and, occasionally, outside) the polis; and dialogic, in that the interlocutor ends by himself confessing ignorance of what he speaks, and *not* to the perpetration of a crime. Although Kurke does not bring this up, this goes once more to the problematic of the irreducible 'torturability' of slaves: Socrates, in flagrant disregard of this practice, is prepared to question absolutely anybody he encounters, including non-legal persons such as the slave boy of the *Meno*, precisely because these are local distinctions of no import with regard to the life of the soul.[55] Socratic questioning – insofar as it takes up Aesop – is therefore a radically new way to transfigure servitude.

Plato's Socrates, in other words, directly assaults the dominant classes of the polis and *their* uses of prose, and he does so by drawing on the prosaic resources made available by Aesop the slave fabulist. As he does so, Socrates transfigures the status of political divisions: 'masters' and 'slaves' are all, in principle, equal in thought; to the extent that they, masters and slaves, remain captives of these political divisions, they all remain, equally, 'slaves'; to the extent that they turn themselves to philosophical inquiry, they all are capable, equally, of true mastery.[56] Plato's

---

[54] Kurke, 'Plato, Aesop, and the Beginnings of Mimetic Prose', p. 33.

[55] A. J. Bartlett has reminded me that the reference to Evenus is 'not a favourable one. In the *Apology* he is the figure Socrates mocks. He earns 500 drachma for his course. Callias is the richest man in Athens, whose money comes from slavery, and who buys Evenus for his sons. Anyway, the slave connection goes deep with sophistry. The money to buy Evenus is from slavery, and the knowledge desired by the slave owner is what Evenus provides'; personal communication. Moreover, Xenophon's *Symposium* and Plato's *Protagoras* are in fact set in Callias's house.

[56] See Page duBois, *Slaves and Other Objects*, especially the chapter provocatively entitled 'The Slave Plato', in which she argues that 'Of course Plato accepts slavery, never questions the institution of slavery, sees it as a fundamental structure, uses it as a metaphor for the relationship between gods and human beings, between one part of the soul and another. Yet there is a fluidity, a slippage imagined between slave and free that would violate the rigid barrier between them erected later by Aristotle and reified in terms of race in New

takeover of Aesopian prose – one might even say Plato's *plagiarism* of Aesop, given that 'plagiarism' has for etymology 'the kidnapping of another's slaves' – is therefore also a covert assault upon the polity as it exists, including (and perhaps especially) the democratic polity: true masters and slaves are not given in political actuality. A slave is just as capable of thought as anybody else; a demagogue is a slave to his passions. Rather than masters and slaves, then, the philosopher's is a regime of masters and disciples.[57] This opens immediately onto the problematic of philosophical pedagogy, which, as A. J. Bartlett has pointed out, is absolutely central to the philosophical enterprise (here, one might also be reminded that a 'pedagogue' was originally a slave who took children to and from school, and was often authorised to beat them if required).[58] For Plato himself, and not just for his Socrates, one can immediately see how useful this philosophical takeover of prose is in his own struggles against sophists, poets and other post-Socratic philosophers. Moreover, as Alain Badiou has pointed out, it enables a 'speculative parricide' of Plato's own philosophical father Parmenides, who himself wrote in verse.[59] But it is also where a real division between Aesop and Socrates is established, between the fabulist and the philosopher. As Kurke demonstrates, 'philosophy achieves the appearance of transcendent form by having Socrates fail. Socrates' failure, the negative of the *elenchos*, ignorance exposed, and the aporia in which Socrates himself claims to participate as much as his interlocutors – all this produces the permanently open space of philosophy.'[60] Socrates's genius is integrally articulated with his failure, his ruination, and not with his triumph; his death-sentence by the Athenian courts arraigns Athens *tout court*, as it enables Socrates to most fully expose his own *parcours*. Aesop's is an art of living-in-servitude, Socrates's the art of dying-in-mastery.

World slavery'; *Slaves and Other Objects* (Chicago: University of Chicago Press, 2003), p. 167. For her part, Patterson comments: 'preparing to separate his own philosophical soul from the body, and to present that separation as a manumission from a slavery to the body, he has nevertheless used as an instrument of that preparation the extremely corporeal and anti-idealistic fables of Aesop, the Phrygian slave'; Patterson, *Fables of Power*, p. 7.

57 For an extended meditation of the problem of slavery in contemporary philosophy, see R. Faber, '"Amid a Democracy of Fellow Creatures" – Onto/Politics and the Problem of Slavery in Whitehead and Deleuze (with an Intervention of Badiou)', in Faber et al. (eds), *Event and Decision: Ontology and Politics in Badiou, Deleuze, and Whitehead* (Newcastle: Cambridge Scholars Press, 2010), pp. 192–237.

58 See A. J. Bartlett, 'Conditional Notes on a New *Republic*', in P. Ashton et al. (eds), *The Praxis of Alain Badiou* (Melbourne: re.press, 2006), pp. 201–42.

59 See A. Badiou, *Conditions* (Paris: Éditions du Seuil, 1992), p. 277.

60 Kurke, 'Plato, Aesop, and the Beginnings of Mimetic Prose', p. 35. DuBois herself says, 'Plato seems to use the mention of Aesop as a figure for the release from slavery, which is for him bound up with the theme of the merely relative freedom possible in material existence'; *Slaves and Other Objects*, p. 181.

Why claim that psychoanalysis is an Aesopic discourse? First, because they share structures of address: (1) the speaker of the fable is foregrounded in its utterance (i.e. there is no disembodied, neutral or third-party utterance); (2) this speaker speaks from the point of the slave, not of the master (i.e. as the repressed of the situation, as without legal standing or proper name within it); (3) the utterance itself is directed towards the situation in which it is uttered (i.e. it is about the status of *this* repression itself); (4) the utterance is necessarily dissimulating (i.e. it is, as Freud says of the symptom, a 'compromise formation'); (5) this dissimulation speaks what everybody knows but doesn't know at the same time (i.e. literally, the body politics of the situation); (6) in doing so, it paradoxically exceeds the situation in which it is uttered. For Freud himself, the very existence of the unconscious entails that conscious life must be nothing other than constrained temporal dissimulation – yet without being able to recognise itself as such. For Freud, dreams, parapraxes, forgettings, jokes and so on – the entire panoply of the psychopathology of everyday life – are in fact telling a truth about you that you cannot yourself bear. So you fabulate: in fact, you are the power against which you struggle, you are the slave and master of yourself. As such, psychoanalysis is directed against the claims of philosophical mastery, once again rendering the latter's epistemophilia subordinate to the fables of the unconscious.

But there is a further issue, again hinging on the peculiar mode of address of the Aesopic. If the Aesopic fable is, indeed, at the 'origin' of philosophical prose, it remains at the same time a very primordial, literally enigmatic mode of address: *aînos*. Here is Gregory Nagy on the topic:

> this ambiguous discourse of the poet, the technical word for which is *aînos*, is not just a negative concept. It can also be a positive social force: when the disguised king Odysseus is begging for food at the feasts of the impious suitors, he is actually speaking not only in the mode of an *aînos* but also in the role of an exponent of *dike*, 'justice.' The role of Aesop, master of the *aînos* in both the general sense and in the specific sense of 'fable,' is analogous: he uses this discourse to indicate cryptically what is right and wrong, and we must keep in mind the *aítion* 'cause' of his death, which was that he ridiculed the ritualised greed of a Delphic rite where meat is being apportioned in a disorderly and frenzied manner. In the praise poetry of Pindar, the technical word for which is likewise *aînos* (in the testimony of the poetry itself), the concept of the *gaster* can again be seen as a positive social force.[61]

---

[61] G. Nagy, *Greek Mythology and Poetics* (Ithaca and London: Cornell University Press, 1990), pp. 274–5; see also his *Pindar's Homer: The Lyric Possession of an Epic Past* (Baltimore: Johns Hopkins University Press, 1997), esp. Chapter 11, and *The Best of the*

Ambivalently linked by commentators to Odysseus, to Apollo and to Marsyas the Satyr, Aesop can be understood as a *pharmakos*, and, indeed, shares this feature with Oedipus, who is also intimately connected with enigmas and their (true-false) solutions.[62] A speculation: Aesop would then be the mythical figure who renders *aînos* prosaic, who tears it from the museum and returns it to the life of the body.

In his seminar of 17 December 1969, Jacques Lacan remarked that: 'If I insisted at length on the difference in level between the utterance [*énonciation*] and the statement [*énoncé*], it was so that the function of the enigma would make sense. An enigma is most likely that, an utterance. I charge you with the task of making it into a statement. Sort that out as best you can – as Oedipus did – and you will bear the consequences. That is what is at issue in an enigma.'[63] Lacan's distinction, which exacerbates the division within every speech act between *what* is said and *that* it is said, is aimed at exposing humanity's irrevocable subjection to something enigmatic in communication, that is, to the indestructible barrier that founds the possibility of speech. The Sphinx, in this conception, is itself the half-body that bespeaks the half-said (*mi-dit*) of the enigma, which cannot ever be fully spoken. The enigma is therefore not a riddle that can be answered; indeed, Oedipus's folly is that he treats the enigma as if it were a riddle, an utterance as if it were a statement. But there is nothing behind the enigma, which simply founds the statement as it disappears, constituting an ever-elusive and vanishing truth. In Giorgio Agamben's words:

> What the Sphinx proposed was not simply something whose signified is hidden and veiled under an 'enigmatic' signifier, but a mode of speech in which the original fracture of presence was alluded to in the paradox of a word that approaches its object while keeping it indefinitely at a distance. The *aînos* (story, fable) of the *ainigma* is not only obscurity, but a more original mode of speaking. Like the labyrinth, like the Gorgon, and like the Sphinx that utters it, the enigma belongs to the sphere of the apotropaic, that is, to a protective power that repels the uncanny by attracting it and assuming it within itself. The dancing path of the labyrinth, which leads into the heart of that which is held at a distance, is the model of this relation with the uncanny that is expressed in the enigma.[64]

Achaeans (Baltimore: Johns Hopkins University Press, 1999), *passim*, but esp. Chapter 12.

[62] In addition to Nagy's work on the *pharmakos* in this context and its links to the *therapon* (which becomes our 'therapist'), see J.-P. Vernant, 'Ambiguity and Reversal: On the Enigmatic Structure of *Oedipus Rex*', *New Literary History*, 9:3 (1978), pp. 475–501. See, too, Jacques Derrida's brilliant essay 'Plato's Pharmacy' in *Dissemination*, trans. B. Johnson (Chicago: University of Chicago Press, 1981), pp. 61–171.

[63] Lacan, *Seminar XVII*, pp. 36–7.

[64] G. Agamben, *Stanzas: Word and Phantasm in Western Culture*, trans. R. L. Martinez (Minneapolis: University of Minnesota Press, 1993), p. 138.

This, then, would be Aesop's success compared to Oedipus: Aesop holds himself within the enigmatic without treating it as having any solution or resolution.

The Aesopic embodies real servitude transfigured through the medium of the fable, whose ultimate enigma is precisely this transfiguring potential itself, that is, its potential to transform the conditions of speaking by speaking about *this* as if it were *that* – and in such a way as if its destiny were to speak to everybody. In addition to its basic characters and narratives, the simple prose of the fable itself encrypts an essential agonistic feature: the Aesopic fable is not a mystical utterance of a poetic or religious kind, which would imply the privilege of a revelation; nor is it founded on linguistic operations directed at ensuring the quasi-secret transmission of an esoteric message meant only for an elite. It is not an utterance that establishes or overthrows a (or the) law. The fable, rather, *simulates dissimulation* as it stages the vicissitudes of speech in tale after tale, often taking the relationships of speaking as its themes. Lions upbraid hares for thinking equality can reside other than in tooth and claw; wolves grasp for excuses that would legitimate their intended acts of terror; foxes cheer themselves up by pooh-poohing what they aimed at but couldn't get; dolphins show themselves incompetent to fulfil contracts on land; and so on. Pretending to pretend, irreducibly ambiguous and ambivalent, the fable plays ceaselessly with the play in power-relations – but never abandons its roots in the constitutive foundation of human communities in servitude and death.

6. Torture, Psychoanalysis and Beyond

> The goal of torture, in effect, is to produce acceptance of a State discourse, through the confession of putrescence. What the torturer in the end wants to extort from the victim he tortures is to reduce him to being no more than that [*ça*], rottenness.
>
> Michel de Certeau[1]

INTRODUCTION: TORTURE AS THE ORIGINARY LANDSCAPE OF THE POLITICAL

In the previous chapter, I examined the problem of slave-speech under the heading of the 'Aesopic': how a slave, whose speech can only have public standing when it is extracted through legal torture, can nonetheless transform the obscenity of such restrictions into inventive utterance. I also argued that psychoanalysis was *the* contemporary discourse that affirms the speech of slaves, against the depredations of authoritarian dispensations. Yet, by this very affirmation, psycho-analysis should also alert us to the centrality of torture in the formation and maintenance of human polities. Torture is historically variable in its means and uses, and, if I have already briefly invoked its relations to the origins of antiphilosophy in a particular antique context, I wish to turn now to its reapparition in the contemporary situation. In doing so, I seek also to show both the power and the limits of psychoanalysis as an antiphilosophy, by extending the account of Giorgio Agamben's work offered in Chapter 4. In the terms of this book, Agamben is a phi-losopher, but one who, having taken psychoanalysis utterly seriously, has gone beyond a limit that inheres in the general antiphilosophical project as such.

---

[1] M. de Certeau, *Heterologies: Discourse on the Other*, trans. B. Massumi, foreword by W. Godzich (Minneapolis and London: University of Minnesota Press, 1986), p. 40.

Torture is the originary landscape of the political. Why? Because torture is, historically, pragmatically and in principle the 'technique' that functions to effect the transition between the living body and the life of the community.[2] It does this not only according to the well-known exigencies of spectacular punishment, the establishment of the grounds for debt reclamation, and festive enjoyment, but, perhaps fundamentally, in its establishment of the conditions of what counts as a legitimate speech act in and for a polity at all. Torture is (literally) the point at which law is articulated with the political. In Kristian Williams's words, 'Torture . . . is not incidental to state power; it is characteristic of that power. Torture doesn't represent a system failure; it *is* the system.'[3] Strangely enough, given the bluntness of this claim, something approximating this thesis has been operative throughout post-Enlightenment philosophy, if in a minor key; it is, moreover, quite directly linked to the centrality of the problematic of language in modern thought. Even a rapid survey of writings by Cesare Beccaria, Jeremy Bentham, Friedrich Nietzsche, Sigmund Freud, Michel Foucault, Michel de Certeau, Judith Butler and Eric Santner, among many others, would have to acknowledge that the problem of torture has a crucial place there.[4] Why? Because part of the problem of accounting for man's essence as a speaking being is, from the eighteenth century onwards, necessarily linked to the question of how man comes to language in the first place. The question 'how does man come to language?' cannot be separated from the question concerning *questioning*, a question whose paradigm is that of torture, judicial torture, the elicitation of speech from a resisting body, and the accompanying implantation and regimentation of

[2] S. C. Carey, Mark Gibney and S. C. Poe, in *The Politics of Human Rights: The Quest for Dignity* (Cambridge: Cambridge University Press, 2010), obviously make a great deal of the Human Rights declarations. They note that no country voted against the Universal Declaration (1948), although eight countries abstained; also many countries were still under colonial rule. Moreover, noting problems with universality, they assert: 'Still, human rights are universal in the sense that all human beings possess human rights by the mere fact of their human existence'; p. 11.

[3] K. Williams, *American Methods: Torture and the Logic of Domination* (Cambridge: South End Press, 2006), p. 3.

[4] See, inter alia, C. Beccaria, *On Crimes and Punishments and Other Writings*, ed. R. Bellamy, trans. R. Davies et al. (Cambridge: Cambridge University Press, 1995); F. Nietzsche, *On the Genealogy of Morality*, ed. K. Ansell-Pearson, trans. C. Diethe (Cambridge: Cambridge University Press, 2007); S. Freud, 'Notes upon a Case of Obsessional Neurosis', in *The Standard Edition of the Complete Psychological Works of Sigmund Freud*, Vol. X (1909), ed. J. Strachey et al. (London: The Hogarth Press, 1955); M. Foucault, *Discipline and Punish: The Birth of the Prison*, trans. A. Sheridan (New York: Vintage, 1979); M. de Certeau, *Heterologies: Discourse on the Other*, trans. B. Massumi, foreword by W. Godzich (Minneapolis and London: University of Minnesota Press, 1986); J. Butler, *Antigone's Claim: Kinship Between Life and Death* (New York: Columbia University Press, 2000); E. Santner, *My Own Private Germany: Daniel Paul Schreber's Secret History of Modernity* (Princeton: Princeton University Press, 1996).

particular kinds of speech. Moreover, this paradigm is linked to what at least initially might seem its absolute other: the elicitation of language from the infant, the one-who-is-not-yet-speaking but whose destiny is always already to be caught in the chains of language.

The question concerning technology is therefore also at the heart of these political questions, particularly the technologies of the body that Foucault himself, in Nietzsche's wake, has so carefully and ingeniously tracked. But I would also want to be very careful about specifying the key technological problematic, necessarily subjacent to the others: the necessity for the elicitation and control of 'speech', understood as the order of language in general. There are of course innumerable different technologies for doing this, and I will discuss some of them shortly. In doing so, I will also say why I think even Foucault can sometimes be a little misleading on the topic. Indeed, the contemporary context – the post-9/11 context in which torture has been explicitly put back on the global political agenda – has already foregrounded this problematic, at any number of levels. Whether it is the interminable scholarly and legal quibblings over its definition, the journalistic furore over whether waterboarding is really torture, or Donald Rumsfeld's little note on the bottom of the notorious memorandum from 2002 authorising extreme interrogation techniques at Guantanamo ('I stand for 8–10 hours a day. Why is standing limited to 4 hours?'), one can immediately see how micro-technologies of the body, the minutiae of physical positions, are imbricated in these calculations.

THE CURRENT INSISTENCE OF THE TICKING-BOMB SCENARIO AS PROSPECTIVE LICENCE FOR PRE-EMPTIVE TORTURE

Let me begin by providing an all-too-familiar example of the contemporary dominant discourses about torture, whose emblem is the sophism of the 'ticking bomb'. In his Heidelberg University lecture of 1992, Niklas Luhmann opened with precisely such an example:

> Imagine: You are a high-level law-enforcement officer. In your country – it could be Germany in the not-too-distant future – there are many left- and right-wing terrorists – every day there are murders, fire-bombings, the killing and injury of countless innocent people. You have captured the leader of such a group. Presumably, if you tortured him, you could save many lives – 10, 100, 1000 – we can vary the situation. Would you do it?[5]

---

[5] N. Luhmann, 'Are There Still Indispensable Norms in Our Society?', *Soziale Systeme*, 14:1 (2008), p. 18.

For Luhmann, there can be no definitive answer to this question: the problem as such is properly undecidable for our societies.[6] If such examples are at once chilling and ludicrous, their very popularity is certainly an index of a kind of *Zeitgeist*. As Costas Douzinas has noted, Luhmann seems to have been extraordinarily prescient in his choice of example: a mere decade after Luhmann's presentation, Wolfgang Daschner, a high-ranking Frankfurt police officer, threatened to harm the key suspect in the kidnapping of Jakob von Metzler, the eleven-year-old son of a prominent banking family.[7] As it happens, the suspect decided to talk without further intervention only ten minutes later: the victim, it transpired, was already dead. But Luhmann's apparent prescience is in fact a little misleading. As Douzinas adds, 'The trick is that we have to say yes or no to an unreal situation that never happens,' concluding that Luhmann's position is tantamount to a depoliticisation.[8] To some extent this is true, but it remains the case that Luhmann's particular formulation of the scenario captures something about torture in the contemporary political space that others, apparently very similar, do not.

For one can no longer ignore how popular this example is for those who clearly think that the topic of torture can be debated like any other, not to mention those who clearly enjoy the possibility of its official return. Hence Michael Levin, in a (repellently influential) 1982 essay titled 'The Case for Torture', lasciviously runs through one version of this scenario after another: 'Suppose a terrorist has hidden an atomic bomb on Manhattan Island which will detonate at noon on July 4 unless ... Someone plants a bomb on a jumbo jet ... Suppose a terrorist group kidnapped a newborn baby from a hospital. . .' Levin even announces, with staggering sang-froid, that 'there are situations in which torture is not merely permissible but morally mandatory'.[9] If Levin still stands behind these arguments today, so do an extraordinary number of other public intellectuals. The best-known contemporary proponent of such views is perhaps the US civil rights lawyer Alan Dershowitz, who – with an enthusiasm verging on the hallucinatory – even denominates this position a 'new realism'.[10]

---

[6] See the responses to Luhmann's article in the same issue of *Soziale Systeme*, especially Niels Werber's 'A Test of Conscience Without Indispensable Norms: Niklas Luhmann's War on Terror' (pp. 83–101) and Costas Douzinas's 'Torture and Systems Theory' (pp. 110–25).

[7] See 'Police Threat Fuels Debate on Torture', *Deutsche Welle*, 24 February 2003, <http://www.dw-world.de/dw/article/0,,785751,00.html> (last accessed 12 October 2012).

[8] Douzinas, 'Torture and Systems Theory', p. 111.

[9] M. Levin, 'The Case for Torture', *Newsweek*, 7 June 1982, p. 13.

[10] See A. Dershowitz, *Why Terrorism Works: Understanding the Threat, Responding to the Challenge* (New Haven, CT: Yale University Press, 2003).

As John Kleinig has noted in an article on the mysterious charm of this generic fiction:

> if it takes the ticking bomb argument to justify torture, we might wonder whether it ever justifies any *actual* torture that we might encounter. For, consider what gives the ticking bomb argument such persuasiveness as it has:
>
> First, it posits a *known* – and not merely a possible or even probable – threat. Second, there is a *pressing* need for action. Third, the threatened evil is of *enormous magnitude*. Fourth, *only* torture is likely to succeed in getting the information needed to avert the evil. Fifth, the person to be tortured is *the perpetrator* of the threat. And finally, as a result of the torture, the evil is *very likely* to be averted.[11]

Kleinig also immediately shows how such a scenario is de facto mobilised to expand the cases under which torture is allegedly legitimately able to be used, and adds that torture is the worst assault imaginable on the dignity of the human being insofar as it effects a 'de-moralisation' of the individual, who is thereby turned against him- or herself. In this, his arguments rejoin those of Elaine Scarry or John Parry, or any of the others who find torture morally repugnant, an assault on dignity and decency, a contravention of fundamental human rights and so on. But they thereby also come to share a peculiar feature with their adversaries. For, as Richard Matthews remarks, 'defenders of torture curiously focus on the ethics of specific decisions or acts of torture', that is, on *individual* decisions.[12] Moreover, as David Luban puts it, 'the ticking bomb begins by denying that torture belongs to liberal culture, and ends by constructing a torture culture'.[13] One can certainly see Luban's diagnosis confirmed in the most recent disquisitions on the subject.

There are several further features of the scenario which need to be addressed. First, it is at once surprising and unsurprising to find the origins of this example in the work of none other than Jeremy Bentham, whose 'Of Torture' – which seems to have been part of a longer work titled *Plan of a Penal Code* dating from the late 1770s – speaks of the utility of torture in recapturing an arsonist who is going to strike again. One can immediately see how torture is unlikely to be excluded from any utilitarian calculations, on the one hand, but, on the other, how Benthamite technologies are strongly dedicated to minimising physical

---

[11] J. Kleinig, 'Ticking Bombs and Torture Warrants', *Deakin Law Review*, 10:2 (2006), p. 616.

[12] R. Matthews, *The Absolute Violation: Why Torture Must Be Prohibited* (Kingston and Montreal: McGill-Queen's University Press, 2008), p. 10.

[13] D. Luban, 'Liberalism, Torture, and the Ticking Bomb', in K. Greenberg (ed.), *The Torture Debate in America* (Cambridge: Cambridge University Press, 2006), p. 36.

punishments in favour of optical-blackmailing ones.[14] It is surely significant to find this example historically linked to democratic modernity itself: it seems that this example arises precisely at the moment when torture was, for the first time, about to disappear officially from Western Europe.

Yet, with the historical emergence of this sophism at the very moment that the conundrum this sophism purports to examine has de facto been excluded from real political actuality, torture is linked to a radical experience of the multiplicity of possible futures, that is, of the opaque heterogeneity of anticipated possibilities. With Romanticism, philosophy – as Foucault himself notes – starts to become first and foremost a philosophy of time, and the future above all as an index and emblem of negativity that hollows out as it necessitates the plans of the present.[15] One derived logic of Romantic modernity is therefore that of *technical assaults on the future* or what is, strictly speaking, a *pre-emptive speculative strike*. This is why Levin, in the article cited above, can so easily announce that 'I am advocating torture as an acceptable measure for *preventing* future evils', and that '[b]etter *precedents* for torture are assassination and *pre-emptive* attack' (my emphases). In accordance with this logic, of course, it is hard to know why you couldn't torture everybody on the planet immediately, just to make sure. But the point stands: torture is a political technique directed against time. It may even function as the repressed paradigm of the modern thinking of technology itself, given that torture is the very model of the effective transformation of bodies into information under extreme time pressure. It is such an unthought solidarity of this technico-legal consideration of torture with a generalised technocratic ethos of risk-management that supports the recurrent fantasy of its proponents that the scenario can constitute a 'realism' at all. Hence another fundamental proposition: *the real exclusion of torture from the legal system immediately gives rise to the conviction that the exclusion of torture is antiquated and anachronistic, 'unrealistic'*. The paradox of the abolition of torture is that its very abolition comes to seem unrealistic in the space that that abolition opens up.

The very calculations made by *dirigeants* – from Bentham's own 'felicific calculus' to the mathematically modelled insurance schema of

---

[14] See also Bob Brecher's book on the subject, entitled *Torture and the Ticking Bomb* (Malden and Oxford: Blackwell, 2007), in which he notes that the 'scenario remains in crucial respects a fantasy; and that the grounds it is said to offer for justifying interrogational torture so as to avoid a putative catastrophe are spurious'; p. x.

[15] M. Foucault, *Power/Knowledge: Selected Interviews 1972–1977*, ed. C. Gordon (New York: Pantheon Books, 1980), pp. 149–50.

'risk society' – depend on their drive to remobilise a forbidden means whose limits thereby vanish. As Bentham admits of this aspect of torture, 'The Quantity of Torture is indeterminate'. What this means is clear, at least, for Bentham: torture can have no particular codification that ensures its effectiveness; its effectiveness can be gauged only by results. As such, the paradox is that, precisely in order to assure oneself of torture's clarity and utility, what constitutes torture in terms of techniques, times, quantities of pain and so on *must* become obscure. It is surely Bentham's own probity of thought in this regard that explains why he vacillated on the benefits of torture throughout his life; and, moreover, why Luhmann, unlike those who proselytise *for* torture on the basis of such scenarios, concludes that it is properly undecidable. Luhmann is in this the true heir to Bentham insofar as he maintains that the scenario *cannot not continue to arise* in functionally differentiated societies such as our own, precisely because systems-operations are and must be irreducible to moral considerations, and that all arguments for or against torture can therefore and thereafter receive no resolution. As A. J. Bartlett has remarked: 'This is also why torture can now "come up for debate" like anything else, but it is neither morality nor management that counts. It is politics which disappears under this binary confederacy.'[16]

I would like to add two further points here. The first involves posing the question: given the ubiquity of and enthusiasm for torture historically, how did people ever come to think that an absolute ban was possible, desirable and necessary? Russell Grigg and I have posed this question from the standpoint of psychoanalysis.[17] On the basis of this approach, Grigg and I answer: the struggle for democracy as equality.[18] To this end, we isolated a number of propositions that we consider historically invariant:

- psychoanalytically speaking, there is nobody who does not enjoy the spectacle of torture, albeit often in the mode of denegation or disavowal;
- torture is politically the paradigm of arbitrary 'exceptional' power;

---

[16] A. J. Bartlett, personal communication, 2 July 2012.
[17] See J. Clemens and R. Grigg, 'A Note on Psychoanalysis and the Crime of Torture', *Australian Feminist Law Journal*, 24 (2006), pp. 159–76; republished in M. Kulkarni (ed.), *Interdisciplinary Perspectives on Political Theory* (Delhi: Sage, 2011), pp. 236–59. See also J. Clemens, 'You Have the Right to Remain Silent', *Heat*, 23 (2010), pp. 7–21.
[18] For exemplary accounts of the actual role played by torture in democracy, see D. M. Rejali, *Torture and Democracy* (Princeton: Princeton University Press, 2007); J. Lokaneeta, *Transnational Torture: Law, Violence, and State Power in the United States and India* (New York: New York Press, 2011).

- freedom of speech is not and should not be the 'right' to 'say any-thing', but rather the capacity *not* to have to speak;
- torture and pre-publication censorship are *essentially* twinned;
- one essential element of democracy is the *exclusion* of torture as its necessary condition;
- the existence of slavery within any society in general is defined by a person's *torturability*;
- one universal wrong of torture is its *confusion-power* (e.g. confusion of sense and reference, aims and ends, actuality and potentiality, persons and voices, etc.).

Let us note that these are not really 'ethical' propositions in the common acceptation of ethics today. They do not speak of the inherent or essential wrong of cruelty to others, of the mutilation of bodies, of the psychological consequences of such practices – although these are of course to be condemned. The point is to speak of the specifically *political* dimensions of torture.

As already flagged, this point is remarkably often occluded in the literature, no doubt sometimes for reasons of legal or philosophical specialisation. It can nonetheless be rendered legible with a slight shift in optic. In the US context, for example, Jeremy Waldron has argued that 'the rule against torture operates in our law as an archetype – that is, as a rule which has significance not just in and of itself, but also as the embodiment of a pervasive principle',[19] and this comes somewhat close to the position offered by José Alvarez in his introduction to 'Torturing the Law': 'Lawyers – of all people – should not be addressing torture and cruel, inhuman, degrading treatment as if this were just another policy choice over which reasonable, civilized people can disagree.'[20] However, and this is one of the significant aspects of the contemporary discussions of torture – in fact, of the post-Romantic discussions more generally – even those against torture reason according to a radical depoliticisation of the theme, indeed, by giving it a 'specifically' philosophical, moral and/or legal treatment.[21] This is as true for Waldron

[19] See J. Waldron, 'Torture and Positive Law: Jurisprudence for the White House', *Columbia Law Review*, 105:6 (October 2005), p. 1,687. One can see evidence of the shift towards Waldron's dystopia in the laws regarding rendition; see A. W. Clarke, 'Rendition to Torture: A Critical Legal History', *Rutgers Law Review*, 62:1 (Fall 2009), pp. 1–74. See also the book version in J. Waldron, *Torture, Terror, and Trade-Offs: Philosophy for the White House* (Oxford: Oxford University Press, 2010).

[20] J. E. Alvarez, 'Torturing the Law', *Case Western Reserve Journal of International Law*, 37:2–3 (2006), p. 175.

[21] Exemplary here would be Henry Shue's moral arguments in 'Torture', *Philosophy and Public Affairs*, 7:2 (1978), pp. 124–43, as well as his response to the ticking-bomb scenario in 'Torture in Dreamland: Disposing of the Ticking Bomb', *Case Western Reserve Journal of International Law*, 37:2–3 (2006), pp. 231–9.

as it is for Levin, for those who take a stringently moral position as for those for whom the ticking-bomb scenario comes to be the only universally recognised exemplum: in other words, *the very democracy that excludes torture also occludes the reasons for such an occlusion from its subjects.*[22] (Falsely, but unsurprisingly then, the 'Enlightenment' is occasionally blamed for this occlusion, for instance by historians such as John Langbein.)

That Grigg and I could only make this point about the political status of torture by means of psychoanalysis is itself significant. How could psychoanalysis, which is so often held to be incapable of dealing with political institutions and problems in any plausible, effective or empirical way, nonetheless be incisive in this particular context? Precisely because psychoanalysis deals essentially with the places at which speech and the body meet. These are self-evidently the same places upon which torture operates. Moreover, this recognition also enables something further to be said about psychoanalysis itself. If democracy requires the exclusion of torture as the fundamental guarantee of free speech, psychoanalysis ratchets up this requirement to its impossible limit: free association, the 'fundamental rule' of psychoanalysis, shows that such free speech necessarily retains traces of the very torture it repudiates, and that the elicitation of such speech comes at a cost that cannot itself be spoken. As such, psychoanalysis is at once the unprecedented exacerbation of democratic principles and their radical subversion.

But this brings me to my second point, the one on which I will focus in the remainder of this chapter: the very popularity of the ticking-bomb scenario and its technical, interrogational, informational arguments for torture mask something that is perhaps more sinister and unspeakable. For it is not that contemporary torturers are able to extract a rapid and effective confession from suspects by the judicious and restricted use of new technologies; it is that the new technologies of torture render all information-gathering impossible by rendering their subjects, in the jargon of military PR, neutralised. In this regard, one would have to say, echoing Luhmann, that we already inhabit thoroughly post-democratic societies, that these societies are indeed without any fundamental norms, and that a new dispensation of the torture-polity articulation is at the heart of these developments. Such a

---

[22] L. M. Johnson has taken up Jacques Derrida's paradox of democracy – whereby *alternatives to democracy* can be presented within democracies as *democratic alternatives* – in the context of terrorism and torture. This is to put torture back into its properly political context; 'Terror, Torture and Democratic Autoimmunity', *Philosophy & Social Criticism*, 38:1 (2012), p. 118.

dispensation is not founded on the elicitation of speech, but upon the absolute obliteration even of its possibility.

I will adduce some evidence, offer some arguments and draw some conclusions about these propositions. To do this, I draw on the work of Giorgio Agamben on the powers of language, and I will give a brief exegesis of three crucial moments in Agamben's work which have a direct bearing on the question of torture: one drawn from his recent short book, *The Sacrament of Language: An Archaeology of the Oath*; one from the short essay 'K', first published in English in a collection I co-edited with Nick Heron and Alexander Murray; and from *Remnants of Auschwitz*, Agamben's study of Holocaust testimony. I will be treating Agamben's extracts in reverse order of their appearance, before concluding with some remarks about the consequences for political life today.

THE SACRAMENT OF LANGUAGE: AN ARCHAEOLOGY OF THE OATH

The role of the oath in the formation of political communities has been well known and well studied for some time. As John Spurr puts it in 'A Profane History of Early Modern Oaths', 'Oaths bind lovers, just as they adjudicate between litigants. They are constitutive of communes, gilds, fraternities, professions and institutions. They are at the heart of covenanting communities and bonds of association.'[23] Oaths are speech-practices that bind individuals to communities, at once sacred and profane. As one might expect, recent studies in the field – suggestively, the most important English-language studies focus on the revolutionary seventeenth century – tend to effect a double move. The first is to mobilise a theory of performatives to account for oaths; the second, connected with the first, is to insist on the situated nature of the use of oaths, which means that part of the point is to avoid undue metaphysical presuppositions or disavowed anachronism.[24] But this sort of historical polemic is foreign to Agamben.

As Agamben notes of the oath in general, it is indissociably an affir-

[23] J. Spurr, 'A Profane History of Early Modern Oaths', in *Transactions of the Royal Historical Society* (Cambridge: Royal Historical Society, 2001), p. 47.

[24] See, for example, 'often unexamined perspectives can impose an anachronistic structure on the past', C. Condren, *Argument and Authority in Early Modern England: The Presupposition of Oaths and Offices* (Cambridge: Cambridge University Press, 2006), p. 11; D. M. Jones, *Conscience and Allegiance in Seventeenth Century England: The Political Significance of Oaths and Engagements* (Rochester: University of Rochester Press, 1999); E. Vallance, *Revolutionary England and the National Covenant: State Oaths, Protestantism, and the Political Nation 1552–1682* (Woodbridge: Boydell Press, 2005).

mation, an invocation and a profanation.[25] As such, the oath precedes received divisions between magic, religion and law that have hitherto governed – and, as Agamben demonstrates, often severely bungled – its study. Agamben typically pinpoints a key problem in the relevant scholarship, showing how this scholarship falsifies its own evidence to the extent that disputes within the scholarship come to mirror each other without realising it. He proceeds to isolate the key features of the problem, and, by way of close analyses of the crucial texts, turns them towards the paradoxes of its invariance. Agamben seeks the exposure of an *arché* within immanence, not the transmission of a hermetic transcendence. As he puts it, 'the *arché* is not a given, a substance, or an event but a field of historical currents stretched between anthropogenesis and the present, ultrahistory and history'.[26] Here this also means: don't think that the truth of words can be found outside words themselves. But it also means: don't think that an attentiveness to allegedly contextual specifics relativises the operations within and upon language.

It is with this principle in hand that Agamben unlocks the enigma of the oath as that primordial function whereby speaking beings try to curtail the irreducible possibility of language's perjuries: the 'proper context of the oath is therefore among those institutions . . . whose function is to performatively affirm the truth and trustworthiness of speech'.[27] As such, an oath can only be an oath of allegiance to a particular office on the basis of this prior operation: the oath is required as a self-reference of language to language within language before any putatively reliable reference to the world can take place. Agamben: 'The oath seems, then, to result from the conjunction of three elements: an affirmation, the invocation of the gods as witnesses, and a curse directed at perjury.'[28]

The oath, a supplemental ritual declaration, expressed as a futile but necessary attempt to stabilise the insuperable rift between words and things, inscribes its own futility in its very expression by means of the curse. Some people care more for grammar than they do for God, Augustine complained; God, as Nietzsche added, *is* a function of grammar. For Agamben, 'God' is a name that humans give to the hope that names can reliably name at all, de jure if not de facto. But God is then the name for the name of everything that cannot not be taken

[25] G. Agamben, *The Sacrament of Language: An Archaeology of the Oath*, trans. A. Kotsko (Stanford: Stanford University Press, 2011).

[26] Agamben, *Sacrament*, p. 11.

[27] Agamben, *Sacrament*, p. 65.

[28] Agamben, *Sacrament*, p. 31.

in vain. For if 'the connection that unites language and the world is broken, the name of God, which expressed and guaranteed this connection based in blessing, becomes the name of the curse, that is, of a word that has broken its truthful relation to things'.[29] As Jacques Lacan constantly essayed to remind his auditors – and Lacan, not to mention psychoanalysis more generally, is, as the current book argues, the true, if well-secreted prime precursor of Agamben's work – you cannot speak without believing in a God you also cannot help but betray in and by that very utterance.[30]

But this leads to a real problem. For if 'every oath swears on the name par excellence, that is on the name of God, because the oath is the experience of language that treats all of language as a proper name',[31] then how can one speak at all without implicitly participating in oath-making (and oath-breaking)? Silence, or showing in silence, can become one attempt to escape this situation; inventive expressions of senselessness is another. But the first, often a favoured tactic of antiphilosophy itself, finds its withdrawal towards muteness becoming indiscernible from that of the victims of the powers it would contest. As for the latter, we find a Romantic problematic of poetry (or artistic creation) establishing the very politics that come to foreclose it. Hence, a third way: the practice of philosophy itself, which, in Agamben's words, 'is constitutively a critique of the oath: that is, it puts in question the sacramental bond that links the human to language, without for that reason simply speaking haphazardly, falling into the vanity of speech'.[32]

Yet it is at this point that the principle of immanence that enables Agamben's insights in this particular work also curbs them, for it forgoes the question of the *crossing* of the body and its speech. For what of those figures who are excluded from swearing an oath at all, but who are nevertheless required to appear as the subjects of a legal process in which testimony can be given only on oath? I am thinking here of the figure of the slave, whose testimony in ancient law could only be admissible if it had been extracted by torture, as Agamben himself has noted elsewhere (of which more below). Yet he does not acknowledge that

[29] Agamben, *Sacrament*, p. 42.
[30] See J. Lacan, *Seminar XX: Encore: The Seminar of Jacques Lacan, Book XX: On Feminine Sexuality: The Limits of Love and Knowledge 1972–1973*, ed. J.-A. Miller, trans. with notes by B. Fink (New York: W. W. Norton & Co., 1998). For Agamben, 'If, in polytheism, the name *assigned to* the god named this or that event of language, this or that specific naming, this or that *Sondergott*, in monotheism God's name names language itself'; *Sacrament*, p. 49.
[31] Agamben, *Sacrament*, p. 53.
[32] Agamben, *Sacrament*, p. 72.

torture and the oath are necessarily, if asymmetrically, bound together: on his own terms, torture must be the shadow bodily accompaniment of the oath, its foundation and truth. It is thus no wonder today, when the oath has fallen into desuetude, that torture is explicitly back on the agenda even for those democratic states which had prided themselves on their thoroughgoing rejection of it. Without any trust in oaths – indeed, having repudiated almost altogether their function and efficacy – our contemporary materialist polities can imagine no other recourse than direct psycho-physical incursions into bodies in a forlorn and ter-rifying attempt to extract 'reliable' 'information'. This enables us to add to our discussion of the ticking bomb another, perhaps unexpected corollary: those who argue for the good of torture today have at once unconsciously registered a serious transformation in the status of lan-guage, the loss of the efficacy of the oath, and, panicked, betray their own impotence and thoughtlessness precisely by trying to reinscribe the lack within the 'natural' 'human' body itself. So if Agamben does not name torture as such as the corporeal underlining of the oath, he has nonetheless implicitly provided a profound explanation for torture's recent re-emergence on a global scale. I now turn to another part of Agamben's *oeuvre*, in which he explicitly discusses the role of torture in law.

K O

It is precisely because Agamben had already dealt with the question of torture that its absence from his book on oaths is so noteworthy. One suspects that this is partially due to the very difficulty of the articulation. Yet, in an essay denominated simply 'K', and dedicated to a doubled reading of Franz Kafka's *Trial* and *The Castle*, Agamben speaks directly of this. Noting that the letter K for *kalumniator* was branded on the forehead of those found guilty of bringing false accu-sations in Roman law, Agamben makes this insight the 'key' to the *Trial*: 'Every man brings a slanderous trial against himself.'[33] In doing so, self-slander 'calls into question the principle itself of the trial: the moment of accusation', 'it puts guilt into question' and arraigns the law itself at the very threshold of its operations. For Agamben, 'the accusa-tion is, perhaps, the juridical "category" par excellence (kategoria, in Greek, means accusation) . . . The law is . . . in its essence, accusation, "category."'[34]

[33] G. Agamben, 'K', in J. Clemens et al. (eds), *The Work of Giorgio Agamben* (Edinburgh: Edinburgh University Press, 2008), p. 14.
[34] Agamben, 'K', p. 15.

The paradox is extraordinary: the false accuser has charged himself; if he is guilty, he is innocent; if innocent, guilty. Or, more precisely, 'guilt does not exist, or rather, the only guilt is self-slander, which consists in accusing oneself of a non-existent guilt (which is to say, of one's own innocence – and this is the comic gesture par excellence).'[35] Agamben even discerns a triple operation in K's actions: he slanders himself; he colludes with himself in the slander; and he gives way on his own self-slander. As such, this is a 'strategy that aims to deactivate and render inoperative the accusation'[36] – *from the point of the accusation itself*.

Such slander, therefore, must be distinguished from confession. As Agamben writes:

> While in the law of the republican era confession was admitted with res-
> ervations and used more to defend the accused, in the imperial era, above
> all for crimes against power (conspiracy, treason, plot, impiety against the
> ruler), but also for adultery, magic and illicit divination, the criminal pro-
> cedure involved the torture of the accused and his slaves in order to extort
> a confession from them. 'To extract the truth' (*veritatem eruere*) is the
> emblem of the new juridical rationality that, tightly binding confession and
> truth, makes torture – in cases of *lèse majesté* extended even to witnesses
> – the probatory instrument par excellence. Hence the name *quaestio* that
> designates it in juridical sources: torture is an inquiry into truth (*quaestio
> veritatis*).[37]

We are thus dealing with not one but two paired, linked oppositions. On a first level, that of linguistic acts, we have the paradox of self-slander, which stalls and evades the operations of law qua law of truth, against the act of confession, which is the paradigm of the action of law. On a second level, that of bodies, we have the peculiar continuation of freedom of movement – K's '"arrested" condition', as Agamben notes, 'does not entail any change in his life'[38] – against, not a death-sentence, but the use of torture. Indeed, speaking of the murderous, malfunction-ing device in Kafka's *In the Penal Colony*, Agamben remarks that 'the true purpose of the machine is . . . torture as *quaestio veritatis*; death, as often happens in torture, is only a collateral effect of the discovery of truth.'[39] A grimly comic struggle ensues between self-slander and self-condemnation, the dissolution of cause and the violent inscription of marks upon the body, in the course of which these antitheses merge and become indistinguishable. Hence the strategy of self-slander fails;

[35] Agamben, 'K', p. 14.
[36] Agamben, 'K', p. 16.
[37] Agamben, 'K', p. 18.
[38] Agamben, 'K', p. 16.
[39] Agamben, 'K', p. 19.

indeed, becomes in turn the strategy by which the law turns its own groundlessness into its justification. The trial opened by the accusation will end inevitably in a confession, or in a torture-death, which comes to the same thing.

Before I proceed to my third example, let me note a few aspects of Agamben's procedure. Above all, he takes literary texts absolutely seriously as providing the most profound analyses of the relation between life and the law. Kafka's text shows precisely what it is unable to say without succumbing to precisely the operations of the law it seeks to evade. In its own failure, it nonetheless enables what it shows to be said philosophically, that is, a saying which seeks to break the bond between law and language without falling into what W. H. Auden might have called 'elderly rubbish' or 'drivel'. Or, to put this another way, philosophy is an experiment with examples of language that exceed the grip of properties (i.e. those phenomena which can be brought under a law identified by science). In doing this, philosophy testifies to a very peculiar experience which it does not itself have, but which it discerns above all in poetry: a split and impossible experience of the non-relation between language and the living body.

THE *MUSLIM* IN AUSCHWITZ

The key text of Agamben's in this regard is *Remnants of Auschwitz*, perhaps the book of his that has come in for the most vocal criticisms. More particularly, the examination that he provides there of the figure widely known as the *Muselmann* has proved especially contentious. So Ruth Leys charges Agamben with an illicit junking of the affect of guilt in favour of an analysis of shame.[40] J. M. Bernstein claims that Agamben aestheticises the *Muselmann*'s 'fate for the sake of a metaphysics of language'.[41] Mesnard and Kahan similarly charge Agamben with misunderstanding the historiographical debate and aestheticising the figure. Marianne Hirsch and Leo Spitzer speak of this 'deeply problematic argument of Giorgio Agamben'.[42] On the other hand, even apparently 'friendly' commentary, such as that of Slavoj Žižek,

---

[40] R. Leys, *From Guilt to Shame: Auschwitz and After* (Princeton: Princeton University Press, 2007), esp. Chapter 5; see also E. M. Vogt, 'Catastrophic Narratives and Why the "Catastrophe" to Catastrophe Might Have Already Happened', in S. Jöttkandt et al. (eds), *The Catastrophic Imperative* (Basingstoke: Palgrave Macmillan, 2009), pp. 26–52.

[41] J. M. Bernstein, 'Bare Life, Bearing Witness: Auschwitz and the Pornography of Horror', *Parallax*, 10:1 (2004), p. 17.

[42] M. Hirsch and L. Spitzer, 'Holocaust Studies/Memory Studies', in S. Redstone (ed.), *Memory: Histories, Theories, Debates* (New York: Fordham University Press, 2010), p. 398.

regularly misses the point.[43] Not only are all these responses radically insufficient (even in the simplest sense of clearly not having read what Agamben has written), but their disorder is precisely symptomatic of what Agamben is trying to analyse.

Indeed, this is one of the first phenomena that Agamben notes in his discussion: 'It is a striking fact that although all witnesses speak of him as a central experience, the *Muselmann* is barely named in the historical studies on the destruction of European Jewry.'[44] Relying on the testimony of witnesses themselves, including Primo Levi and Jean Amery, and not only or primarily upon subsequent historiography, Agamben attempts to bring to light some of the consequences of the appearance of such a creature. As survivors such as Levi testify, if the Nazis perpetrated mass industrial genocide in the death camps, another kind of personage emerged as an unintended, unexpected by-product. Often denominated the '*Muselmann*' – although there were regional variations in the jargons of different camps – this personage is crucial for Agamben insofar as what philosophy had always maintained was the essence of the human (its capacity for language) had been fully stripped from the *Muselmänner*. The *Muselmann* survived as a biological organism, but could no longer be tolerated as human not only by the Nazis, but by fellow camp inmates themselves. The classical figure that Levi invokes in this regard is that of the Gorgon, the creature that to look on directly entails one's own paralysis and destruction, and he defines the *Muselmann* as 'he who has seen the gorgon'. Agamben in fact reads the apparition of this figure as an absolute limit, 'the final biopolitical substance to be isolated in the biological continuum'.[45] Why? Because the Western philosophical tradition had always considered the 'essence of man' to be the animal with language – it is precisely this characterisa-

---

[43] On this point, see J. Clemens, 'The Politics of Style in the Works of Slavoj Žižek', in G. Boucher et al. (eds), *Traversing the Fantasy: Critical Responses to Slavoj Žižek* (Aldershot: Ashgate, 2005), pp. 3–22. In recent works, Žižek has become progressively more abusive and insinuating about Agamben's position, yet still without getting it right. In *The Monstrosity of Christ*, Žižek even asserts that Agamben makes an implicit distinction between 'good' and 'bad' *homines sacres*, to the extent that Agamben's image of happiness, 'limbo', 'sounds uncannily close to the dream of a "good" concentration camp'; J. Milbank and S. Žižek, *The Monstrosity of Christ: Paradox or Dialectic?* (Cambridge: MIT, 2009), p. 293. Strangely enough, Žižek's claims, without any footnotes or other references, here repeat, almost verbatim, Jacques Derrida's objections to Walter Benjamin's theses on 'divine violence', objections that Agamben has himself in turn criticised in – what else? – the book *Homo Sacer*. See J. Derrida, 'Force de loi: Le "Fondement mystique de l'autorité"', *Cardozo Law Review*, 11:5–6, (1990), pp. 919–1,045; G. Agamben, *Homo Sacer: Sovereign Power and Bare Life*, trans. D. Heller-Roazen (Stanford: Stanford University Press, 1998).

[44] G. Agamben, *Remnants of Auschwitz: The Witness and the Archive*, trans. D. Heller-Roazen (New York: Zone Books, 1999), p. 34.

[45] Agamben, *Remnants of Auschwitz*, p. 85.

tion that Agamben had visited in an earlier text, *Language and Death*[46] – what the *Muselmann* literally incarnates is that a creature, the 'human', a biological creature endowed with language, can be stripped of its essence in actuality. This is why Agamben can remark that 'The *Muselmann* is not only or not so much a limit between life and death; rather, he marks the threshold between the human and the inhuman'.[47] The human being can thereafter be consigned by the most extreme expressions of sovereign power (the camps, contemporary torture) to a kind of undead, unspeaking subsistence. The potential for speech (to speak or not) had therefore been expropriated from the *Muselmänner*; it would be impossible for a *Muselmann* to say 'I am a *Muselmann*'. As a consequence, survivor testimonies exhibit an extraordinary structure. They testify in language to an experience which the writers state that they did not and could not have had, that is, the experience of being stripped of the possibility of having an experience at all (i.e. language). This at once reveals something essential about the relationship between human language-use and political power (human beings can be separated by power from their own essence) as they contest it (the witness confronts and resists this possibility).[48]

All the other extreme procedures familiar from the literature – mass extermination, selections, scientific experiments upon inmates, the organisation of the *Sonderkommando* – had had precedents elsewhere, and did not in themselves constitute a radical novelty, but an expansion and intensification of existing political techniques.[49] What the *Muselmann* shows is that the 'ethical lesson' of the camps is not simply a matter of numbers or of intention or of technology. Leaving aside the well-known difficulties of such accountancy procedures, it is the question of a *remnant* – that which has gone almost undiscussed in nearly seventy years since Auschwitz. What Auschwitz constituted that was radically and irreversibly new was not simply human corpses in unprecedented numbers, but a structure which inadvertently produced humans-who-were-no-longer-human as a kind of industrial waste-product. Unfortunately, this also means that – however desperately one would like to keep to these ideals – 'dignity', 'human rights' and 'rule of law' are no longer viable categories for thinking through what actually

---

[46] See G. Agamben, *Language and Death: The Place of Negativity*, trans. K. E. Pinkus with M. Hardt (Minneapolis: University of Minnesota Press, 1991).

[47] Agamben, *Remnants of Auschwitz*, p. 55.

[48] This paragraph extends part of my entry for 'Language' in A. Murray and J. Whyte (eds), *The Agamben Dictionary* (Edinburgh: Edinburgh University Press, 2011), pp. 118–19.

[49] However, see also J.-C. Milner, *Les Penchants criminels de l'Europe démocratique* (Paris: Verdier, 2003), in which he notes that the 'Jew' was in fact that creature for whom a new technology (of destruction) was invented.

happened, for what has been actualised and cannot be wished away. As Agamben says: 'This is also why Auschwitz marks the end and the ruin of every ethics of dignity and conformity to a norm. The bare life to which human beings were reduced neither demands nor conforms to anything. It itself is the only norm; it is absolutely immanent.'[50] The equal and inalienable rights which derive from the inherent dignity of the human person cannot be viably sustained, even as a legal fiction: the problematic of the survivor has exceeded the frame of the trial, including in the projective forms of reparation- or war-crimes tribunals.

One of the unbearable revelations of Auschwitz is that the *Muselmann*-witness dyad is fundamental to being human: that the human biopolitical substance can be irremediably separated from language as such, from what makes it human. As Jessica Whyte writes,

> Agamben, unlike Heidegger, does not therefore see Auschwitz as simply one among a list of manifestations of technological nihilism, but as something radically new – and what was new was not so much the mass industrial production of death as the creation of the *Muselmann*, as the final point on a biopolitical continuum, beyond which 'there is only the gas chamber.'[51]

I truly cannot see how this is an 'aestheticization'. What was created inadvertently was subsequently captured technologically: US interrogation techniques are now allegedly able to destroy anyone as a person forever within one hundred hours.[52]

PHILOSOPHY AND ANTIPHILOSOPHY IN THE WAKE OF THE SEPARATION OF LANGUAGE AND THE BODY

We have recently seen the reinstrumentalisation of the spectre of torture as a device for turning the panic of contingency attendant on the contemporary crisis of state legitimacy into the licensing of arbitrary state power as the solution to this crisis. Indeed, this intention clearly underwrites the circulation of the Abu Ghraib photographs. Such images are not based on any natural language, and hence are able to convey their message of universal torturability universally, that is, technically; or, to put this differently, they teach a lesson at the level of perceptibility, not language. Coterminously, torture has now been explicitly legiti-

---

[50] Agamben, *Remnants of Auschwitz*, p. 69.
[51] See J. Whyte, *Catastrophe and Redemption: The Political Thought of Giorgio Agamben* (Albany: State University of New York Press, 2013).
[52] This is through a combination of sensory deprivation, drugs, noise, 'dietary management', 'sleep management', electroshock, neurosurgery and so on. See, for a rare public notice of these techniques, N. Klein, 'The US Psychological Torture System is Finally on Trial', *The Guardian*, 23 February 2007, p. 41.

mated in the oldest democracies through its legal-medical redefinition. Between 2002 and 2006, the Office of Legal Counsel for the US Justice Department, exemplified by the notorious 'Bybee memo', enabled torture to emerge 'under the color of law'.[53] If it is not so well known, it is a salient fact that the Bybee memo drew on the 'health benefits' clause of the non-US Citizens Statute Title 8 USC Sec. 1369, from the section 'Emergency Medical Condition', to define what separated the cruel, inhumane or degrading from torture, namely:

> For purposes of this section, the term 'emergency medical condition' means a medical condition (including emergency labor and delivery) manifesting itself by acute symptoms of sufficient severity (including severe pain) such that the absence of immediate medical attention could reasonably be expected to result in –
> (1) placing the patient's health in serious jeopardy,
> (2) serious impairment to bodily functions, or
> (3) serious dysfunction of any bodily organ or part.

So only death, organ failure or serious impairment of bodily functions now counted as torture under this redescription, a redescription which therefore licenses all other practices up to those points. Note that in these cases, all the contemporary available terms for any public debate concerning torture – the ticking bomb, the necessity to urgently extract information that will save the lives of innocents – have no role to play here whatsoever. Except, that is, for the fact of legitimising torture by legitimising discussion about torture.

So the relation between torture and the political that I began by sketching seems, in the wake of Agamben's demonstrations – and all the evidence – exactly as the defenders of torture often suggest, if for completely different reasons, archaic. We no longer live in active polities, but in administrative waste-management societies. If democracy has historically defined itself by its repression of torture in order to enable 'free speech' – not simply to be able to say anything in public, but to be able to speak, publicly or not, in one's own name, without coercion – it is now essentially over. Contemporary torture is no longer about the *extraction* of speech from the body, but the absolute and irreversible *separation* of speech from the body. Perhaps this feature alone is enough to render the whole 'debate' utterly otiose. In any case, it seems that Agamben's diagnoses are substantially correct, insofar as they reconstruct a logic for apparently diverse phenomena (the

---

[53] I owe details regarding the Bybee memo and its usage to an unpublished paper by Peter Hutchings, 'Invented Sovereignty and the Bush Presidency', conference paper, Australasian Society for Continental Philosophy Annual Conference, La Trobe University, 14 December 2011.

ticking-bomb debate, the use of testimony and oaths, etc.), while also illuminating certain occlusions, opacities and undecidabilities of the situation. If this is indeed the case, then existing means of political contestation will hardly be adequate to the challenge of our own torturing present.

Agamben's own 'solution' – which bears primarily on an ingenious reconstruction of the practice of testimony – is dissatisfactory in this context insofar as it does not essentially go beyond what I called the 'Aesopic' in the previous chapter. Agamben thereby repeats as solution that which his own analysis has demonstrated nugatory. This conclusion is horrifying, and its implications go far beyond the self-circumscribed scope of this book. Given that, as I have been arguing throughout, psychoanalysis has also always located itself at the intersection of the body and its languages, it too is thoroughly disabled by this new political situation. If bodies and languages can no longer be held to intersect necessarily with each other, then psychoanalysis is literally finished as a viable practice. It therefore becomes necessary to pose the question with urgency, as in a state of emergency: what becomes of psychoanalysis when its very foundation in the slave animal tortured by the signifier can no longer be assured? It is to this problem that I now turn.

7. *Man is a Swarm Animal*

Socrates: I seem to be in great luck, Meno; while I am looking for one virtue, I have found you to have a whole swarm of them.

Plato, *Meno*, 72a[1]

It is clear that man is a social animal more than the bee or any other gregarious creature.

Aristotle, *Politics*, 1253a7[2]

For looke you vpon the face of this common wealth, and you shall find it in as bad or worse state, than was the state of the common wealth of the Israelites in the time of Ezechiel, or rather woorse concerning religion. For Atheistes. Papistes, & blasphemers of Gods holie name, swarme as thick as butter flies, without checke or controlment.

John Hooker[3]

A 'PUNCEPT'

The previous chapter ended with a dilemma: if the human is that 'living being' which can actually be separated from what once was held to be its essence, that is, 'language', what possible effectivity – whether of diagnosis or treatment – is left to psychoanalysis? The ongoing psychiatric, pharmaceutical and philosophical assault against psychoanalysis is one thing; the loss of its very basis for being is quite another. The first, as I have shown throughout this book, is hardly the threat to

---

[1] Plato, *Meno*, in *Complete Works*, ed. with intro. and notes by J. M. Cooper (Indianapolis: Hackett, 1997), p. 872.

[2] Aristotle, *The Politics*, trans. T. A. Sinclair, rev. T. J. Saunders (Harmondsworth: Penguin, 1986).

[3] J. Hooker, *A pamphlet of the offices, and duties of euerie particular sworne officer, of the citie of Excester: collected by Iohn Vowell alias Hoker, Gentleman & chamberlaine of the same* (London: Henrie Denham, 1584).

psychoanalysis that it is often supposed to be; but the second would be fatal. The second, in fact, is tantamount to an experience of what we could telegraphically call 'the renaturalisation of man', and its effects are patent across the universe of discourse. To advert to the terms offered by Giorgio Agamben and discussed in the previous chapter, this is the epoch in which sovereign power has finally effected the isolation and separation of 'bare life' as such.

In this chapter, I examine a radical revision of psychoanalysis from within psychoanalysis itself, which at once registers the unprecedented extremity of this situation and attempts to respond to it. Significantly enough, this revision begins with a pun, and with a relatively bad pun too. The reader will not be surprised to hear that this is a pun of Jacques Lacan's: S_1, *l'essaim*; S-one, the swarm. Just as significantly, this pun has to date, at best, been taken as a suggestive metaphor; at worst, as just another meaningless word-game, entirely typical of Lacan. My argument is that – if indeed a pun is sometimes just a pun – this pun is more than that. In fact, it provides a concept that bears centrally upon the relationship between technology, politics, language and psychoanalytic formalisation. I trace the aetiology of this pun-concept (or 'puncept'[4]) and examine the significance of its emergence at a particular historical moment – not to mention at a very particular moment in Lacan's own conceptual development – in order to suggest what sort of problems it responds to and what sort of theoretical consequences it entails, especially in regard to the revision of Lacan's own revision of Hegel's master-slave dialectic which I discussed in Chapter 2.

THE PREPOLITICAL

What is it about 'man' that makes him a candidate for politics and the political? What makes human being-together a properly political question and not just a question of species-activity or genetic determinism? Man, says Aristotle, is the only animal with politics and language. For Aristotle, these features are integrally connected. But such formulas still don't answer the question: what makes the human a candidate for politics at all? A 'candidate' only, given that a human being can rise above or fall from politics (e.g. Aristotle's 'man without community', either a beast or a god). So the question remains: what is specific

---

[4] A 'puncept' is not a philosophical concept but an elementary psychoanalytic notion; perhaps it would be better phrased as a 'puneme' or 'calemboureme', on the same model as a 'mytheme' or 'matheme'. See Lacan's remarks on Democritus in *Seminar XI: The Four Fundamental Concepts of Psychoanalysis*, trans. A. Sheridan, intro. by D. Macey (London: Penguin, 1994), pp. 63–4.

about humanity's matter such that a human can come to function as a political animal, indeed, the political animal *par excellence*? Every philosopher has provided his own answer to this question. Let's provide a stupid list.

Aristotle: man is a mimetic animal.[5]
Judeo-Christianity: man is a fallen animal.[6]
Machiavelli: man is a tricky animal.[7]
Hobbes: man is a fearful animal.[8]
Locke: man is a social animal.[9]
Voltaire: man is a sensible animal.[10]
Rousseau: man is a contracting animal.[11]
Kant: man is a maturing animal.[12]
Hegel: man is a historical animal.[13]

[5] 'The instinct for imitation is inherent in man from his earliest days; he differs from other animals in that he is the most imitative of creatures, and he learns his earliest lessons by imitation. Also inborn in all of us is the instinct to enjoy works of imitation'; Aristotle, *On the Art of Poetry*, in *Classical Literary Criticism*, trans. with intro. by T. S. Dorsch (London: Penguin, 1988), p. 35.

[6] Stupid as it is to say so, there are no politics in Eden, precisely because it is sexual difference as such that distributes social labour, and there is no polity. If the snake is the +1 that introduces desire into the mix, then that triangulation is the condition of the political.

[7] N. Machiavelli, *The Prince*, trans. G. Bull, intro. by A. Grafton (London: Penguin, 2003), e.g. 'One can make this generalization about men: they are ungrateful, fickle, liars, and deceivers, they shun danger and are greedy for profit; while you treat them well, they are yours'; p. 54.

[8] 'The passions that incline men to peace are fear of death, desire of such things as are necessary to commodious living, and a hope by their industry to attain them'; T. Hobbes, *Leviathan*, ed. A. P. Martinich (Ontario: Broadview, 2002), p. 97.

[9] 'God, having made man such a creature that, in His own judgment, it was not good for him to be alone, put him under strong obligations of necessity, convenience, and inclination, to drive him into society, as well as fitted him with understanding and language to continue and enjoy it'; J. Locke, *Two Treatises of Government* (London: Everyman, 1986), pp. 154–5. See also 'God having designed Man for a sociable Creature, made him not only with an inclination, and under a necessity to have fellowship with those of his own kind; but furnished him also with Language, which was to be the great Instrument, and common Tye of Society'; *An Essay Concerning Human Understanding*, ed. P. H. Nidditch (Oxford: Clarendon Press, 1985), Book III, Chapter 1, p. 402.

[10] 'Among the Romans *sensus communis* meant not only common sense, but humanity, sensibility. Since we are not up to the Romans this word means only half as much to us as it did to them'; Voltaire, *Philosophical Dictionary*, ed. and trans. T. Besterman (Harmondsworth: Penguin, 1972), pp. 376–7. Or, again, 'the man who is not a beast and does not think he is an angel'; p. 376. One can easily see why Alain Badiou recently denominated Voltaire 'one of the most considerable thinkers of humanitarian mediocrity', *Le Siècle* (Paris: Éditions du Seuil, 2005), p. 177.

[11] See J.-J. Rousseau, *Discourse on Political Economy; and The Social Contract*, trans. with intro. and notes by C. Betts (Oxford: Oxford University Press, 1994).

[12] '*Enlightenment is man's emergence from his self-incurred immaturity*'; I. Kant, *Political Writings*, ed. H. Reiss, trans. H. B. Nisbet (Cambridge: Cambridge University Press, 1991), p. 54.

[13] G. W. F. Hegel, *The Phenomenology of Spirit*, trans. A. V. Miller, foreword by J. N. Findlay (Oxford: Oxford University Press, 1977).

Bentham: man is a useful animal.[14]
The Romantic poets: man is a baby animal.[15]
Hazlitt: man is a toad-eating animal.[16]
De Quincey: man is an addictive animal.[17]
Hegel: man is a prestigious animal.[18]
Marx: man is a labouring animal.[19]
Nietzsche: man is a herd animal.[20]
Freud: man is a horde animal.[21]

These adjectives do not provide the *essence* of what these thinkers consider to be the *political* being of man; they rather specify something that founds the *possibility* of the political in man, the conditions for man to be or become political. After all, if there is one proposition that almost every Western philosopher shares, in one way or another, it is this: man presents as a mutable being which cannot know a priori what it is capable of. These answers are therefore directed towards a seizure of that mutability insofar as it can be crystallised in a concept that can be articulated with the political. The problem is that the articulation is precisely the problem. There is simply no 'fundamental' 'categorical pair' of concepts (whether friend/enemy, as Carl Schmitt would have it, or *zoe/bios*, as Giorgio Agamben argues) that founds political thought in the West. Yet the tradition also agrees that man is the only animal with politics *and* language.

It is into this tradition that Lacan intervenes when broaching his own investigations into language. It is why he maintains: 'That the symptom institutes the order in which our politics emerges, implies, moreover, that everything that articulates itself of this order is susceptible to interpretation. This is why we are right to put psychoanalysis at the

---

[14] J. Bentham, *An Introduction to the Principle of Morals and Legislation*, ed. J. H. Burns and H. L. A. Hart (London and New York: Methuen, 1980).
[15] See Carl Schmitt's fury at this formation in *Political Romanticism*, trans. G. Oakes (Cambridge: MIT, 1986), p. 69.
[16] 'Man is a toad-eating animal. The admiration of power in others is as common to man as the love of it in himself: the one makes him a tyrant, the other a slave'; W. Hazlitt, *Selected Writings* (Harmondsworth: Penguin, 1989), p. 378.
[17] T. De Quincey, *Confessions of an English Opium Eater*, ed. A. Hayter (London: Penguin, 1986).
[18] This, at least, would be what Alexandre Kojève takes from and extends in Hegel: the primacy of the struggle for prestige as founding the political sphere.
[19] See K. Marx, *Capital*, Vol. 1, trans. B. Fowkes, intro. by E. Mandel (Harmondsworth: Penguin, 1976).
[20] F. Nietzsche, *The Anti-Christ, Ecce Homo, Twilight of the Idols, and Other Writings*, ed. A. Ridley and J. Norman (Cambridge: Cambridge University Press, 2005).
[21] S. Freud, *Group Psychology and the Analysis of the Ego*, in *The Standard Edition of the Complete Psychological Works of Sigmund Freud*, Vol. XVIII (1920–1922), ed. J. Strachey et al. (London: The Hogarth Press, 1955), p. 121.

head [*chef*] of politics.'[22] However serious Lacan may be about such a programme, it is also the case that his position on language – and therefore also the political – develops throughout his career. I focus here on a period that lasts barely a handful of years, from about 1969 to 1972, and which is, in any case, hardly very perspicuous. It is a transitional period for Lacan, and it is the nature of that transition that I will try to capture here under the heading of 'the swarm'. Indeed, I want to add to the list above that, *chez* Lacan – at least for a certain period in his thought – 'man is a swarm animal'.

S_1 = SWARM

To my knowledge, Lacan explicitly generates a clinical significance from this pun for the first time in *Seminar XVII: The Other Side of Psychoanalysis*. In the opening session of 26 November 1969, Lacan introduces his four discourses, those of the Master, Hysteric, Analyst and University, with their accompanying algebraic letters of $ (the barred subject), S_1 (the master-signifier), S_2 (knowledge) and a (the object). The S_1, the master-signifier, is homophonic in French with *l'essaim*, the swarm, so whenever S_1 is pronounced, that is what you hear; or, more likely, you don't, you overlook it, or rather 'overhear' it. That's too bad. In fact, most of those who have noted the pun seem to have taken it entirely in their stride, as an entirely typical instance of Lacan's oneiric style that doesn't have to disrupt whatever mission they're already on.

In other words, the swarm appears only to disappear at once. The hilarious compilation *789 néologismes de Jacques Lacan* excludes it, presumably on the basis that: 'With only three exceptions (*seconder*, *verge* and *soir*), the words of this glossary don't contribute to a semantic neology, that is, through adding signification to an existing word.'[23] The instructions immediately proceed to confess, alarmingly, how difficult it was to decide on inclusions and exclusions to the volume given Lacan's relentless linguistic inventiveness. Whatever the reason, the word *essaim* doesn't make it in. Too boring, perhaps, too opportunistic, too ordinary.

Neither, to my knowledge, does 'swarm' make it as a concept into any of the dictionaries, handbooks, companions or readers currently available on Lacan, and often not even into the indices. To take only one recent, authoritative instance of such an omission, we find, in the

[22] J. Lacan, 'Lituraterre', in *Autres Écrits* (Paris: Éditions du Seuil, 2001), p. 18.
[23] Y. Pélissier, 'Glossaire mode d'emploi', in Pélissier et al. (eds), *789 néologismes de Jacques Lacan* (Paris: EPEL, 2002), p. x.

index to the *Cambridge Companion to Lacan*, despite the presence of such Lacanian coinages as *linguisterie* and *parlêtre*, that 'swarm' is nowhere to be found – although, as I've already stated, you can't pronounce S₁ in French without hearing *essaim*.[24] As American cultural theorists like to ask, waving their hands in wheedling disbelief: 'Where's the swarm in this text?'

It was therefore something of a shock to find, not 'swarm' itself, but a cognate, *Schwärmerei*, listed in the index to the recent complete English translation of *Écrits*, where, in the 'Index of Freud's German Terms', it is referenced to page 773 (the French page numbers reproduced in the translation, not the English ones).[25] The *écrit* in question turns out to be nothing other than 'Kant with Sade', where the context is Lacan's discussion of how the Marquis de Sade's boudoir education provides the truth of Immanuel Kant's abstemious moral law.

Now this is a particularly odd contribution of Lacan's. Unlike most of the other *écrits*, it was not delivered as a public performance before being written up for publication. Neither does it have a strictly psychoanalytic provenance. Rather, it was commissioned as a preface to Sade's tract *Philosophy in the Bedroom*, slated to appear in a new edition of his works with Éditions du Cercle. Rejected by the editors, Lacan's essay then found a home as 'a review of the edition of Sade's works for which it was intended' (in *Critique*, no less!); finally, after the success of the *Écrits* themselves in 1966, the piece was 'recommissioned' and 'included as a postface in the same publisher's 1966 edition of Sade's *Oeuvres complètes*'.[26] Phew.

Something else is significant here: this is a text on perversion. Just as Freud had treated psychosis primarily through Judge Schreber's testimony and not, like Jung or Lacan himself, in clinical settings, Lacan – though he had dealings with a surfeit of hysterics, obsessionals, paranoics, schizophrenics and so on – doesn't seem to have spent a lot of time with perverts. There are perhaps a number of reasons for this. Above all, as J.-A. Miller says,

[24] J.-M. Rabaté (ed.), *The Cambridge Companion to Lacan* (Cambridge: Cambridge University Press, 2003); note also the absence of 'swarm' in the index to J. Clemens and R. Grigg (eds), *Jacques Lacan and the Other Side of Psychoanalysis* (Durham, NC: Duke University Press, 2006), where it does not appear under 'master-signifier', nor under 'S₁', nor in its own right.

[25] J. Lacan, *Écrits*, trans. B. Fink et al. (New York: W. W. Norton & Co., 2006), p. 870. I would also like to point out two typos in the publishing details, all the more peculiar when read together: instead of the French publisher of Lacan's texts being listed as *Éditions du Seuil* (lit. 'Threshold Publishing'), it is here *Éditions du Deuil* ('Bereavement Publishing'); Lacan's name appears further down the same page, with his birthdate (1901–), but no termination, as if he hadn't yet died. This seems like a paradigm case of a veritable refusal to mourn!

[26] Lacan, *Écrits*, p. 645.

Few perverts ask to undergo analysis. We might conclude that perverts are unanalysable, but the fact is that they simply don't come asking to undergo analysis. They don't come to seek out the lost object; thus, it is just plain common sense to believe that, in some way, they have found it and can expect nothing from analysis. The effect known since Lacan as the 'subject supposed to know' doesn't arise with a true pervert, demonstrating that the subject supposed to know always arises in the place of sexual enjoyment.[27]

The paradox here is that, if psychoanalysis is precisely the discourse that introduced the notion of perversion as basic to human sexuality *tout court* – Freud positing an infantile 'polymorphous perversity' at the root of all sexuality – perverts evade the clinic of psychoanalysis more successfully than neurotics or psychotics.

I will come back to this problem of perversion later, to some of the consequences of the fact that Lacan's major published discussion of perversion emerges from an extra-clinical commission, and that it is linked to a particular problem in the theorisation of *jouissance*. Indeed, 'Kant with Sade' comprises one of Lacan's most extended early accounts of *jouissance*. But I first want to identify a passage determining for Lacan's later puncept of the swarm.

The passage in question is at once an exclamation and a mission statement: 'But humph! *Schwärmereien*, black swarms – I chase you away in order to return to the function of presence in the Sadean fantasy.'[28] Just as hysteria's peculiar structure of address enables the lineaments of desire to emerge with the greatest force and clarity, here the pervert's peculiar structure of enjoyment enables the lineaments of fantasy to emerge in the most scandalous fashion. Unlike desire, fantasy seems to be most clearly revealed in its inversion or perversion: according to the Lacanian matheme, the pervert's fantasy is not formalised as $\$\Diamond a$, but as $a\Diamond\$$. This is to say that the pervert – exemplified here by the Sadean master – places himself in the position of the object, in order that the splitting of desire is visited upon the other, not himself. Yet, it seems, in order to outline this fantasy, one has to avoid the philosophical confusion of *Schwärmereien*. This proves to be more difficult than one might think.

The translator's endnotes give the following gloss: '*Schwärmereien* means fanaticism, mysticism, and enthusiasm; *Schwärme* means swarms, and the French *essaims* (swarms) is pronounced like Lacan's matheme S_1. See *Critique of Practical Reason*, 94, 110, and 204.'[29] The

[27] J.-A. Miller, 'On Perversion', in R. Feldstein et al. (eds), *Reading Seminars I and II* (Albany: State University of New York Press, 1996), pp. 309–10.
[28] Lacan, *Écrits*, p. 652.
[29] Lacan, *Écrits*, p. 832.

complexity doesn't stop there, however, as the book sports yet another index denominated 'Freud's German Terms', which in turn includes such classic Freudian favourites as *Durcharbeiten, Fort! Da!* and *Trieb*. What is peculiar about this is that we also find listed, not *Freud's* German terms at all, but a term allegedly deriving from Immanuel Kant (who goes unnamed in the note proper), that is, *Schwärmerei*. Lest you think this is a failure of the English translator, one finds the same entry in the French version under the same heading, *sans* the reference to Kant, and initialled by 'J.L.' himself. A closer look at these German terms reveals others that have nothing particularly to do with Freud himself, but a great deal to do with late-eighteenth- and early-nineteenth-century German philosophy and poetry: *Aufhebung, Bildung, Dichtung* (and *Wahrheit*) and so on.

SCHWÄRMEREI UND ENTHUSIASMUS

We might say then that Lacan himself is responsible for, or at least signs off on, authorises, the illegitimate importation of a swarm of foreign words under cover of a Freudian alibi. With respect to *Schwärmerei* in particular, it is not just any word whatsoever. In fact, it is one of the key political terms of the German *Aufklärung*. Introduced into German theologico-political discourse by Martin Luther in the 1520s, *Schwärmerei* quickly came to be distinguished from a near-synonym: *Enthusiasmus*. Whereas *Enthusiasmus* had had a glorious Greek prehistory (from Plato's *Ion* onwards), *Schwärmerei* was something a little less elevated.

As Peter Fenves remarks:

> *Schwärmerei* derives from the swarming of bees. The likeness between the aggregates of swarming bees and the congregations of swarming churchmen gives *Schwärmerei* its highly amorphous and irreducibly figural shape. A commonality between human beings and animals – not human beings and God – is implied in every use of the word. Like bees, *Schwärmer* fly through the air on erratic paths, and, again like bees, they hover there without any easily understood means of support.[30]

---

[30] P. Fenves, 'A Note on the Translation of Kant', in Fenves (ed.), *Raising the Tone of Philosophy: Late Essays by Immanuel Kant, Transformative Critique by Jacques Derrida* (Baltimore and London: Johns Hopkins University Press, 1993), p. xi. As Anthony La Vopa puts it, '*Schwärmerei* . . . drew on the sights and sounds of agricultural life, and these made it resonant with images that gave contagion and mass violence a palpable presence'; 'The Philosopher and the *Schwärmer*: On the Career of a German Epithet from Luther to Kant', *Huntington Library Quarterly*, 60:1–2 (1997), p. 88. The term *Schwärmerei* entered medicine in the course of the eighteenth century, and hence, as La Vopa suggests, philosophers began to use the term by analogy: doctors deal with the health of the physical body, philosophers with that of the ethico-political body.

In fact, almost everyone who was anyone ended up contributing to the late-eighteenth-century German debate around *Schwärmerei*.[31] From Christoph Martin Wieland, who in 1775 had called on the public to try to fix the linguistically unfixed nature of the word, to Lessing, Herder, Kant, Hölderlin and Schelling, *Schwärmerei* denominated a *topos* whose limits could not quite be fixed or formalised.[32] In Fenves's words, '*Schwärmerei* names the aporetic condition of a coordinated disorderliness'.[33] In English, *Schwärmerei* has been translated as 'fanaticism', 'mysticism', 'enthusiasm', 'zealotry' and 'exaltation', all of which seem unsatisfactory.[34] But the difficulty is irreducible, for *Schwärmerei* is an exemplarily equivocal term.

In his own reconstruction of the debate, Anthony La Vopa notes that '*Schwärmerei* assumed new (though still familiar) shapes in the ideological arena created by the French revolution', and that it thereafter 'became a commonplace of German antirevolutionary discourse that philosophical *Schwärmerei* was assuming especially virulent forms in the rhetoric of radical intellectuals and in the frenzy of violent mobs'.[35] So: the problem of *Schwärmerei* is the problem of the articulation of radical political action and abstract philosophy, of the fixing and un-fixing of the limits of reason with respect to the being-together of human beings.[36]

If Fink's note (quite rightly) sends us then to the *Critique of Practical Reason*, which is, after all, Lacan's central explicit reference in this text, the final sentence of 'Kant avec Sade' clearly alludes to another of Kant's works. Lacan, in his summing up of the case of Sade, writes, 'What is announced about desire here, in this mistake based on an encounter, is at most but a tone of reason.'[37] Think of Kant's late text, 'On a Newly Arisen Superior Tone in Philosophy' (1796), itself a response to the conservative Johann Georg Schlosser's annotated translation of Plato, *Plato's letters on the revolution in Syracuse with a historical introduction and notes* (1795). There Kant speaks of the philosophising of

---

[31] See P. Fenves, *A Peculiar Fate: Metaphysics and World-History in Kant* (New York: Cornell University Press, 1991).

[32] One of Hölderlin's juvenile poems is entitled, precisely, 'Schwärmerei'; there is another poem by Sophie Friederike Mereau-Brentano entitled 'Schwärmerei der Liebe'.

[33] P. Fenves, 'The Scale of Enthusiasm', *Huntington Library Quarterly*, 60:1–2 (1997), p. 121.

[34] In addition to Fink and Fenves, see Nisbet's footnote to 'What is orientation in thinking?' ('Was heisst: Sich im Denken orientieren?') in Kant, *Political Writings*, p. 284.

[35] La Vopa, 'The Philosopher and the *Schwärmer*', p. 91, p. 103.

[36] In fact, the metaphor of the swarm extends far beyond the German scene. See M. Bull, 'The Limits of Multitude', *New Left Review*, 35 (September/October 2005), p. 32. Bull argues that, from Hobbes through Mandeville and Smith to Hayek to Hardt and Negri, the image of the swarm serves to found a philosophically conservative naturalisation of man.

[37] Lacan, *Écrits*, p. 667.

mathematics as consisting in the feeling and enjoyment of swarming ('im Gefühl und Genuß zu schwärmen'), of the mistuning of heads in swarming ('Verstimmung der Köpfe zur Schwärmerei') and so on. Lacan's implication is surely that this philosophical tone is really a *drone*.

In fact, Kant's work of this time swarms with swarms. In 'Conjectures on the Beginning of Human History' (1786), he writes of the establishment of human imperialism and colonialism in the struggle between agrarian settlements and nomadic tribespeople:

> The human race could multiply and, like a beehive, send out colonists in all directions from the centre – colonists who were already civilised. This epoch also saw the beginning of human inequality, that abundant source of so much evil but also of everything good; this inequality continued to increase hereafter. So long as the nations of nomadic herdsmen, who recognise only God as their master, continued to swarm around the town-dwellers and farmer, who are governed by a human master or civil authority, and as declared enemies of all land ownership, treated the latter with hostility and were hated by them in turn, the two sides were continually at war, or at least at constant risk of war.[38]

But this war between the swarms of nomads and the permanent settlements of the village communities is also one of the guarantees of internal freedom for Kant: after all, 'perpetual peace' stinks of the grave. A fundamental asymmetry is at stake whenever a swarm begins to form.

Speaking of his *Schema 2* in 'Kant with Sade', Lacan notes that Sade's declaration of the universal rights of *jouissance* doesn't have a symmetrical structure. Rather, the commands and tortures inflicted upon sufferers are such that 'it can be seen that the subject's division does not have to be reunited in a single body'.[39] There is more than a hint of the swarm in this phrase: the subject's division can be distributed across 1+ bodies. In other words, perversion is something that reveals how a subject tends towards an indeterminate proliferation of bodies without any concomitant obliteration, proliferation or dispersion of the subject. It is at this point that Lacan finds himself (conscious of) having to 'chase off' the black swarms of letters that confuse the issue of fantasy.

So the Lacanian swarm has almost-but-not-quite-emerged with

---

[38] Kant, *Political Writings*, p. 230. Earlier in his career, 'Kant ha[d] criticised Boehme and Swedenborg as mystics who had fallen prey to *Schwärmereien* – wild and unaccountable enthusiasm'; J.-M. Rabaté, *Jacques Lacan: Psychoanalysis and the Subject of Literature* (London: Palgrave, 2001), p. 97. Fenves notes that 'After the publication of the first *Critique*, Kant's polemics against *Schwärmerei* cease to be so closely bound up with attempts to explain the phenomenon through recourse to physiology; instead, Kant almost always returns to the history of philosophy and thus alters the basis of explanation from biological causality to historical and genealogical nexes'; *Raising the Tone of Philosophy*, p. 112, n. 1.

[39] Lacan, *Écrits*, p. 657, trans. modified.

respect to the clinical problem of perversion; to the problem of the relation between philosophy and non-pathological actions; to the problem
of the theorisation of *jouissance* – only to vanish nearly immediately
as a term. But that doesn't mean the idea's not still active in Lacan's
work.[40] Indeed, it is my thesis here that this first, fleeting, quasi-
emergence of the black swarms sees them immediately disperse, only to
regroup some time later, under completely different circumstances, and
in a clarified form.

FREUDIAN *SCHWÄRMEREI*

If *Schwärmerei* isn't a strictly Freudian concept, why does Lacan insert
it into the German glossary of *Écrits* under that heading? Is this merely
another case of an arbitrary Lacanian fiat, whim or parapraxis? I don't
think so, again for good political – not to mention psychoanalytical –
reasons. For if *Schwärmerei* is not a particularly Freudian word, nor
a particularly Freudian concept, it is not entirely absent from Freud's
work. Certainly, it would be a surprise *not* to find it at least somewhere in Freud, not only because it is a standard German word, but
also because it would seem eminently appropriate to a man who traces
all knowledge, even the most elevated and refined, back to its sources
in infantile fantasies and biophysical drives. On the other hand, it is
also a word that comes overdetermined with pre-analytic significance,
enmeshed in a politico-theological genealogy that might well make it
inappropriate for Freudian redeployment.

So when the word does appear – as it does at significant moments in
Freud's work – it proves to be used consistently, although without ever
attaining the rigour of a true concept. Symptomatically, *Schwärmerei*
and its cognates receive unreliable attention in the relevant indices to the
Gesammelte Werke (and none at all in the *Standard Edition*).[41] There is

---

[40] Significantly, the word *Schwärmerei* has already cropped up in Lacan's work in a tangential way, e.g. in 1960 he declares that 'Plato's *Schwärmerei* consists in having projected the
idea of the Supreme Good on that which I name the impenetrable void'; *Le Séminaire, livre
VIII: Le transfert* (Paris: Éditions du Seuil, 2001), p. 35.

[41] Indeed, the disappearance of *Schwärmerei* from English-language psychoanalysis has
been close to complete. When I searched the Psychoanalytic Electronic Publishing archive
(which, as their publicity has it, 'contains the full text of the Standard Edition of the
Complete Psychological Works of Sigmund Freud and the full text of eighteen premier
journals in psychoanalysis'), I found only three occurrences of the word in the tens of thou-
sands of articles available outside of nine other references to the *Gesammelte Werke* itself:
in E. J. Hárnik, 'Pleasure in Disguise, the Need for Decoration, and the Sense of Beauty',
Psychoanalytic Quarterly, 1 (1932), pp. 216–64; A. De Marchi, 'Fanatismi', *Rivista di
Psicoanalisi*, 51 (2005), pp. 1,195–204; G. W. Pigman, 'The Dark Forest of Authors:
Freud and Nineteenth-Century Dream Theory', *Psychoanalysis and History*, 4 (2002),
pp. 141–65.

no listing for *Schwärmerei* in the indices to the key *Gesammelte Werke* Volumes X, XII and XIII, and only one listing in the index for Volume V. In Volume XVIII, the *Gesamtregister*, however, we find a far more extensive entry.[42] Following these references is of extreme interest in the present context.

In *Three Essays on the Theory of Sexuality* (1905), we find *Schwärmerei* under the heading 'Die Umgestaltungen der Pubertät' ('The Transformations of Puberty'), where Freud remarks: 'Dessoir hat mit Recht daruf aufmerksam gemacht, welche Gesetzmäßigkeit sich in den schwärmerischen Freundschaften von Jünglingen und Mädchen für ihresgleichen verrät.'[43] The *Standard Edition* translates: 'Dessoir [1894] has justly remarked upon the regularity with which adolescent boys and girls form sentimental friendships with others of their own sex.'[44] Note the peculiarity, first, of the translation, and, second, of Freud's use of the word. As the *Vocabulaire européen des philosophies* explains, in a short entry, 'La "*Schwärmerei*" chez Freud':

> [*Schwärmerei*] does not designate, for the founder of psychoanalysis, any form of delirium, nor any belief, but the stories recounted by adolescents when they devote an exalted love towards a person of the same sex as themselves . . . These whims or fervours generally dissolve as if by magic, as Freud says in *Three Essays on Sexuality*, and in particular when love for a person of the other sex takes form.[45]

For Freud, then, the word is not used in its familiar, polemical conceptual sense, but merely in passing, as an adjectival specification, to designate a transitory inversion, a momentary swerve towards an (idealised) homosexual object-choice.

---

[42] 'Schwärmerei [Schwärmen, schwärmerische Liebe] (s.a. Verliebtheit), V 130f.; homosexuelle, V 130f.; XII 110, 272, 278, 295; hysterische beim Mann V 221 beim Weib V 220f., 223f.; bei Normalen (s.a. Schwärmerei, i.d. Pubertät), V 130f.; XII 297f; f. Künstler, XIII 133; i.d. Masse, XIII 132f.; Mitleids-, X 325, 333; XIV 503 f.; i.d. Pubertät, V 130f., XII 297f., XIII 123-25; religiöse u. Mätyertum, V 297 u. Perversion u. Mystik (s.a. Mystik), X 77; f. Soldaten, XII 100.'

[43] S. Freud, *Gesammelte Werke*, Vol. V (London: Imago, 1942), p. 130.

[44] S. Freud, *The Standard Edition of the Complete Psychological Works of Sigmund Freud*, Vol. V (1900–1901), ed. J. Strachey et al. (London: The Hogarth Press, 1953), p. 229.

[45] B. Cassin (ed.), *Vocabulaire européen des philosophies: Dictionnaire des intraduisibles* (Paris: Éditions du Seuil/Dictionnaires Le Robert, 2004), p. 456. Though the *Vocabulaire* gives *Psychische Behandlung* (1890), *Drei Abhandlungen zur Sexualtheorie* (1905), *Zur Geschichte der psychoanalytischen Bewegung* (1914) and *Über die Psychogenese eines Falles von weiblicher Homosexualität* (1920) as references, it does not, for reasons that are obscure, note the apparition of the term in a number of other places, including 'Thoughts for the Time on War and Death' and the *Massenpsychologie*. Freud also uses the word in *Interpretation of Dreams* to designate his own youthful *enthusiasm* for Hannibal, 'the Carthaginian General'. Although the following discussion does not identify the word as such, it does make a case for the abiding importance of the identification throughout Freud's life: W. J. McGrath, 'Freud as Hannibal: The Politics of the Brother Band', *Central European History*, 7:1 (1974), pp. 31–57.

Freud will also use the word in passing in such texts as 'On the History of the Psycho-Analytic Movement' in the context of the perverse eroticism of religious enthusiasts, the preparedness of martyrs to suffer for their God (and it is also noteworthy that that text is concerned with the religious backslidings of psychoanalytic renegades such as Adler and Jung).[46] If such use may seem to reunite Freud not only with the political and philosophical, but also with the physiological genealogy of the word, it remains the case that he gives the word a directly *sexual* significance that it has hitherto lacked. *Schwärmerei* emerges to designate a transitional sexual phase between the pre-pubescent interregnum and the full-blown emergence of adult sexuality, in which an intense yet unfulfilled homoerotic attraction manifests itself. Yet it also refers to an excessive capacity for self-sacrifice, to an extraordinary submission to an ideal.

These features remain operative in Freud's most liberal use of the word, in a famous case-study of 1920, *Über die Psychogenese eines Falles von weiblicher Homosexualität* ('The Pychogenesis of a Case of Homosexuality in a Woman').[47] The word (or cognate) appears at least seven times in this text. Let me quote liberally from both the German and the *Standard Edition*'s translation:

> *Wie weit es zwischen ihrer Tochter und jener zweifelhaften Dame gekommen ist, ob die Grenzen einer zärtlichen Schwärmerei bereits überschritten worden sind, wissen die Eltern nicht.*[48]
> The parents could not say to what lengths their daughter had gone in her relations with the questionable lady, whether the limits of devoted admiration had already been exceeded or not.[49]

> *Es war nur klar, daß sie die Schwärmerei ihrer Tochter nicht so tragisch nahm und sich keineswegs so sehr darüber entrüstete wie der Vater.*[50]
> All that was clear was that she did not take her daughter's infatuation so tragically as did the father, nor was she so incensed at it.[51]

> *Bei keinen der Objekte ihrer Schwärmerei hatte sie mehr als einzelne Küsse und Umarmungen genossen, ihre Genitalkeuschheit, wenn man so sagen darf, war unversehrt geblieben.*[52]

46 See 'Zur Geschichte der psychoanalytischen Bewegung' in *Gesammelte Werke*, Vol. X (London: Imago, 1946), p. 77, and 'Zeitgemäßes über Krieg und Tod' in the same volume, e.g. 'die meisten Mitleidsschwärmer, Menschenfreunde, Tierschütze, haben sich aus kleinen Sadisten und Tierquälern entwickelt'; p. 333.
47 S. Freud, *Gesammelte Werke*, Vol. XII (London: Imago, 1947), pp. 269–302; 'The Psychogenesis of a Case of Homosexuality in a Woman' (1920), in *Standard Edition*, Vol. XVIII, pp. 145–72. Unless otherwise indicated, all further German and English in-text references will be to these volumes.
48 Freud, *Gesammelte Werke*, p. 272.
49 Freud, *Standard Edition*, p. 148.
50 Freud, *Gesammelte Werke*, p. 274.
51 Freud, *Standard Edition*, p. 149.
52 Freud, *Gesammelte Werke*, p. 278.

> With none of the objects of her adoration had the patient enjoyed anything
> beyond a few kisses and embraces; her genital chastity, if one may use such
> a phrase, had remained intact.[53]

What are the hallmarks of Freud's use of the word here? Above all, it
refers to an a-sexual devotion, an 'inversion' or 'perversion'. It is central
in Freud's account of this case that the young woman rejects those of
her sex with whom she might actually enjoy direct sexual (genital) satisfaction. Indeed, she insists on refusing or renouncing such satisfaction
– with a concomitant, extraordinary idealisation of her love-object – up
to and beyond the point of self-sacrifice and self-abnegation, indeed, to
the point of (attempted) suicide. In his own commentary on this case in
Seminar IV – a seminar in which the interpretation of perversion is centrally at stake – Lacan doesn't hesitate to identify the young woman's
love for her Lady with the intricacies of courtly love. The young
woman, for Lacan, is aiming *beyond* her apparent object, at the phallus
itself.[54] What I want to underline again here, however, are the triple
aspects of *Schwärmerei* – transient inversion, idealisation of the object,
and propensity for self-sacrifice – that seem implicitly bound together
for Freud in his uses of the word, which also hints at the phylogenetic
regression suggested by the standard political sense of the term.

Yet what would usually go under the name of *Schwärmerei* takes
another route in Freud, especially in his later theories of group behaviour. Let us turn to his *New Introductory Lectures on Psychoanalysis*
which, though denominated 'Lectures', were in fact never delivered and
which, though dated 1933, in fact appeared in 1932. In Lecture XXX
of that volume, titled 'Dreams and Occultism', we find the following
extraordinary statement:

> The telepathic process is supposed to consist in a mental act in one person
> instigating the same mental act in another person. What lies between these
> two mental acts may easily be a physical process into which the mental one
> is transformed at one end and which is transformed back once more into the
> same mental one at the other end. The analogy with other transformations,
> such as occur in speaking and hearing by telephone, would then be unmis-
> takable. And only think if one could get hold of this physical equivalent of
> the psychical act! It would seem to me that psycho-analysis, by inserting the
> unconscious between what is physical and what was previously called 'psy-
> chical,' has paved the way for the assumption of such processes as telepathy.
> If only one accustoms oneself to the idea of telepathy, one can accomplish a

[53] Freud, *Standard Edition*, p. 153. See also pp. 288/160, 288/161, 295/166, 297/170 of
Gesammelte Werke/Standard Edition. Note that the variations in the *Standard Edition*
make it impossible to recognise – let alone reconstruct – the vicissitudes of the word in
English translation, and, a fortiori, whatever import it may have for psychoanalysis.
[54] See J. Lacan, *Le Séminaire, livre IV: La relation d'objet* (Paris: Éditions du Seuil, 1994),
p. 109.

great deal with it – for the time being, it is true, only in imagination. It is a familiar fact that *we do not know how the common purpose comes about in the great insect communities* [my emphasis]: possibly it is done by means of a direct psychical transference of this kind. One is led to a suspicion that this is the original, archaic method of communication between individuals and that in the course of phylogenetic evolution it has been replaced by the better method of giving information with the help of signals which are picked up by the sense organs. But the older method might have persisted in the background and still be able to put itself into effect under certain conditions – for instance, in passionately excited mobs.[55]

There are a number of features of this passage to which I would like to draw attention. First, Freud is returning to something that will prove a little embarrassing, if not for him, at least for such *bien pensant* followers as Ernest Jones: the topic of telepathy. He has brought it up several times before, most notably in 1921/1922, when completing the essays 'Psychoanalysis and Telepathy' (1921, but unpublished until 1941) and 'Dreams and Telepathy' (1922). What is noteworthy about its reappearance here is the direct link that Freud makes between telepathy and materiality. If thoughts are material events, then it is perhaps possible that they are able to be transmitted according to as-yet-unknown biophysical processes. A good materialist cannot a priori exclude the possibility of telepathy.

Second, Freud's analogy here is with the telephone, a piece of relatively new communications technology. In this context, it is significant that Freud opened the entire series of 'Lectures' with another famous analogy, that of his one-time 'phonographic memory' (now, lamentably, not quite what it used to be, although still pretty impressive). As ever, Freud is extremely sensitive to the psychopathology of technological life (His Master's Voice, and all that).

Third, Freud wants to suggest not only that evolutionary developments don't simply supplant archaic formations, but that these archaic characteristics of the organism are always liable to be revivified in raw forms under certain extreme conditions. In this instance, Freud suggests that the enigmatic communicational powers of insect communities – which are presumably prior to any form of psychological individuation – may well account for the peculiarities exhibited by 'passionately excited mobs'. Freud thereby proposes that there may be a direct link between the possibility of telepathy and group psychology.

Four, Freud thereby binds materialist rationalism, telepathy, modern

---

[55] S. Freud, *New Introductory Lectures on Psychoanalysis*, in *The Standard Edition of the Complete Psychological Works of Sigmund Freud*, Vol. XXII (1932–1936), ed. J. Strachey et al. (London: The Hogarth Press, 1964), p. 55.

telecommunications, mass psychology and the most archaic forms of socio-biological organisation together in a single concept. As ever, he sees no principled difference between human beings and other forms of life, no matter how allegedly lowly. Indeed, we find this procedure throughout Freud's later work, where the links between technology, biology and politics are ceaselessly re-examined, and concepts developed to unite them.

Yet where else does one find such an explicit reference to 'passionately excited mobs' but in the *Group Psychology and the Analysis of the Ego* of 1921 (a piece that Freud is writing, moreover, just after the case of the young homosexual woman)? *Group Psychology* was itself written in the wake of a major theoretical shift. Freud had just altered his theory of the drives in *Beyond the Pleasure Principle*. This alteration had forced him to return to his existing theoretical concerns and rethink them according to the new problematic of the death-drive. The basic point is this: if libidinal economy is not sufficient to account for the entirety of psychic organisation, then how does the non-libidinal part contribute to such an organisation? In *Group Psychology*, the central problem is to explain how psychologically complex individuals can form into larger aggregates with qualities radically different from those of the individuals that compose them. What triggers the formation of a mob? How do the individuals that comprise it communicate amongst themselves? Why is there such a serious diminution in the intellectual level of an individual's mental functioning when subsumed in a group?

Freud draws heavily on the work of Gustave Le Bon, the conservative French writer whose work on crowds of 1895 was extremely influential in the early twentieth century.[56] For Le Bon, the crowd suppresses individuality, is irrational, and is closer to a kind of racial unconscious than at other times. Le Bon gives three main reasons for the alterations in psychology in groups: (1) from sheer *force of numbers*, the individual develops a sense of personal invincibility; (2) *contagion* (for Le Bon, a phenomenon 'of a hypnotic order'), which enables an individual to sacrifice 'personal interest to the collective interest'; (3) the most important, the *hypnotic suppression of ego* to the point of becoming an automaton.

While these reasons won't entirely wash for Freud, the problems raised by Le Bon of 'contagion' and 'hypnotic suppression' are pre-eminently psychoanalytic problems. This raises the problem of telepathy once more, and, whatever you make of Freud's speculations in

---

[56] G. Le Bon, *The Crowd: A Study of the Popular Mind*, ed. R. K. Merton (New York: Penguin, 1977). See also B. Marpeau, *Gustave Le Bon: Parcours d'un intellectuel 1841–1931* (Paris: CNRS, 2000), for some suggestive details about the circumstances in which Le Bon penned his masterpiece, including sales of his books.

this regard, there is a very good reason for him pursuing the idea in this context: how *do* groups hang together? Telepathy becomes the focus of interest for Freud at precisely the same time that he is studying group behaviour ('Psychoanalysis and Telepathy' (1941/1921) and 'Dreams and Telepathy' (1922), as well as 'Some Additional Notes on Dream-Interpretation as a Whole' (1925) and the aforementioned 'New Introductory Lectures, XXX' (1933)). But the possibility of telepathy remains mere speculation, and so Freud finds himself having to generate a new theory of identification to explain the emergence of a wide variety of groups. This theory hinges on the concept of 'the unary trait' ('ein einziger Zug'). As Alenka Zupančič glosses it, the unary trait 'is very different from imaginary imitation of different aspects of the person with which one identifies: in it, the unary trait itself takes over the whole dimension of identification'.[57]

It is at a hinge point of this text that the word *Schwärmerei* re-emerges for Freud. In Chapter VIII, 'Being in Love and Hypnosis', and Chapter IX, 'The Herd Instinct' (in fact, 'Der Herdentrieb', 'the herd-drive'), the word recurs, along with the same problematic I noted above. In Chapter VIII, we read: 'Der Mann zeigt schwärmerische Neigungen zu hochgeachteten Frauen, die ihn aber zum Liebesverkehr nicht reizen, und ist nur potent gegen andere Frauen, die er nicht "liebt," geringschätzt oder selbst verachtet' ('A man will show a sentimental enthusiasm for women whom he deeply respects but who do not excite him to sexual activities, and he will only be potent with other women whom he does not "love" and thinks little of or even despises').[58] We have met with this 'universal tendency to debasement in the sphere of love' before, with its characteristic aim-inhibited drives and sexual over-valuation. Here, however, Freud is preparing a new kind of explanation.[59]

---

[57] A. Zupančič, 'When Surplus-Enjoyment Meets Surplus-Value', in Clemens and Grigg (eds), *Jacques Lacan*, p. 156.

[58] S. Freud, *Gesammelte Werke*, Vol. XIII (London: Imago, 1940), p. 123; *Standard Edition*, Vol. XVIII, p. 112. In Chapter IX, Freud writes: 'Man denke an die Schar von schwärmerisch verliebten Frauen und Mädchen die den Sänger oder Pianisten nach seiner Produktion umdrängen'(*GW*, XIII, p. 133); 'We have only to think of the troop of women and girls, all of them in love, in an enthusiastically sentimental way, who crowd round a singer or pianist after his performance'(*SE*, XVIII, p. 120).

[59] Note that, following the passage cited, Freud soon realises how problematic the situation is, and begins to run through explanatory possibilities very quickly. Is it the case that, first, *'The object has been put in place of the ego ideal'* (p. 113)? Is it that, in identification, the ego has 'enriched itself' with the object, whereas, in the extreme 'fascination' and 'bondage' of certain loves, the object has been substituted for the ego itself? Can it be that, in identification, the object has been lost or renounced, but set up again in the ego, which now has partially modelled itself after the lost object, whereas, in fascination, there is rather a hypercathexis of the object (traces of 'Mourning and Melancholia' are at play here)? Or is the question whether the object has been put in place of the ego *or* of the ego ideal? It is such questions that the new theory of identification is to resolve.

For Freud, the earlier 'group psychology' of *Totem and Taboo*, in which the murder of the father founds the community of brothers, is no longer enough to account for the artificial, temporary or spontaneous nature of certain group formations. Instead, Freud now has to supplement the earlier account with one better able to explain, say, mass hysteria at a girl's school. Freud thus gives the following summary:

> First, identification is the original form of emotional tie with an object; secondly, in a regressive way it becomes a substitute for a libidinal object-tie, as it were by means of introjection of the object into the ego; and thirdly, it may arise with any new perception of a common quality shared with some other person who is not an object of the sexual instinct.[60]

Instead of telepathy, then, we have a new account of identification. The aggregations made possible by the mechanism of the unary trait are no longer the primal hordes of the earlier study, but far more volatile, transient, intense and (apparently) irrational mobs. And we also find a Freudian anticipation of just the characteristics I have tried to emphasise in Lacan's 'Kant avec Sade': mob behaviour is bound up with transient perversion, idealisation and self-sacrifice. In a word, *Schwärmerei*.

THE PLACE OF SEMINAR XVII

If the swarm had only briefly caught Lacan's attention, by the time of Seminar XVII all is flux (to invoke Heraclitus). First, the political situation: May '68 has happened, which seems to have unleashed an entirely new form of political action. Second, the socio-economic situation: the law, the family, work, all seems to be in crisis. Lacan himself alludes to the events with his famous, ironical remarks about pot-smoking, nudist homosexuals. Third, the institutional situation: Lacanian psychoanalysis is entering the university of the French state, itself undergoing massive and rapid expansion (thanks, in part, to the administrative labours of one Michel Foucault). Fourth, the theoretical situation: Lacan is no longer happy with his idiosyncratic structuralist account of language that has, with constant minor divergences, sustained him until now. There are both immanent and external reasons for this unhappiness, for example, in the shift to post-structuralism then under way with Foucault, Derrida and Deleuze, all of whom are at that time elaborating serious critiques of the classical Saussurean doctrine. Fifth, the clinical situation is itself changing: psychoanalysis doesn't seem to be working as effectively as it once did.[61] Sixth, the technological situation

---

[60] Freud, *Standard Edition*, Vol. XVIII, pp. 107–8.
[61] 'Lacan's inaugural point of departure, in 1952, is the assertion, "There is psychoanalysis."

is changing too: not only genetics, but post-WWII forms of telecommunications are now clearly shifting the relationship between humans and their environment (e.g. television and computing).

It is my contention that the 'swarm' now returns as part of Lacan's attempt to respond to this situation. As such, it is a puncept that attempts to account for political, technological, social, institutional, theoretical and clinical change *at once*. This programme is entirely in line with psychoanalysis as it had been bequeathed by Freud: as we have seen, Freud himself had recourse to an insect metaphor in order to think the problem of groups in a time of political, socio-economic, institutional, theoretical, clinical and technological crisis.

As a result of this ferment, what, in terms of Lacanian dogma, gets reworked in Seminar XVII? The nature of the unary trait, the master, identification, the object and enjoyment. The father is separated from the master. The master is now the master-signifier, and, in being separated from the father, is no longer: (1) the locus of law; (2) the phallus; (3) the father; (4) diacritically defined. As Lacan puts it in this Seminar, the father has only 'the most distant of relationships' with the master. The Oedipus complex is, moreover, a myth. The master himself doesn't give the law in knowing what he wants and knowing what he wants to say, but in his very incoherence and opacity. Yet this master 'not only induces but determines castration'. This master will later become the foundations for the doctrine of *lalangue*. But here the work of separation is beginning in earnest: $S_1 \neq$ phallus $\neq$ *nom-du-père* $\neq$ unary trait.

The unary trait, for instance, which had previously 'filled the invisible mark that the subject draws from the signifier', that 'alienated the subject in the primary identification that forms the ideal ego',[62] and which was 'the mark of a primary identification that will function as ideal',[63] is now given a different spin. First appearing as such in Seminar VIII ('The Transference'), then taken up in earnest in Seminar IX ('Identification'), the unary trait continues to shift its significance. In Seminar XIV, 'The Logic of Fantasy', Lacan says the act can only be defined 'on the foundation of the double loop, in other words, of repetition . . . It is this repetition in a single line (trait) that I designated earlier by this cut that it is possible to make in the centre of the Moebius strip' (15 February 1967). It is here that one can discern that the 'one' of the 'unary trait' is essentially the 'one' of repetition, that is, of what I am arguing becomes the one-multiple of the *essaim*.

It exists, it works . . . His arrival point is "psychoanalysis doesn't work," and to ask himself why it doesn't'; J.-A. Miller, 'Six Paradigms of Jouissance', *Lacanian Ink*, 17 (2000), p. 41.

[62] Lacan, *Écrits*, p. 808.

[63] J. Lacan, 'Comptes rendus d'enseignement 1964–1968', *Ornicar?*, 29 (1984), p. 10.

As for the algebra (not the concept) of S_1, it first appears, to my knowledge, in 1967, for example in the 'Proposition of 9 October 1967 on the Psychoanalyst of the School', where it has a rather different significance, being merely one element in the denominator of the formula of the transference.[64] But it is not until Seminar XVII that the S_1 achieves its canonical form as the master-signifier. Prior to this, as I have shown in Chapter 2, the master most clearly had a role in Lacan's reading of Hegel, and by which it was often associated with a major function of the ego (e.g. 'Le moi est une fonction de maîtrise').

Without fully reconstructing this conceptual trajectory, it would remain difficult to determine the relation that S_1 and the unary trait bear to each other in Lacan. Indeed, the difficulties have led to dissension on the part of various authorities. Mark Bracher says that the *trait unaire*:

> is the earliest significance through which the child experiences itself – as a result of significations attributed to it by the Other (mother, father, and ultimately society at large). This constitutes the subject's primary identification . . . But the *trait unaire* established by primary identification is supplemented and extended by various secondary identifications that serve as its avatars. It is, in fact, only through these secondary identifications that the primary identification manifests itself. And these secondary identifications, which are certain (usually collective) values or ideals, play a crucial role in discourse. They are what Lacan calls master signifiers, S_1.[65]

Gilbert Chaitin's opinion is that: 'the unitary trait is a sign rather than a signifier; unlike the signifier, which can function only in opposition to other signifiers, it operates alone, without entering into relation with a "battery of signifiers".'[66] For his part, Paul Verhaeghe thinks that 'Subject formation derives from an S_1 that stems from a unary trait that needs to be repeated over an underlying absence.'[67] For Ellie Ragland, 'Miller has spoken of this signifier [S_1] as commensurate with the unary trait. Identification with the father is identification with him as the voice of difference.'[68] For his part, Dominiek Hoens has written: 'in *Seminar XVII* Lacan is again dealing with the unary trait (introduced in the final part of *Seminar VIII* and developed in *Seminar IX*), neither distinguish-

[64] One can also find S_1 making a very brief appearance in *Seminar XI*, where it is linked with S_2 as 'the first dyad of signifiers' (p. 236) along with a diagram (p. 238), where it surmounts the algebra 'S(i(a, a', a'', a''',. . .))' for a series of identifications; Lacan, *Seminar XI: The Four Fundamental Concepts*.

[65] M. Bracher, 'On the Psychological and Social Functions of Language: Lacan's Theory of the Four Discourses', in Bracher et al. (eds), *Lacanian Theory of Discourse: Subject, Structure, and Society* (New York and London: New York University Press, 1994), p. 111.

[66] G. D. Chaitin, *Rhetoric and Culture in Lacan* (Cambridge: Cambridge University Press, 1996), p. 129.

[67] P. Verhaeghe, 'Enjoyment and Impossibility', in Clemens and Grigg (eds), *Jacques Lacan*, p. 56.

[68] E. Ragland, 'The Hysteric's Truth', in Clemens and Grigg (eds), *Jacques Lacan*, p. 99.

ing it from nor identifying it with the master-signifier S_1.'[69] In another account, Lorenzo Chiesa writes: 'the one as unary trait is the "*instrument*" by means of which identification is made possible: the unary trait is not a one but an operation, a count, that constitutes "the *foundation of the one*" of identification with the signifier.'[70]

I have quoted these commentators in order to show how Lacan's text is clearly anything but clear on how the *trait unaire* and S_1 relate, or what their precise functions might be. I would like to suggest that the problem can be both explained and resolved by recourse to the swarm. Indeed, the difficulties experienced by commentators in deciding the precise relationship between the unary trait and master signifier are a result of the difficulty of the puncept itself. My own account is this: the S_1 derives from the originary multiplication of unary traits into a swarm, i.e. an equivocal mess of foreign lines of imaginary identification that have been cut into the body: 'Repetition is the precise denotation of a trait that I have uncovered for you in Freud's text as identical with the unary trait, with the little stick, with the element of writing, of a trait in so far as it is the commemoration of an irruption of enjoyment.'[71] So the unary trait must be re-marked (or re-marks itself); it is only 'unary', one, by being so re-marked; as it is re-marked, it becomes a swarm, the S_1, the precondition of language in the subject, what emerges between imaginary and symbolic as the trace of the real (*jouissance*).

So an S_1 is *literally* a 'swarm' of unary traits that have been incised into a living body and which have acquired a kind of 'critical mass'. When it is no longer possible to define the foundations of signification on the basis of a primordial diacritical difference (as had previously been the case for Lacan's theory of signification), Lacan is forced to come up with a new response. This S_1-unary-trait theory is an important part of his answer. For the S_1 is not a diacritically defined signifier, but emerges from an irreducibly equivocal reiteration prior to meaning, inseparable from the identificatory stigmata of the unary traits.[72]

---

[69] D. Hoens, 'Towards a New Perversion: Psychoanalysis', in Clemens and Grigg (eds), *Jacques Lacan*, pp. 124–5.

[70] L. Chiesa, 'Count-as-one, Forming-into-one, Unary Trait, S_1', in P. Ashton et al. (eds), *The Praxis of Alain Badiou* (Melbourne: re.press, 2006), p. 154. Chiesa continues: 'the S_1 is the unary trait as repressed'; p. 173.

[71] J. Lacan, *Seminar XVII: The Other Side of Psychoanalysis*, trans. R. Grigg (New York: W. W. Norton & Co., 2007), p. 89. As Lacan also says, 'Here I will borrow something from Freud's text and give it a sense that is not highlighted there, namely, the function of the unary trait, that is, of the simplest form of mark, which properly speaking is *the origin of the signifier*'; p. 52 (my emphasis). He immediately adds: 'everything that interests us analysts as knowledge originates in the unary trait'; p. 52.

[72] See J. Lacan, *Seminar XX: Encore: The Seminar of Jacques Lacan, Book XX: On Feminine Sexuality: The Limits of Love and Knowledge 1972–1973*, ed. J.-A. Miller, trans. with notes by B. Fink (New York: W. W. Norton & Co., 1998), p. 143.

The swarm of the S_1 thus at once conditions and envelops knowledge; knowledge, *pace* Kant, cannot escape *Schwärmerei*. The swarm *must* be prior to sexual differentiation, so the origin cannot be a Father, Name-of-the-Father, or phallus. In fact, a swarm is – as recent scientific research has suggested – autotaxic (i.e. without leader or external directives), non-linear, omnidirectional, transient, a one-multiple composed of indiscriminable elements.[73]

Swarms are highly unpredictable in their movements, varying in the length, scale, dimensionality, velocity and acceleration of individuals. One notable feature is that the scale of the relations between the creatures comprising the swarm is necessarily smaller than the swarm itself (that is, no creature can communicate across the extent of the swarm, only with its immediately proximate neighbours). There is no leader, organising structure, clear aim or end to a swarm. Why, then, do creatures swarm? Usually it is considered: a defence against predators, e.g. lizard predators turn out to be averse to gregarious but not solitarious locusts and there is less chance of any individual being eaten due to sheer force of numbers; a defence against environmental change (the phase-shifts of locusts enable rapid adaptation to different environments); there are mating and feeding swarms ('love and hunger'), and so on. Yet swarms are inevitably destroyed (e.g. locust swarms starve or are blown out to sea). So there is also an adaptive problem posed by the swarm: what is the evolutionary point? Moreover, swarm creatures are diphasic creatures, that is, 'split subjects', and, if the swarm is not any kind of Dionysian orgy (i.e. a self-destructive melding with others), it still bears clear links to the death-drive. The swarm is thus irreducibly equivocal.

Moreover, why Lacan considers 'the master' to be 'a swarm' seems to me determined by the lines I have been tracing: the problem of pre-linguistic foundation and the problem of pre-political community meet on the terrain of the swarm. We no longer have a phallus, but *traits unaires*, bundles of little sticks, letter-scar-stigmata of primal identifications; meaningless in themselves, they constitute the S_1 as a one-multiple. We no longer have enjoyment as transgression of the law (which now becomes a secondary phenomenon, itself just a *semblant*), but sophisticated technical apparatuses (soon denominated *lathouses* by Lacan) for extracting *lichettes*, tiny amounts of *jouissance*. The limits of existence are no longer given by primal bands of guilty broth-

---

[73] See such accounts as E. Bonabeau, M. Dorigo and G. Theraulaz, *Swarm Intelligence: From Natural to Artificial Systems* (New York: Oxford University Press, 1999). What is striking about the models proposed by such naturalists is that they continue to rely on a very basic Empedoclean model: a swarm is held together by both attractive and repulsive forces.

ers, nor by highly organised, hierarchical mass societies of repression, but by stochastic drifts of unleashed particles that sporadically and unpredictably erupt into vast destructive swarms that are both pre- and trans-individual.

With the swarm, then, Lacan not only rethinks more traditional psychoanalytic concepts, but anticipates and formalises a notion that is today everywhere in science, technology and cultural studies. The swarm is now a staple quasi-notion in communication-theory, a function of 'a creeping shift from an era of centralized communication dominated by commercial mass communication to an emergent era of decentralized communication dominated by mobile mass communication'.[74] This is then one great psychoanalytic contribution to the study of technology. Contemporary technology isn't going to lead to any transcendence of consciousness, as MIT robotics researchers are idiotically wont to declare, but rather uncovers something profoundly archaic, uncanny: humans are swarm animals. Technology, as 'the highest means for the lowest ends', today inserts its connections directly into the organism, without having to pass through 'language' *per se* or the mediation of the vocal apparatus. Thus the Lacanian swarm undoes the distinction between human and animal – but without a simple reduction to the natural. The polymorphous perversity of the human is now shown to be correlated with a primal master that is a swarm. And where Lacan differs from many others who praise the swarm is in his refusal to idealise it. One can see also how Lacan continually attempts to make mathemes out of the material hazards of literality itself. When 'language' can no longer be considered to be the 'essence of man', the antiphilosophy that is psychoanalysis seeks new singularities, new fixed points upon which to operate and from which to proceed. I have tried to suggest several ethical practices which emerge from Lacan's attempt. Moreover, the reconstructed swarm raises once again the problem of un-binding in psychoanalysis, that is, a problem

[74] J. A. Nicholson, 'FCJ-030 Flash! Mobs in the Age of Mobile Connectivity', *The Fibreculture Journal*, 6 (2005), <http://journal.fibreculture.org/issue6/issue6_nicholson. html> (last accessed 27 September 2012). See also J. Arquilla and D. Ronfeldt, *Swarming and the Future of Conflict* (Santa Monica: RAND, 2000) (military affairs); J. Kennedy and R. C. Eberhart with Y. Shi, *Swarm Intelligence* (San Diego: Academic Press, 2001) (academic psychology); E. C. Brown (ed.), *Insect Poetics* (Minneapolis: University of Minnesota Press, 2006) (cultural history); J. Parikka, 'Politics of Swarms: Translations Between Entomology and Biopolitics', *Parallax*, 14:3 (2008), pp. 112–24. A strong interpretation has been given by Eugene Thacker, in 'Networks, Swarms, Multitudes' (in two parts), in *ctheory* (2004), <http://www.ctheory.net/articles.aspx?id=422> (last accessed 15 October 2012). Thacker argues that 'networks can form a collectivity, through connectivity, while swarms can initiate a connectivity, but only through collectivity'. His thesis, moreover, makes the crucial (anti-socio-biological) point that the relation between 'pattern' and 'purpose' is at once irreducible yet inevitably elided in naturalising accounts.

that psychoanalysis from the beginning considered under the rubric of *love*.

CODA: TERMINABLY INTERMINABLE

The problem of love, present from the first, emerges in fits and starts until it becomes the very heart of psychoanalytical theory and clinical practice. As I discussed in Chapter 2, it is the transference as an organ of crisis that delivers psychoanalysis's ontology, an ontology that at once prevents psychoanalysis from ever being able to settle comfortably into the warm embrace of the sciences, on the one hand, or into the clammy hands of philosophical ontologies, on the other. If it is true that psychoanalysis is the greatest modern theory of love, it is also true that psychoanalysis, in the course of its ceaseless development and re-elaboration, constantly seems to forget the love at its heart. Such a forgetting means that psychoanalysis constantly forgets itself, an unfortunate situation for an enterprise supposedly founded on the therapeutic powers of anamnesis. Hence the consequences of transference's crisis-status within analysis, as can be verified by the attempts of all sorts of post-Freudian orientations to reduce transference's field of operations to those of egoistic defence, to animal ethology, to power-games of resistance, or to games of proper distancing. Yet it is also the case that the great innovators of psychoanalysis have also always returned to the powers of love.

As I have argued throughout this book, such a situation is par for the psychoanalytic course. Psychoanalysis is an antiphilosophy only insofar as it takes love as an index of a subject's slavery to a master (an ideal, a trait, a swarm), and attempts to leverage this love against itself to the point where a particular kind of suspension of this master can emerge for the subject itself. As Lacan affirmed: 'In the beginning of analytic experience . . . was love.'[75] It is by means of love as a practice that analysts reformalise the status of subjects *as* their own formalisation, and analysands find that, in their reformulations of their singular non-relation to their master, that that master's contingency can emerge as such. Science, literature and love against servitude, torture and love – this is psychoanalysis as antiphilosophy.

[75] Lacan, *Le Séminaire, livre VIII*, p. 12.

Bibliography

Abraham, N., and M. Torok, *The Shell and the Kernel, Vol. 1*, trans. and intro. by N. Rand (Chicago: University of Chicago Press, 1994).

Acosta-Hughes, B., and R. Scodel, 'Aesop *Poeta*: Aesop and the Fable in Callimachus' *Iambi*', in A. Harder, R. F. Regtuit and G. C. Wakker (eds), *Callimachus II* (Leuven: Peeters Publishers, 2002), pp. 1–21.

Acton, W., *The Functions and Disorders of the Reproductive Organs in Youth, in Adult Age, and in Advanced Life Considered in their Physiological, Social, and Psychological Relations*, 2nd edn (London: John Churchill, 1858).

Adorno, T., *Prisms*, trans. S. and S. Weber (Cambridge, MA: MIT, 1995).

Agamben, G., *The Coming Community*, trans. M. Hardt (Minneapolis: University of Minnesota Press, 1993).

Agamben, G., *Homo Sacer: Sovereign Power and Bare Life*, trans. D. Heller-Roazen (Stanford: Stanford University Press, 1998).

Agamben, G., *The Idea of Prose*, trans. M. Sullivan and S. Whitsitt (Albany: State University of New York Press, 1995).

Agamben, G., *Infancy and History: The Destruction of Experience*, trans. L. Heron (London: Verso, 1993).

Agamben, G., 'K', in J. Clemens, N. Heron and A. W. Murray (eds), *The Work of Giorgio Agamben* (Edinburgh: Edinburgh University Press, 2008), pp. 13–27.

Agamben, G., *Language and Death: The Place of Negativity*, trans. K. E. Pinkus with M. Hardt (Minneapolis: University of Minnesota Press, 1991).

Agamben, G., *Means Without End: Notes on Politics*, trans. V. Bineti and C. Casarino (Minneapolis: University of Minnesota Press, 2000).

Agamben, G., *Potentialities: Collected Essays in Philosophy*, ed. and trans. with intro. by D. Heller-Roazen (Stanford: Stanford University Press, 1999).

Agamben, G., *Profanations*, trans. J. Fort (New York: Zone Books, 2007).

Agamben, G., *Remnants of Auschwitz: The Witness and the Archive*, trans. D. Heller-Roazen (New York: Zone Books, 1999).

Agamben, G., *The Sacrament of Language: An Archaeology of the Oath*, trans. A. Kotsko (Stanford: Stanford University Press, 2011).

Agamben, G., *Stanzas: Word and Phantasm in Western Culture*, trans. R. L. Martinez (Minneapolis: University of Minnesota Press, 1993).

168

Bibliography

Agamben, G., *The Time That Remains: A Commentary on the Letter to the Romans*, trans. P. Dailey (Stanford: Stanford University Press, 2005).

Albrand, L., 'Freud et le panegyrique de la cocaine', in P. Spiriot (ed.), *Sigmund Freud et la drogue* (Monaco: Éditions du Rocher, 1987), pp. 24–44.

Alexander, B., 'Going Nomadic: Mobile Learning in Higher Education', *Educause Review*, September/October 2004, pp. 29–35.

Allhoff, F., *Terrorism, Ticking Time-bombs, and Torture: A Philosophical Analysis* (Chicago: University of Chicago Press, 2012).

Alvarez, J. E., 'Torturing the Law', *Case Western Reserve Journal of International Law*, 37:2–3 (2006), pp. 175–223.

Anidjar, G., *The Jew, The Arab: A History of the Enemy* (Stanford: Stanford University Press, 2003).

Appignanesi, L., and J. Forrester, *Freud's Women* (London: Weidenfeld and Nicolson, 1992).

Aristotle, *On the Art of Poetry*, in *Classical Literary Criticism*, trans. with intro. by T. S. Dorsch (London: Penguin, 1988).

Aristotle, *The Politics*, trans. T. A. Sinclair, rev. T. J. Saunders (Harmondsworth: Penguin, 1986).

Armintor, M. N., *Lacan and the Ghosts of Modernity: Masculinity, Tradition, and the Anxiety of Influence* (New York: Peter Lang, 2004).

Arquilla, J., and D. Ronfeldt, *Swarming and the Future of Conflict* (Santa Monica: RAND, 2000).

Ashton, P., A. J. Bartlett and J. Clemens, 'Masters and Disciples: Institution, Philosophy, Praxis', in Ashton, Bartlett and Clemens (eds), *The Praxis of Alain Badiou* (Melbourne: re.press, 2006), pp. 3–12.

Avtonomova, N., et al. (eds), *Lacan avec les philosophes* (Paris: Albin Michel, 1991).

Badiou, A., *The Adventure of French Philosophy*, trans. B. Bosteels (London: Verso, 2012).

Badiou, A., *Being and Event*, trans. O. Feltham (London: Continuum, 2005).

Badiou, A., *Conditions* (Paris: Éditions du Seuil, 1992).

Badiou, A., *Conditions*, trans. S. Corcoran (London: Continuum, 2008).

Badiou, A., *Handbook of Inaesthetics*, trans. A. Toscano (Stanford: Stanford University Press, 2005).

Badiou, A., 'Lacan and the pre-Socratics', in S. Zizek (ed.), *Lacan's Silent Partners* (London: Verso, 2006), pp. 7–16.

Badiou, A., *Logics of Worlds*, trans. A. Toscano (London: Continuum, 2009).

Badiou, A., *Le Siècle* (Paris: Éditions du Seuil, 2005).

Badiou, A., *Theoretical Writings*, ed. and trans. R. Brassier and A. Toscano (London: Continuum, 2004).

Badiou, A., 'Who is Nietzsche?', *Pli*, 11 (2001), pp. 1–11.

Badiou, A., *Wittgenstein's Antiphilosophy*, trans. B. Bosteels (London: Verso, 2011).

Badiou, A., J. Bellassen and L. Mossot, *The Rational Kernel of the Hegelian*

Dialectic: Translations, Introductions and Commentary on a Text by Zhang Shiying, trans. T. Tho (Melbourne: re.press, 2011).

Bahti, T., *Ends of the Lyric: Direction and Consequence in Western Poetry* (Baltimore: Johns Hopkins University Press, 1996).

Bakalar, J., and L. Grinspoon, *Cocaine: A Drug and Its Social Evolution* (New York: Basic Books, 1976).

Barnard, S., and B. Fink (eds), *Reading Seminar XX: Lacan's Major Work on Love, Knowledge, and Feminine Sexuality* (Albany: State University of New York Press, 2002).

Bartlett, A. J., 'Conditional Notes on a New *Republic*', in P. Ashton, A. J. Bartlett and J. Clemens (eds), *The Praxis of Alain Badiou* (Melbourne: re.press, 2006), pp. 201–42.

Bartlett, A. J., and J. Clemens (eds), *Alain Badiou: Key Concepts* (Durham: Acumen, 2010).

Baudrillard, J., *Fragments: Cool Memories III 1991–1995* (Paris: Éditions Galilée, 1995).

Beccaria, C., *On Crimes and Punishments and Other Writings*, ed. R. Bellamy, trans. R. Davies, V. Cox and R. Bellamy (Cambridge: Cambridge University Press, 1995).

Benjamin, W., *Reflections: Essays, Aphorisms, Autobiographical Writings*, ed. with intro. by P. Demetz, trans. E. Jephcott (New York: Schocken Books, 1986).

Bentham, J., *An Introduction to the Principle of Morals and Legislation*, ed. J. H. Burns and H. L. A. Hart (London and New York: Methuen, 1980).

Berlin, H. A., and C. Koch, 'Neuroscience Meets Psychoanalysis', *Scientific American Mind*, April/May 2009, pp. 16–19.

Bernheimer, C., and C. Kahane (eds), *In Dora's Case: Freud, Hysteria, Feminism* (London: Virago, 1985).

Bernstein, J. M., 'Bare Life, Bearing Witness: Auschwitz and the Pornography of Horror', *Parallax*, 10:1 (2004), pp. 3–19.

Berridge, V., and G. Edwards, *Opium and the People: Opiate Use in Nineteenth-Century England* (New York: Allen Lane/St. Martin's Press, 1981).

Beye, C. R., *Ancient Greek Literature and Society*, 2nd edn (Ithaca and London: Cornell University Press, 1987).

Bloom, H., *Agon: Towards a Theory of Revisionism* (Oxford: Oxford University Press, 1982).

Blunt, A. F., 'Poussin and Aesop', *Journal of the Warburg and Courtauld Institutes*, 29 (1966), pp. 436–7.

Bonabeau, M., M. Dorigo and G. Theraulaz, *Swarm Intelligence: From Natural to Artificial Systems* (New York: Oxford University Press, 1999).

Borch-Jacobsen, M., 'Psychotropicana', *London Review of Books*, 11 July 2002, pp. 17–18.

Borch-Jacobsen, M., *Remembering Anna O.: A Century of Mystification*, trans. K. Olson with X. Callahan and the author (New York: Routledge, 1996).

Bosteels, B., 'Alain Badiou's Theory of the Subject: Part I. The Recommencement of Dialectical Materialism?', *Pli*, 12 (2001), pp. 200–29.

Bosteels, B., 'Radical Antiphilosophy', *Filozofski Vestnik*, 29:1 (2008), pp. 155–87.

Bouveresse, J., *Wittgenstein Reads Freud: The Myth of the Unconscious*, trans. C. Cosman, foreword by V. Descombes (Princeton: Princeton University Press, 1995).

Bowie, M., *Freud, Proust and Lacan: Theory as Fiction* (Cambridge: Cambridge University Press, 1987).

Bowra, C. M., *Ancient Greek Literature* (London: Oxford University Press, 1964 [1933]).

Bozovic, M., 'The Body and *Psycho*; or, of "Farther Uses of the Dead to the Living"', *Umbr(a)* (2000), pp. 81–98.

Bracher, M., M. W. Alcorn Jr, R. J. Corthell and F. Massardier-Kenney (eds), *Lacanian Theory of Discourse: Subject, Structure, and Society* (New York and London: New York University Press, 1994).

Brecher, R., *Torture and the Ticking Bomb* (Malden and Oxford: Blackwell, 2007).

Breger, L., *Freud: Darkness in the Midst of Vision* (New York: John Wiley, 2000).

Breuer, J., and S. Freud, *Studies in Hysteria*, in *The Standard Edition of the Complete Psychological Works of Sigmund Freud*, Vol. II (1893–1895), ed. J. Strachey with A. Freud, A. Strachey, A. Tyson, J. Breuer and S. Freud (London: The Hogarth Press, 1955).

Brillat-Savarin, J.-A., *The Physiology of Taste*, trans. A. Drayton (London: Penguin, 1994).

Brito, V., 'The Desert Island and the Missing People', *Parrhesia*, 6 (2009), pp. 7–13.

Brown, E. C. (ed.), *Insect Poetics* (Minneapolis: University of Minnesota Press, 2006).

Buck-Morss, S., 'Aesthetics and Anaesthetics: Walter Benjamin's Artwork Essay Reconsidered', *October*, 62 (1992), pp. 3–41.

Bull, M., 'The Limits of Multitude', *New Left Review*, 35 (September/October 2005), pp. 19–39.

Butler, J., *Antigone's Claim: Kinship Between Life and Death* (New York: Columbia University Press, 2000).

Butler, J., *Gender Trouble* (New York: Routledge, 1989).

Butler, J., *The Psychic Life of Power: Theories in Subjection* (Stanford: Stanford University Press, 1997).

Byck, R., 'Introduction: Sigmund Freud and Cocaine', in S. Freud, *Cocaine Papers*, ed. R. Byck (New York: Stonehill Publishing, 1974).

Carey, S. C., M. Gibney and S. C. Poe, *The Politics of Human Rights: The Quest for Dignity* (Cambridge: Cambridge University Press, 2010).

Carson, A., *Eros the Bittersweet* (Dalkley Archive Press, 1998).

Cassin, B., *Jacques le sophiste: Lacan: Logos et psychanalyse* (Paris: EPEL, 2012).

Cassin, B. (ed.), *Vocabulaire européen des philosophies: Dictionnaire des intra-duisibles* (Paris: Éditions du Seuil/Dictionnaires Le Robert, 2004).

Celan, P., *Threadsuns*, trans. Pierre Joris (Copenhagen and Los Angeles: Green Integer, 2005).

Certeau, M. de., *Heterologies: Discourse on the Other*, trans. B. Massumi, foreword by W. Godzich (Minneapolis and London: University of Minnesota Press, 1986).

Chaitin, G. D., *Rhetoric and Culture in Lacan* (Cambridge: Cambridge University Press, 1996).

Chiesa, L., 'Count-as-one, Forming-into-one, Unary Trait, S_1', in P. Ashton, A. J. Bartlett and J. Clemens (eds), *The Praxis of Alain Badiou* (Melbourne: re.press, 2006), pp. 147–76.

Chiesa, L., *Subjectivity and Otherness: A Philosophical Reading of Lacan* (Cambridge: MIT, 2007).

Clark, R., *Freud: The Man and the Cause* (London: Jonathan Cape, 1980).

Clarke, A. W., 'Rendition to Torture: A Critical Legal History', *Rutgers Law Review*, 62:1 (Fall 2009), pp. 1–74.

Classen, C., D. Howes and A. Synnott, *Aroma: The Cultural History of Smell* (London: Routledge, 1994).

Clemens, J., 'Letters as the Condition of Conditions for Alain Badiou', *Communication and Cognition*, 36:1–2 (2003), pp. 73–102.

Clemens, J., 'Only Psychoanalysis Can Make You Really Unhappy', *Cosmos and History: The Journal of Natural and Social Philosophy*, 1:2 (2005), pp. 357–66.

Clemens, J., 'The Politics of Style in the Works of Slavoj Žižek', in G. Boucher, J. Glynos and M. Sharpe (eds), *Traversing the Fantasy: Critical Responses to Slavoj Žižek* (Aldershot: Ashgate, 2005), pp. 3–22.

Clemens, J., 'The Purloined Veil: Notes on an Image', *(a)*, 4:1 (2004), pp. 75–88.

Clemens, J., 'You Have the Right to Remain Silent', *Heat*, 23 (2010), pp. 7–21.

Clemens, J., and R. Grigg (eds), *Jacques Lacan and the Other Side of Psychoanalysis* (Durham, NC: Duke University Press, 2006).

Clemens, J., and R. Grigg, 'A Note on Psychoanalysis and the Crime of Torture', *Australian Feminist Legal Journal*, 24 (2006), pp. 159–76.

Cohen, L., *Various Positions* (Passport Records, 1984).

Compton, T., 'The Trial of the Satirist: Poetic Vitae (Aesop, Archilochus, Homer) as Background for Plato's *Apology*', *The American Journal of Philology*, 111:3 (1990), pp. 330–47.

Condren, C., *Argument and Authority in Early Modern England: The Presupposition of Oaths and Offices* (Cambridge: Cambridge University Press, 2006).

Constantine, D., *Hölderlin* (Oxford: Clarendon Press, 1988).

Crelinsten R., and A. P. Schmid (eds), *The Politics of Pain: Torturers and their Masters* (Boulder: Westview Press, 1995).

Damasio, A., *The Feeling of What Happens: Body, Emotion, and the Making of Consciousness* (New York: Random House, 2000).

Danner, M., *Torture and Truth: America, Abu Ghraib and the War on Terror* (New York: New York Review of Books, 2004).

Darwin, C. R., *Journal of researches into the natural history and geology of the countries visited during the voyage of H.M.S. Beagle round the world, under the command of Capt. Fitz Roy R.N.* (London: John Murray, 1860).

Deleuze, G., and F. Guattari, *A Thousand Plateaus: Capitalism and Schizophrenia*, trans. and foreword by B. Massumi (Minneapolis: University of Minnesota Press, 1987).

De Marchi, A., 'Fanatismi', *Rivista di Psicoanalisi*, 51 (2005), pp. 1,195–204.

De Quincey, T., *Confessions of an English Opium Eater*, ed. A. Hayter (London: Penguin, 1986).

De Quincey, T., 'Style', in *De Quincey as Critic*, ed. J. E. Jordan (London: Routledge and Kegan Paul, 1973).

Derrida, J., *Acts of Literature*, ed. D. Attridge (New York: Routledge, 1992).

Derrida, J., *Dissemination*, trans. B. Johnson (Chicago: University of Chicago Press, 1981).

Derrida, J., 'Force de loi: Le "Fondement mystique de l'autorité"', *Cardozo Law Review*, 11:5–6 (1990), pp. 919–1,045.

Derrida, J., *Given Time: I Counterfeit Money*, trans. P. Kamuf (Chicago: University of Chicago Press, 1992).

Derrida, J., *Positions*, trans. A. Bass (Chicago: University of Chicago Press, 1987).

Derrida, J., *Resistances of Psychoanalysis*, trans. P. Kamuf, P.-A. Brault and M. Naas (Stanford: Stanford University Press, 1998).

Derrida, J., 'The Rhetoric of Drugs: An Interview', *differences*, 5:3 (1993), pp. 1–25.

Dershowitz, A., *Why Terrorism Works: Understanding the Threat, Responding to the Challenge* (New Haven, CT: Yale University Press, 2003).

Douzinas, C., 'Torture and Systems Theory', *Soziale Systeme*, 14:1 (2008), pp. 110–25.

duBois, P., *Slaves and Other Objects* (Chicago: University of Chicago Press, 2003).

duBois, P., *Torture and Truth* (London: Routledge, 1991).

Düttmann, A. G., 'Integral Actuality: On Giorgio Agamben's *Idea of Prose*', in J. Clemens, N. Heron and A. W. Murray (eds), *The Work of Giorgio Agamben* (Edinburgh: Edinburgh University Press, 2008), pp. 28–42.

Eaglestone, R., *The Holocaust and the Postmodern* (Oxford: Oxford University Press, 2004).

Ebert, T., 'Why is Evenus Called a Philosopher at *Phaedo* 61c?', *The Classical Quarterly*, New Series, 51:2 (2001), pp. 423–34.

Einolf, C. J., 'The Fall and Rise of Torture: A Comparative and Historical Analysis', *Sociological Theory*, 25:2 (2007), pp. 101–21.

Faber, R., '"Amid a Democracy of Fellow Creatures" – Onto/Politics and the Problem of Slavery in Whitehead and Deleuze (with an Intervention of Badiou)', in Faber, H. Krips and D. Pettus (eds), *Event and Decision: Ontology and Politics in Badiou, Deleuze, and Whitehead* (Newcastle: Cambridge Scholars Press, 2010), pp. 192–237.

Felman, S., *Jacques Lacan and the Adventure of Insight* (Cambridge: Harvard University Press, 1987).

Fenves, P., *A Peculiar Fate: Metaphysics and World-History in Kant* (New York: Cornell University Press, 1991).

Fenves, P. (ed.), *Raising the Tone of Philosophy: Late Essays by Immanuel Kant, Transformative Critique by Jacques Derrida* (Baltimore and London: Johns Hopkins University Press, 1993).

Fenves, P., 'The Scale of Enthusiasm', *Huntington Library Quarterly*, 60:1–2 (1997), pp. 117–52.

Ferenczi, S., *Thalassa: A Theory of Genitality*, trans. H. A. Bunker (London: Maresfield Library, 1989).

Fine, R., *A History of Psychoanalysis* (New York: Columbia University Press, 1979).

Fink, B., *A Clinical Introduction to Lacanian Psychoanalysis: Theory and Technique* (Cambridge: Harvard University Press, 1997).

Finke, M., 'Puškin, Pugačev, and Aesop', *The Slavic and East European Journal*, 35:2 (1991), pp. 179–92.

Flusser, V., 'The City as Wave-Trough in the Image-Flood', *Critical Inquiry*, 31 (2005), pp. 320–8.

Forrester, J., 'Lessons from the Freud Wars', unpublished manuscript.

Fotopoulou, A., D. Pfaff and M. Conway (eds), *From the Couch to the Lab: Trends in Psychodynamic Neuroscience* (Oxford: Oxford University Press, 2012).

Foucault, M., *Discipline and Punish: The Birth of the Prison*, trans. A. Sheridan (New York: Vintage, 1979).

Foucault, M., *Power/Knowledge: Selected Interviews 1972–1977*, ed. C. Gordon (New York: Pantheon Books, 1980).

Freud, S., *Case Histories I: 'Dora' and 'Little Hans'*, trans. A. and J. Strachey (Harmondsworth: Penguin, 1977).

Freud, S., *Civilization and its Discontents*, trans. J. Riviere, rev. J. Strachey (London: The Hogarth Press, 1963).

Freud, S., *Cocaine Papers*, ed. R. Byck (New York: Stonehill Publishing, 1974).

Freud, S., *The Complete Introductory Lectures on Psychoanalysis*, trans. J. Strachey (Cambridge: The Belknap Press, 1971).

Freud, S., *The Complete Letters of Sigmund Freud to Wilhelm Fliess, 1887–1904*, ed. J. Masson (Cambridge: The Belknap Press, 1985).

Freud, S., *Gesammelte Werke*, Vol. V (London: Imago, 1942).

Freud, S., *Gesammelte Werke*, Vol. X (London: Imago, 1946).

Freud, S., *Gesammelte Werke*, Vol. XII (London: Imago, 1947).

Freud, S., *Gesammelte Werke*, Vol. XIII (London: Imago, 1940).

Freud, S., *The Interpretation of Dreams*, trans. J. Strachey (Harmondsworth: Penguin, 1985).

Freud, S., *Letters of Sigmund Freud 1873–1939*, ed. E. L. Freud (London: The Hogarth Press, 1961).

Freud, S., *The Standard Edition of the Complete Psychological Works of Sigmund Freud*, Vol. II (1893–1895), ed. J. Strachey with A. Freud, A. Strachey, A. Tyson, J. Breuer and S. Freud (London: The Hogarth Press, 1955).

Freud, S., *The Standard Edition of the Complete Psychological Works of Sigmund Freud*, Vol. V (1900–1901), ed. J. Strachey with A. Freud, A. Strachey and A. Tyson (London: The Hogarth Press, 1953).

Freud, S., *The Standard Edition of the Complete Psychological Works of Sigmund Freud*, Vol. VII (1901–1905), ed. J. Strachey with A. Freud, A. Strachey and A. Tyson (London: The Hogarth Press, 1953).

Freud, S., *The Standard Edition of the Complete Psychological Works of Sigmund Freud*, Vol. X (1909), ed. J. Strachey with A. Freud, A. Strachey and A. Tyson (London: The Hogarth Press, 1955).

Freud, S., *The Standard Edition of the Complete Psychological Works of Sigmund Freud*, Vol. XI (1910), ed. J. Strachey with A. Freud, A. Strachey, A. Tyson and A. Richards (London: The Hogarth Press, 1957).

Freud, S., *The Standard Edition of the Complete Psychological Works of Sigmund Freud*, Vol. XII (1911–1913), ed. J. Strachey with A. Freud, A. Strachey and A. Tyson (London: The Hogarth Press, 1958).

Freud, S., *The Standard Edition of the Complete Psychological Works of Sigmund Freud*, Vol. XIV (1914–1916), ed. J. Strachey with A. Freud, A. Strachey and A. Tyson (London: The Hogarth Press, 1957).

Freud, S., *The Standard Edition of the Complete Psychological Works of Sigmund Freud*, Vol. XVIII (1920–1922), ed. J. Strachey with A. Freud, A. Strachey and A. Tyson (London: The Hogarth Press, 1955).

Freud, S., *The Standard Edition of the Complete Psychological Works of Sigmund Freud*, Vol. XXI (1927–1931), ed. J. Strachey with A. Freud, A. Strachey and A. Tyson (London: The Hogarth Press, 1961).

Freud, S., *The Standard Edition of the Complete Psychological Works of Sigmund Freud*, Vol. XXII (1932–1936), ed. J. Strachey with A. Freud, A. Strachey, A. Tyson and A. Richards (London: The Hogarth Press, 1964).

Freud, S., *The Standard Edition of the Complete Psychological Works of Sigmund Freud*, Vol. XXIII (1937–1939), ed. J. Strachey with A. Freud, A. Strachey and A. Tyson (London: The Hogarth Press, 1964).

Gagarin, M., and P. Woodruff (eds), *Early Greek Political Thought from Homer to the Sophists* (Cambridge: Cambridge University Press, 1995).

Gay, P., *Freud: A Life for Our Time* (New York: W. W. Norton & Co., 1988).

Gilman, S., *Disease and Representation: Images of Illness from Madness to AIDS* (Ithaca: Cornell University Press, 1988).

Glynos, J., and Y. Stavrakakis (eds), *Lacan & Science* (London: Karnac, 2002).

Gogol, N., *The Diary of a Madman and Other Stories*, trans. A. R. MacAndrew (New York: Signet Classics, 1961).

Goldhill, S., *The Invention of Prose* (Oxford: Oxford University Press, 2002).

Greenberg, K. (ed.), *The Torture Debate in America* (Cambridge: Cambridge University Press, 2006).

Greenberg, K., and J. L. Dratel (eds), *The Torture Papers: The Road to Abu Ghraib* (New York: Cambridge University Press, 2005).

Grey, S., *Ghost Plane: The True Story of the CIA Torture Program* (New York: St. Martin's Press, 2006).

Grigg, R., *Lacan, Language, and Philosophy* (Albany: State University of New York Press, 2008).

Groys, B., *Introduction to Antiphilosophy*, trans. D. Fernbach (London: Verso, 2012).

Hallward, P. (ed.), *Think Again: Alain Badiou and the Future of Philosophy* (London and New York: Continuum, 2004).

Harbury, J. K., *Truth, Torture, and the American Way: The History and Consequences of US Involvement in Torture* (Boston: Beacon Press, 2005).

Hárnik, E. J., 'Pleasure in Disguise, the Need for Decoration, and the Sense of Beauty', *Psychoanalytic Quarterly*, 1 (1932), pp. 216–64.

Hauff, W., *Dwarf Long-Nose*, trans. D. Orgel, pictures M. Sendak (London: The Bodley Head, 1979).

Hawking, S., *A Brief History of Time* (New York: Random House, 2011).

Hazlitt, W., *Selected Writings* (Harmondsworth: Penguin, 1989).

Head, T. (ed.), *Is Torture Ever Justified?* (Detroit: Greenhaven Press, 2005).

Healy, D., *Let Them Eat Prozac: The Unhealthy Relationship between the Pharmaceutical Industry and Depression* (New York: New York University Press, 2004).

Heath, J., *Torture and English Law: An Administrative and Legal History from the Plantagenets to the Stuarts* (Westport: Greenwood Press, 1982).

Hecht, B., *A Guide for the Bedevilled* (New York: Garden City Publishing Co., 1945).

Hegel, G. W. F., *Aesthetics: Lectures on Fine Art*, trans. T. M. Knox (Oxford: Oxford University Press, 1975).

Hegel, G. W. F., *The Phenomenology of Spirit*, trans. A. V. Miller, foreword by J. N. Findlay (Oxford: Oxford University Press, 1977).

Hegel, G. W. F., *Reading Hegel: The Introductions*, ed. A. Singh and R. Mohapatra (Melbourne: re.press, 2008).

Heidegger, M., *Poetry, Language, Thought*, trans. A. Hofstadter (New York: Harper and Row, 1971).

Heidegger, M., *The Question Concerning Technology and Other Essays*, trans. with intro. by W. Lovitt (New York: Harper and Row, 1977).

Heller, Z., and R. Porter, 'The Chemistry of Happiness', in S. Dunn, B. Morrison and M. Roberts (eds), *Mind Readings: Writers' Journeys Through Mental States* (London: Minerva, 1996), pp. 165–75.

Hirsch, M., and L. Spitzer, 'Holocaust Studies/Memory Studies', in S. Redstone (ed.), *Memory: Histories, Theories, Debates* (New York: Fordham University Press, 2010), pp. 390–405.

Hobbes, T., *Leviathan*, ed. A. P. Martinich (Ontario: Broadview, 2002).

Hoens, D., and E. Pluth, 'What If the Other is Stupid? Badiou and Lacan on "Logical Time"', in P. Hallward (ed.), *Think Again: Alain Badiou and the Future of Philosophy* (London: Continuum, 2004), pp. 182–90.

Hoens, D., and E. Pluth, 'Working Through as a Truth Procedure', *Communication and Cognition*, Vol. 37, Nos. 2–3 (2004), pp. 279–92.

Hooker, J., *A pamphlet of the offices, and duties of euerie particular sworne officer, of the citie of Excester: collected by Iohn Vowell alias Hoker, Gentleman & chamberlaine of the same* (London: Henrie Denham, 1584).

Hopkins, K., 'Novel Evidence for Roman Slavery', in R. Osborne (ed.), *Studies in Ancient Greek and Roman Society* (Cambridge: Cambridge University Press, 2004), pp. 206–25.

Hulten, P. (ed.), *Marcel Duchamp* (London: Thames and Hudson, 1993).

Hutchings, P., 'Invented Sovereignty and the Bush Presidency', conference paper, Australasian Society for Continental Philosophy Annual Conference, La Trobe University, 14 December 2011.

Johnson, L. M., 'Terror, Torture and Democratic Autoimmunity', *Philosophy & Social Criticism*, 38:1 (2012), pp. 105–24.

Johnston, A., 'This Philosophy Which Is Not One', *S*, 3 (2010), pp. 137–58.

Jones, D. M., *Conscience and Allegiance in Seventeenth Century England: The Political Significance of Oaths and Engagements* (Rochester: University of Rochester Press, 1999).

Jones, E., *Sigmund Freud: Life and Work. Volume One: The Young Freud 1856–1900* (London: The Hogarth Press, 1956).

Jöttkandt, S., *First Love* (Melbourne: re.press, 2010).

Joyce, C., 'The Idea of "Anti-Philosophy" in the Work of F. R. Leavis', *The Cambridge Quarterly*, 38:1 (2009), pp. 24–44.

Kant, I., *Political Writings*, ed. H. Reiss, trans. H. B. Nisbet (Cambridge: Cambridge University Press, 1991).

Keenan, T., *Fables of Responsibility: Aberrations and Predicaments in Ethics and Politics* (Stanford: Stanford University Press, 1997).

Kennedy, J., and R. C. Eberhart with Y. Shi, *Swarm Intelligence* (San Diego: Academic Press, 2001).

Kesel, M. de, *Eros and Ethics: Reading Lacan's Seminar VII*, trans. S. Jöttkandt (Albany: State University of New York Press, 2009).

King, K. C., '*Torture and Truth* by Page duBois (review)', *Comparative Literature*, 47:3 (1995), pp. 261–3.

Klein, N., *The Shock Doctrine: The Rise of Disaster Capitalism* (London: Penguin, 2008).

Klein, N., 'The US Psychological Torture System is Finally on Trial', *The Guardian*, 23 February 2007, p. 41.

Kleinberg, E., *Generation Existential: Heidegger's Philosophy in France, 1927–1961* (New York: Cornell University Press, 2007).

Kleinig, J., 'Ticking Bombs and Torture Warrants', *Deakin Law Review*, 10:2 (2006), pp. 614–27.

Klemperer, V., *The Language of the Third Reich*, trans. M. Brady (London: Continuum, 2006).

Koestenbaum, W., *Double Talk: The Erotics of Male Literary Collaboration* (New York: Routledge, 1989).

Kojève, A., *Introduction to the Reading of Hegel*, ed. A. Bloom, trans. J. H. Nichols (New York and London: Basic Books, 1969).

Kulkarni, M. (ed.), *Interdisciplinary Perspectives on Political Theory* (Delhi: Sage, 2011).

Kurke, L., *Aesopic Conversations: Popular Tradition, Cultural Dialogue, and the Invention of Greek Prose* (Princeton: Princeton University Press, 2011).

Kurke, L., 'Plato, Aesop, and the Beginnings of Mimetic Prose', in *Representations*, 94 (2006), pp. 6–52.

Lacan, J., *Autres Écrits* (Paris: Éditions du Seuil, 2001).

Lacan, J., 'Comptes rendus d'enseignement 1964–1968', *Ornicar?*, 29 (1984), p. 10.

Lacan, J., *Écrits* (Paris: Éditions du Seuil, 1966).

Lacan, J., *Écrits*, trans. B. Fink with H. Fink and R. Grigg (New York: W. W. Norton & Co., 2006).

Lacan, J., *Je parle aux murs* (Paris: Éditions du Seuil, 2011).

Lacan, J., 'Lecture on the Body', *Scilicet* 6/7 (1976), pp. 38–41.

Lacan, J., *Le Séminaire, livre I: Les écrits techniques de Freud* (Paris: Éditions du Seuil, 1975).[1]

Lacan, J., *Seminar III: The Psychoses: The Seminar of Jacques Lacan Book III, 1955–1956*, trans. R. Grigg (London: Routledge, 1993).

Lacan, J., *Le Séminaire, livre IV: La relation d'objet* (Paris: Éditions du Seuil, 1994).

Lacan, J., *Le Séminaire, livre V: Les formations de l'inconscient, 1957–1958* (Paris: Éditions du Seuil, 1998).

Lacan, J., *Seminar VII: The Ethics of Psychoanalysis (1959–1960)*, trans. D. Porter (London: Routledge, 1992).

Lacan, J., *Le Séminaire, livre VIII: Le transfert* (Paris: Éditions du Seuil, 2001).

Lacan, J., 'Seminar IX: Identification', unpublished seminar.

Lacan, J., *Le Séminaire, livre X: L'angoisse* (Paris: Éditions du Seuil, 2004).

Lacan, J., *Seminar XI: The Four Fundamental Concepts of Psychoanalysis*, trans. A. Sheridan, intro. by D. Macey (London: Penguin, 1994).

Lacan, J., *Seminar XVII: The Other Side of Psychoanalysis*, trans. R. Grigg (New York: W. W. Norton & Co., 2007).

Lacan, J., 'Seminar XIV: The Logic of Fantasy', unpublished seminar.

Lacan, J., *Seminar XX: Encore: The Seminar of Jacques Lacan, Book XX: On*

[1] Note that, in accordance with orthodox Lacanian practice, I have referred to Lacan's seminars first and foremost by their number, a practice which does not always conform to the publishers' titles. This practice, however, should not prevent anybody from locating the relevant texts.

Feminine Sexuality: The Limits of Love and Knowledge 1972–1973, ed. J.-A. Miller, trans. with notes by B. Fink (New York: W. W. Norton & Co., 1998).

Lacan, J., *Le Séminaire, livre XXIII: Le sinthome, 1975–1976* (Paris: Éditions du Seuil, 2005).

LaCapra, D., *History in Transit: Experience, Identity, Critical Theory* (Ithaca: Cornell University Press, 2004).

Langbein, J. H., *Torture and the Law of Proof: Europe and England in the Ancien Régime* (Chicago and London: University of Chicago Press, 1977).

La Vopa, A., 'The Philosopher and the *Schwärmer*: On the Career of a German Epithet from Luther to Kant', *Huntington Library Quarterly*, 60:1–2 (1997), pp. 85–115.

Lear, J., *Freud* (New York and London: Routledge, 2005).

Lear, J., *Love and Its Place in Nature: A Philosophical Interpretation of Freudian Psychoanalysis* (New York: Farrar, Strauss, and Giroux, 1990).

Lear, J., *Therapeutic Action: An Earnest Plea for Irony* (New York: The Other Press, 2003).

Leavis, F. R., *The Critic as Anti-Philosopher*, ed. G. Singh (London: Chatto and Windus, 1982).

Leavis, F. R., *Thought, Words and Creativity: Art and Thought in Lawrence* (London: Chatto and Windus, 1976).

Le Bon, G., *The Crowd: A Study of the Popular Mind*, ed. R. K. Merton (New York: Penguin, 1977).

Lesky, A., *A History of Greek Literature*, trans. J. Willis and C. de Heer (New York: Thomas Y. Crowell, 1966).

Leupin, A. (ed.), *Lacan and the Human Sciences* (Lincoln and London: University of Nebraska Press, 1991).

Levin, M., 'The Case for Torture', *Newsweek*, 7 June 1982, p. 13.

Levinson, S., 'Slavery and the Phenomenology of Torture', *Social Research*, 74:1 (2007), pp. 149–68.

Levinson, S. (ed.), *Torture: A Collection* (Oxford: Oxford University Press, 2004).

Leys, R., *From Guilt to Shame: Auschwitz and After* (Princeton: Princeton University Press, 2007).

Locke, J., *An Essay Concerning Human Understanding*, ed. P. H. Nidditch (Oxford: Clarendon Press, 1985).

Locke, J., *Two Treatises of Government* (London: Everyman, 1986).

Lokaneeta, J., *Transnational Torture: Law, Violence, and State Power in the United States and India* (New York: New York Press, 2011).

Loraux, N., *The Children of Athena: Athenian Ideas about Citizenship and the Division Between the Sexes*, trans. C. Levine (Princeton: Princeton University Press, 1994).

Luhmann, N., 'Are There Still Indispensable Norms in Our Society?', *Soziale Systeme*, 14:1 (2008), pp. 18–37.

McGrath, W. J., 'Freud as Hannibal: The Politics of the Brother Band', *Central European History*, 7:1 (1974), pp. 31–57.

Machiavelli, N., *The Prince*, trans. G. Bull, intro. by A. Grafton (London: Penguin, 2003).

Mahony, P., *Freud as a Writer*, expanded edition (New Haven, CT: Yale University Press, 1987).

Malabou, C., *The New Wounded: From Neurosis to Brain Damage* (New York: Fordham University Press, 2012).

Marin, L., 'The "Aesop" Fable-Animal', in M. Blonsky (ed.), *On Signs* (Baltimore: Johns Hopkins University Press, 1985), pp. 334–40.

Marpeau, B., *Gustave Le Bon: Parcours d'un intellectuel 1841–1931* (Paris: CNRS, 2000).

Marsh, D., 'Aesop and the Humanist Apologue', *Renaissance Studies*, 17:1 (2003), pp. 9–26.

Marx, K., *Capital*, Vol. 1, trans. B. Fowkes, intro. by E. Mandel (Harmondsworth: Penguin, 1976).

Masson, J., *The Assault on Truth: Freud's Suppression of the Seduction Theory* (Harmondsworth: Penguin, 1985).

Matthews, R., *The Absolute Violation: Why Torture Must Be Prohibited* (Kingston and Montreal: McGill-Queen's University Press, 2008).

Merback, M. B., *The Thief, the Cross and the Wheel: Pain and the Spectacle of Punishment in Medieval and Renaissance Europe* (London: Reaktion Books, 1999).

Milbank, J., and S. Žižek, *The Monstrosity of Christ: Paradox or Dialectic?* (Cambridge: MIT, 2009).

Miller, J., and R. Koral (eds), *White Rabbit: A Psychedelic Reader* (San Francisco: Chronicle Books, 1995).

Miller, J.-A., 'The Analytic Experience', in M. Bracher and E. Ragland-Sullivan (eds), *Lacan and the Subject of Language* (New York and London: Routledge, 1991), pp. 83–99.

Miller, J.-A., 'A Discussion of Lacan's "Kant with Sade"', in R. Feldstein, B. Fink and M. Jaanus (eds), *Reading Seminars I and II* (Albany: State University of New York Press, 1996), pp. 212–37.

Miller, J.-A., 'On Perversion', in R. Feldstein, B. Fink and M. Jaanus (eds), *Reading Seminars I and II* (Albany: State University of New York Press, 1996), pp. 309–10.

Miller, J.-A., 'Six Paradigms of Jouissance', *Lacanian Ink*, 17 (2000), pp. 10–47.

Millet, K., *The Politics of Cruelty: An Essay on the Literature of Political Imprisonment* (New York and London: W. W. Norton & Co., 1994).

Milner, J.-C., *Constats* (Paris: Gallimard, 2002).

Milner, J.-C., 'The Doctrine of Science', *Umbr(a)* (2000), pp. 33–63.

Milner, J.-C., *Les Noms indistincts* (Paris: Éditions du Seuil, 1983).

Milner, J.-C., *L'Oeuvre claire: Lacan, la science, la philosophie* (Paris: Éditions du Seuil, 1995).

Milner, J.-C., *Les Penchants criminels de l'Europe démocratique* (Paris: Verdier, 2003).

Milner, J.-C., A. Banfield and D. Heller-Roazen, 'Interview with J.-C. Milner', *S*, 3 (2010), pp. 4–21.

Milton, J., *The Poems of Milton*, ed. J. Carey and A. Fowler (London: Longmans, 1968).

Murray, A., and J. Whyte (eds), *The Agamben Dictionary* (Edinburgh: Edinburgh University Press, 2011).

Nagy, G., *The Best of the Achaeans* (Baltimore: Johns Hopkins University Press, 1999).

Nagy, G., *Greek Mythology and Poetics* (Ithaca and London: Cornell University Press, 1990).

Nagy, G., *Pindar's Homer: The Lyric Possession of an Epic Past* (Baltimore: Johns Hopkins University Press, 1997).

Nancy, J.-L., *The Sense of the World*, trans. with foreword by J. S. Librett (Minneapolis: University of Minnesota Press, 1997).

Nancy, J.-L., and P. Lacoue-Labarthe, *The Title of the Letter: A Reading of Lacan*, trans. F. Raffoul and D. Pettigrew (Albany: State University of New York Press, 1992).

New Formations, special themed issue, 'Psychoanalysis, Money and the Global Financial Crisis', 72 (2011).

Nicholson, J. A., 'FCJ-030 Flash! Mobs in the Age of Mobile Connectivity', *The Fibreculture Journal*, 6 (2005), <http://journal.fibre-culture.org/issue6/issue6_nicholson.html> (last accessed 27 September 2012).

Nietzsche, F., *The Anti-Christ, Ecce Homo, Twilight of the Idols, and Other Writings*, ed. A. Ridley and J. Norman (Cambridge: Cambridge University Press, 2005).

Nietzsche, F., *The Gay Science*, ed. B. Williams, trans. J. Nauckhoff (Cambridge: Cambridge University Press, 2001).

Nietzsche, F., *On the Genealogy of Morality*, ed. K. Ansell-Pearson, trans. C. Diethe (Cambridge: Cambridge University Press, 2007).

Nietzsche, F., *Twilight of the Idols/The Antichrist*, trans. with intro. by R. J. Hollingdale (Harmondsworth: Penguin, 1968).

Palladino, P., 'Life . . . On Biology, Biography, and Bio-power in the Age of Genetic Engineering', *Configurations*, 11:1 (2003), pp. 81–109.

Parikka, J., 'Politics of Swarms: Translations Between Entomology and Biopolitics', *Parallax*, 14:3 (2008), pp. 112–24.

Patterson, A., *Censorship and Interpretation: The Conditions of Writing and Reading in Early Modern England* (Madison: University of Wisconsin Press, 1984).

Patterson, A., *Fables of Power: Aesopian Writing and Political History* (Durham, NC: Duke University Press, 1991).

Patterson, A., *Reading Between the Lines* (Madison: University of Wisconsin Press, 1993).

Peirce, C. S., *Philosophical Writings of Peirce*, ed. J. Buchler (New York: Dover Publications, 1955).

Pélissier, Y., M. Benabou, L. Cornaz and D. de Liège (eds), *789 néologismes de Jacques Lacan* (Paris: EPEL, 2002).

Pelling, C. (ed.), *Characterisation and Individuality in Greek Literature* (Oxford: Clarendon Press, 1990).

Pelling, C., *Literary Texts and the Greek Historian* (London and New York: Routledge, 2000).

Peters, E., *The Magician, the Witch, and the Law* (Philadelphia: University of Pennsylvania Press, 1978).

Peters, E., *Torture*, exp. edn (Philadelphia: University of Pennsylvania Press, 1996).

Phillips, A., *Promises, Promises: Essays on Psychoanalysis and Literature* (London: Faber and Faber, 2000).

Pigman, G. W., 'The Dark Forest of Authors: Freud and Nineteenth-Century Dream Theory', *Psychoanalysis and History*, 4 (2002), pp. 141–65.

Plato, *Complete Works*, ed. with intro. and notes by J. M. Cooper (Indianapolis: Hackett, 1997).

Posner, R., *Not a Suicide Pact: The Constitution in the Time of National Emergency* (Oxford: Oxford University Press, 2006).

Rabaté, J.-M. (ed.), *The Cambridge Companion to Lacan* (Cambridge: Cambridge University Press, 2003).

Rabaté, J.-M., *Jacques Lacan: Psychoanalysis and the Subject of Literature* (London: Palgrave, 2001).

Ragland, E., *Essays on the Pleasures of Death: From Freud to Lacan* (New York: Routledge, 1995).

Rancière, J., *The Aesthetic Unconscious*, trans. D. Keates (Cambridge: Polity, 2009).

Reddy, P., *Torture: What You Need to Know* (Charnwood: Ginninderra Press, 2005).

Redfield, M., '*Fables of Responsibility: Aberrations and Predicaments in Ethics and Politics* (review)', *MLQ*, June 1999, pp. 287–9.

Regnault, F., 'L'Antiphilosophie selon Lacan', *Conférences d'esthétique lacanienne* (Paris: Agalma, 1997).

Rejali, D. M., *Torture and Democracy* (Princeton: Princeton University Press, 2007).

Roazen, P., 'Freud's Patients: First-Person Accounts', in T. Gelfand and J. Kerr (eds), *Freud and the History of Psychoanalysis* (London: The Analytic Press, 1992), pp. 289–306.

Ronell, A., *Crack Wars: Literature, Addiction, Mania* (Lincoln: University of Nebraska Press, 1992).

Ronell, A., *Dictations: On Haunted Writing* (Lincoln: University of Nebraska Press, 1986).

Roth, K., M. Worden and A. D. Bernstein (eds), *Torture: Does It Make Us Safer? Is It Ever OK?* (New York: New Press, 2005).

Roth, M. S., 'A Problem of Recognition: Alexandre Kojève and the End of History', *History and Theory*, 24:3 (1985), pp. 293–306.

Rothwell, K. S. Jr, 'Aristophanes' *Wasps* and the Sociopolitics of Aesop's Fables', *The Classical Journal*, 90:3 (1995), pp. 233–54.

Roudinesco, E., 'Anti-Freudian Revisionism Triumphant in the United States', trans. A. Lewis, *Virtuosity: The Newsletter of the Australasian Society for Continental Philosophy*, 4 (March 1997), p. 4.

Rousseau, J.-J., *Discourse on Political Economy; and The Social Contract*, trans. with intro. and notes by C. Betts (Oxford: Oxford University Press, 1994).

Rushdie, S., *Midnight's Children* (London: Vintage, 2011).

Sacks, O., *The Man Who Mistook His Wife for a Hat* (London: Picador, 1985).

Saïd, S., M. Trédé and A. Le Boulluec, *Histoire de la littérature grecque* (Paris: Presses Universitaires de France, 2004).

Santner, E., *My Own Private Germany: Daniel Paul Schreber's Secret History of Modernity* (Princeton: Princeton University Press, 1996).

Scarry, E., *The Body in Pain: The Making and Unmaking of the World* (Oxford: Oxford University Press, 1985).

Schmitt, C., *The Concept of the Political*, trans. G. Schwab and J. Harvey Lomax, with L. Strauss's notes on Schmitt's essay (Chicago: University of Chicago Press, 1996).

Schmitt, C., *Political Romanticism*, trans. G. Oakes (Cambridge, MA: MIT, 1986).

Sedgwick, E. K., *Tendencies* (Durham, NC: Duke University Press, 1993).

Self, W., *The Quantity Theory of Insanity* (London: Penguin, 1994).

Serres, M., *The Parasite*, trans. L. R. Schehr (Minneapolis: University of Minnesota Press, 2007).

Sharpe, M., *Slavoj Žižek, A Little Piece of the Real* (London: Ashgate, 2004).

Shue, H., 'Torture', *Philosophy and Public Affairs*, 7:2 (1978), pp. 124–43.

Shue, H., 'Torture in Dreamland: Disposing of the Ticking Bomb', *Case Western Reserve Journal of International Law*, 37:2–3 (2006), pp. 231–9.

Sloterdijk, P., *Derrida, an Egyptian: On the Problem of the Jewish Pyramid*, trans. W. Hoban (Cambridge: Polity, 2009).

Smith, M. E., 'Aesop, a Decayed Celebrity: Changing Conception as to Aesop's Personality in English Writers Before Gay', *PMLA*, 46:1 (1931), pp. 225–36.

Soler, C., 'Lacan en antiphilosophie', *Filozofski Vestnik*, 28:2 (2006), pp. 121–44.

Solms, M., 'Freud Returns', *Scientific American*, May 2004, pp. 82–8.

Solms, M., 'What is Consciousness?', *JAPA*, 45:3 (1996), pp. 681–703.

Spiriot, P., 'Psychanalyse, drogue: le malentendu', in Spiriot (ed.), *Sigmund Freud et la drogue* (Monaco: Éditions du Rocher, 1987).

Spurr, J., 'A Profane History of Early Modern Oaths', in *Transactions of the Royal Historical Society* (Cambridge: Royal Historical Society, 2001), pp. 37–63.

Sterne, L., *Tristram Shandy* (New York: Modem Library, n.d.).

Stoltzfus, B., *Lacan and Literature: Purloined Pretexts* (Albany: State University of New York Press, 1996).

Strauss, L., *Persecution and the Art of Writing* (Glencoe: The Free Press, 1952).

Süskind, P., *Perfume*, trans. J. Woods (London: Penguin, 1986).

Taran, L., 'Plato, *Phaedo*, 62A', *The American Journal of Philology*, 87:3 (1966), pp. 326–36.

Thacker, E., 'Networks, Swarms, Multitudes' (two parts), *ctheory* (2004), <http://www.ctheory.net/articles.aspx?id=422> (last accessed 15 October 2012).

Thornton, E. M., *The Freudian Fallacy* (New York: The Dial Press, 1983).

Tlatli, S., *Le Psychiatre et ses poètes: essai sur le jeune Lacan* (Paris: Tchou, 2000).

Tomsic, S., 'The Invention of New Love in Psychoanalysis', *Filozofski Vestnik*, 31:2 (2010), pp. 189–204.

Topaz, C. M., and A. L. Bertozzi, 'Swarming Patterns in a Two-Dimensional Kinematic Model for Biological Groups', *Siam Journal of Applied Mathematics*, 65:1 (2004), pp. 152–74.

Trilling, L., *Beyond Culture: Essays on Literature and Learning* (Harmondsworth: Penguin, 1967).

Tromans, N., 'The Iconography of Velázquez's Aesop', *Journal of the Warburg and Courtauld Institutes*, 59 (1996), pp. 332–7.

Twining, W. L., 'Bentham on Torture', *Northern Ireland Legal Quarterly*, Vol. 24:3 (1973), pp. 307–56.

Tyutyanov, Y., I. Senina and R. Arditi, 'Clustering Due to Acceleration in the Response to Population Gradient: A Simple Self-Organization Model', *The American Naturalist*, 164:6 (2004), pp. 722–35.

Tzara, T., *Seven Dada Manifestos and Lampisteries*, trans. B. Wright, illustrations F. Picabia (London: John Calder, n.d.).

Vallance, E., *Revolutionary England and the National Covenant: State Oaths, Protestantism, and the Political Nation 1552–1682* (Woodbridge: Boydell Press, 2005).

Van Dijk, J. G. M., 'The Function of Fables in Graeco-Roman Romance', *Mnemosyne*, fourth series, 49:5 (1996), pp. 513–41.

Vernant, J.-P., 'Ambiguity and Reversal: On the Enigmatic Structure of *Oedipus Rex*', *New Literary History*, 9:3 (1978), pp. 475–501.

Virno, P., 'Natural-Historical Diagrams: The "New Global" Movement and the Biological Invariant', in Lorenzo Chiesa and Alberto Toscano (eds), *The Italian Difference: Between Nihilism and Biopolitics* (Melbourne: re.press, 2009), pp. 131–48.

Vogt, E. M., 'Catastrophic Narratives and Why the "Catastrophe" to Catastrophe Might Have Already Happened', in D. Hoens, S. Jöttkandt and G. Buelens (eds), *The Catastrophic Imperative* (Basingstoke: Palgrave Macmillan, 2009), pp. 26–52.

Voltaire, *Philosophical Dictionary*, ed. and trans. T. Besterman (Harmondsworth: Penguin, 1972).

Waldron, J., 'Torture and Positive Law: Jurisprudence for the White House', *Columbia Law Review*, 105:6 (October 2005), pp. 1,681–750.

Waldron, J., *Torture, Terror, and Trade-Offs: Philosophy for the White House* (Oxford: Oxford University Press, 2010).

Werber, N., 'A Test of Conscience Without Indispensable Norms: Niklas Luhmann's War on Terror', *Soziale Systeme*, 14:1 (2008), pp. 83–101.

Whitmarsh, T., *Ancient Greek Literature* (Cambridge: Polity, 2004).

Whyte, J., *Catastrophe and Redemption: The Political Thought of Giorgio Agamben* (Albany: State University of New York Press, 2013).

Williams, B., *Shame and Necessity* (Berkeley: University of California Press, 1993).

Williams, K., *American Methods: Torture and the Logic of Domination* (Cambridge: South End Press, 2006).

Wittgenstein, L., *Philosophical Investigations*, trans. G. E. M. Anscombe, P. M. S. Hacker and J. Schulte (Oxford: Wiley-Blackwell, 2009).

Wittgenstein, L., *Zettel*, ed. G. E. M. Anscombe and G. H. von Wright (Berkeley: University of California Press, 1967).

Wollheim, R., 'Freud and the Understanding of Art', in J. Neu (ed.), *The Cambridge Companion to Freud* (Cambridge: Cambridge University Press, 1991), pp. 249–66.

Wright, C. M., *The Maze and the Warrior: Symbols in Architecture, Theology and Music* (Cambridge: Harvard University Press, 2001).

Young-Bruehl, E., *Where Do We Fall When We Fall in Love?* (New York: Other Press, 2003).

Zaretsky, E., *Secrets of the Soul: A Social and Cultural History of Psychoanalysis* (New York: Knopf, 2004).

Žižek, S., *Interrogating the Real*, ed. R. Butler and S. Stephens (London and New York: Continuum, 2006).

Žižek, S. (ed.), *Lacan: The Silent Partners* (London: Verso, 2006).

Žižek, S., *Less Than Nothing: Hegel and the Shadow of Dialectical Materialism* (London: Verso, 2012).

Žižek, S., *The Sublime Object of Ideology* (London: Verso, 1989).

Žižek, S., *Tarrying with the Negative: Kant, Hegel, and the Critique of Ideology* (Durham, NC: Duke University Press, 1993).

Zupančič, A., *Ethics of the Real: Kant, Lacan* (London: Verso, 2000).

Index

EU representative:
Easy Access System Europe
Mustamäe tee 50, 10621 Tallinn, Estonia
Gpsr.requests@easproject.com

www.ingramcontent.com/pod-product-compliance
Lightning Source LLC
Chambersburg PA
CBHW050444280326
41932CB00013BA/2240